JEWS IN SUBURBIA

By Albert I. Gordon

With a foreword by Oscar Handlin

Beacon Press   Beacon Hill   Boston

Table of Contents

To
David
Judith
and
Lennard

Foreword

The move to the suburbs has been one of the most striking phenomena of recent American life. Although there are precedents for the spread of urban population away from the city centers, even in the nineteenth century, the movement of the past twenty years has been of such a magnitude as to demand serious examination. Surely this trend reflects important changes in the character of society and in the system of values in the United States.

Among the most striking circumstances of the shift of population has been the extent to which the newer ethnic groups have participated in it. In the past, escape from the city was the refuge of those who wished to avoid contact with the minorities. Now, however, the minorities are themselves involved in the migration. For, to some degree, the suburban style of life has become, for them too, a symbol of Americanization and of their acceptance in the culture of the United States.

American Jews, who are preponderantly the children of immigrants who arrived in the New World after 1890, have been among the groups most affected by this change. The way in which they have participated in the dispersal of urban population is a product of the special social situation. But in their case, the transition has altered long-established patterns of thought and behavior, and deserves very serious examination.

Rabbi Gordon's work is the first effort to look seriously into the heart of this phenomenon in search of a meaning. It treats the Jews involved dispassionately and yet sympathetically. It raises important questions about their development as a group and as a significant segment of American society. In dealing with these problems, Rabbi Gordon has drawn upon a variety of social materials, carefully collected and arranged, and he has handled them with the understanding and skill derived from his personal contacts and observations of the group. His work should prove of interest to Jews and to all those concerned with this important change in American society.

OSCAR HANDLIN

Acknowledgments

After completing this study, I tried to determine the number of persons to whom I had turned for information, guidance and assistance at some time or other while this work was in progress. My records indicated that over nine hundred men and women in over eighty different communities had responded to my inquiries concerning Jews in suburbia. Of these, five hundred ninety-nine men and women, residents of suburban communities throughout America, had replied to my specific questions about themselves and their lives as Jews in the suburbs. They, their eighty-one Rabbis, lay leaders, secular organizational heads and that unusual group of men and women who possess professional training and specialized knowledge about American Jewish life provided me with a fund of information, conjectures, theories and insights. Though so many of these persons must remain anonymous, I want, nevertheless, to acknowledge with sincere thanks and deep appreciation my debt of gratitude to each of them. Without their cooperation, this book could not have been completed.

The experience, not alone of the central city or the local community, but of many national Jewish organizations as well, was readily made available to me. In many instances, specific and detailed information on a variety of important themes was thus uncovered. I am particularly indebted to Mr. Oscar Cohen, National Program Director of the Anti-Defamation League of B'nai B'rith, whose knowledge of the subject of prejudice in suburbia proved invaluable. Reports of field men and regional directors of the ADL in all parts of the nation were studied for an insight into the problems of Jewish suburbia as the suburbanite himself sees them. To each of these remarkable men, I express my appreciation.

The Council of Jewish Federations and Welfare Funds; its Director, Mr. Philip Bernstein; and his able associates, each a specialist in important phases of American Jewish community life, were most helpful in providing what material was already available and in suggesting visits with numerous persons with valuable professional training and expert knowledge. The opportunity to examine certain unpublished material gathered by Dr. Marshall Sklare, Director of Research for the American Jewish Committee, has also been helpful and is hereby acknowledged with thanks.

Discussions with my revered teachers, Dr. Louis Finkelstein, Chancellor of the Jewish Theological Seminary of America, and Professor Mordecai M. Kaplan, founder of the Jewish Reconstructionist Movement, have helped me to understand their particular positions and attitudes with respect to religion and religious life among American Jews today. My thoughts on this and other subjects have, since my early years at the Seminary, been influenced by these brilliant personalities. I shall always be grateful for their numerous contributions to my spiritual development. I must say, however, that my thoughts on the subject of the Jewish religion have, on many occasions, taken turns of which they might not approve, yet which, I am convinced, need to be recorded.

Mr. Robert Segal, Director of the Jewish Community Council of Greater Boston; Mr. Sidney Cohen, Director of the Combined Jewish Appeal of Boston; Mr. Isaac Seligson, Associate Director of the Combined Jewish Appeal of Boston; and Mr. Sol Kolack of the Boston Anti-Defamation League of B'nai B'rith; Messrs. Julius Bisno, Executive Secretary of the Los Angeles Jewish Community Council, Charles Zibbell, Assistant Executive Secretary, and Fred Massarik, Director of Research Service Bureau—all of Los Angeles; and Messrs. Henry L. Zucker, Director of the Jewish Community Federation of Cleveland, Judah Rubenstein, Research Director in that office, as well as Norman Dockman, Executive Secretary of the Minneapolis Federation for Jewish Service, devoted many hours of their valuable time to this project by answering my numerous questions and offering their suggestions and comments for my consideration. My indebtedness to each of these good people is hereby acknowledged, and my thanks are expressed to the men and women serving on congregational boards in many suburbs all through

America for the time they took to meet with me and discuss Jewish suburbia. I am particularly indebted to the officers and board members of Temple Beth David of Temple City, California, whose pride in their congregation, its beautiful new temple and their fine Rabbi Ephraim F. Einhorn was so evident.

I am grateful to Miss Gloria R. Adelson, my secretary, who painstakingly typed the first draft of my manuscript.

The Mayor of Newton, Howard Whitmore, Jr., and Mr. Monte Basbas, Clerk of the City of Newton, whose cooperation made it possible for me to gain so much information about my home community, have been particularly helpful.

I wish to thank the following authors and their publishers for permission to reprint and quote from their works:

Marshall Sklare and Marc Vosk, *The Riverton Study*, published in May, 1957, by The American Jewish Committee, as well as an as yet unpublished study on Riverton, completed in 1958; Leo Pfeffer, *Creeds in Competition*, and A. H. Maslow, *Motivation and Personality*, both published by Harper and Brothers; Max Lerner, *America as a Civilization*, by Simon and Schuster, Mark Zborowski and Elizabeth Herzog, *Life is with People*, by International University Press; Herbert W. Schneider, *Religion in 20th Century America*, by Harvard University Press; Mordecai M. Kaplan, *Questions Jews Ask*, by the Reconstructionist Press, his books, *New Directions for Zionism* and *The Future of the American Jew*, by Macmillan Co.; Rabbi Henry Kagan's article on "The Jewish Family," in the *CCAR Journal*, published by the Central Conference of American Rabbis; Abraham Heschel's essay on "The Hazzan," included in *Conservative Judaism*; Arthur Schlesinger, Jr.'s article in *Saturday Review* (June 8, 1957); Bill Cunningham, columnist in the *Boston Herald* (August 31, 1957); The Christian Century Foundation, copyright, 1956; Martin M. Cohen's article in *The Jewish Social Service Quarterly* (Fall, 1955); Isadore Chein in *Jewish Social Studies* (July, 1955); Eric Fromm, *Escape from Freedom*, published by Rinehart & Co.; Norman B. Ryder in *The Annals of the American Academy of Political and Social Science* (March,

1958); and Evelyn Rothschild, both in her publications and in personal conversations, about her "home" community of Sharon, Mass.

I am also indebted to the following organizations from whose studies I have quoted:

The Jewish Community Council of Greater Washington, Dr. Isaac Franck, Executive Director, sponsors of *The Jewish Population of Greater Washington*, edited by Stanley Bigman; *Self-Survey of the Minneapolis Jewish Community*, published by the Minneapolis Federation for Jewish Service; *A Study of Natick Jewry* (June, 1957), sponsored by the Associated Jewish Philanthropies and Combined Jewish Appeal of Greater Boston; Dr. Gordon F. Bloom served as Chairman of this study. *Survey of Niles Township* (February, 1956) and its supplement (March, 1957), sponsored by the Jewish Community Centers of Chicago, Illinois; *Jewish Suburban Population Movement in Cleveland,* a report prepared by Dr. Judah Rubenstein, Research Director of the Jewish Community Federation of Cleveland (May, 1957); *The Jewish Population of Greater Lynn, Mass.,* prepared by The Jewish Community Federation of Greater Lynn (1956), and "A Look at the Los Angeles Jewish Community —1958," part of the *1958 Jewish Population Study* undertaken by the Los Angeles Jewish Community Council, whose research is directed by Dr. Fred Massarik.

I am grateful also to my friends, Dr. Ira Eisenstein, Rabbi of Anshe Emet Congregation, Chicago, Illinois; Dr. Theodore Friedman, Rabbi of Beth El Congregation, South Orange, New Jersey; and Dr. Abba Hillel Silver of Cleveland, Ohio, for permission to quote from their writings.

I am indebted also to many colleagues in all parts of the nation for their assistance in providing needed information about their communities. I refer particularly to Rabbis Tzvi H. Porath of Chevy Chase, Lewis Weintraub of Silver Spring and Leon Adler of Kensington, Maryland; Rabbis David Aronson, Albert G. Minda and Stanley Rabinowitz of Minneapolis, Minnesota; Rabbis Max Vorspan, Morton Bauman, Jacob Pressman and Ephraim F. Einhorn of Los Angeles and environs; Rabbis David Weiss of Sharon, Mass.,

Melvin L. Goldstine of Skokie, Illinois, and Rudolph Adler of Euclid, Ohio. I am grateful, too, for the assistance that was provided by my colleagues who responded to my written questionnaire, personal letters and phone calls, and to all who welcomed me into their community to witness at first hand their congregations and their communities "in action."

Professor Oscar Handlin of Harvard University, to whom I first turned for counsel and guidance shortly after I had begun the task of writing this book, proved to be something more than a critic and counselor. Through all the months during which this study was being prepared, his gentle, friendly guidance, encouragement and suggestions have meant more to me than words can say. To him, I extend my heartfelt thanks.

My dear wife, Dorothy Davis Gordon, has contributed to this study in many ways. In addition to her valued and detailed criticism of each of these chapters, her understanding and encouragement through the long period when this book was taking form have assisted me beyond measure. She is, in fact, as her name suggests, "the gift of God."

Albert I. Gordon, Rabbi of Temple Emanuel in Newton, Massachusetts, since 1950, has had thirty years' experience in the Rabbinate. A former Executive Director of the United Synagogue of America, The National Organization of Conservative Congregations, he has traveled and lectured extensively throughout the United States. As a result, he has gained an intimate knowledge of American Jews in both their secular and religious life.

A native of Cleveland, Ohio, and a graduate of New York University, Rabbi Gordon holds an M.A. in sociology and a Ph.D. in anthropology from the University of Minnesota. In 1929 he received the degrees of Rabbi and M.H.L. from the Jewish Theological Seminary of America in New York. From 1930 to 1946 he was the Rabbi of Adath Jeshurun Synagogue in Minneapolis, Minnesota.

Vice President of the Massachusetts Board of Rabbis, Dr. Gordon is an active member of numerous other Jewish and community-wide organizations. Since 1952 he has been a lecturer on Judaism at the Andover-Newton Theological School. He has been a labor arbitrator in a variety of industries since 1934, and in 1943 was appointed a public panel representative for the National War Labor Board.

Rabbi Gordon is the author of several other published works, among them JEWS IN TRANSITION (1949), a well-known sociological study of changes in Jewish cultural life and religious practices from the immigrant to the American-born generations.

Introduction

Suburbanism has been described as a "way of life," [1] distinctive and even unique as compared with life in the big city. The differences between city and suburb consist not only of such factors as population size, density and heterogeneity, but of social-psychological factors as well. Indeed, we may say that Park's [2] description of the big city as a "state of mind" also characterizes the suburb. Most suburbanites are young married couples, often with two or more children. Members of the middle class in our society, they are mostly homeowners, anxious to improve their economic and social status; they are given to neighboring and friendly personal contacts in a casual, though not wholly relaxed, setting, and look forward to the joys of leisurely living. Suburbia has become, for so many, the symbol of Utopia—the middle-class Shangri-La.

The suburb offers ample opportunity to examine and study the many-faceted lives of the men, women and children who reside there.

Jews—especially the young couples, seekers of the good life—have, particularly since World War II, established themselves in America's suburban communities in vast numbers. Members of the middle class and long known as urban dwellers, they are convinced that by moving to the suburb and carrying on business or profession in the big city, they can have "the best of both worlds." [3] They have, as a result, changed the location and often the character of Jewish community life in America.

This study seeks to discover answers to some basic questions about the Jews in suburbia: How are Jews faring in suburbia? What is happening to their family life, their children, their religious values and practices? How do they relate to their Christian neighbors, and how do these in turn relate to the Jews?

It is not always a simple matter to identify that entity we know as "Jew." Chein [4] has correctly indicated that he may be identified in many different ways.

There are the contending interpretations of the Jewish religion, the watering down of observance, whatever the interpretation, and the Jews who will have no truck with any kind of religion; there are the Yiddishists, Hebraists and Englishists who advocate one or another aspect of secular Jewish culture; the varieties of Zionists, non-Zionists and anti-Zionists; the competing Jewish organizations; the "out-of-pocket" Jews who feel they have lived Jewishly when they have contributed to some Jewish philanthropy; or the "gastronomic" Jews when they have dined on "Jewish" foods, or the "cardiac" Jews when they have experienced "in their heart" that they are Jews; and there are the many who, while identifying themselves as Jews, just do not care about anything Jewish. For better or for worse, there is no longer a single model of Jewishness.

It has seemed wise, therefore, to adopt the definition which Warner [5] has used so effectively with respect to "ethnics." He writes: "The term 'ethnic' refers to any individual who considers himself, or is considered to be, a member of a group with a foreign culture and who participates in the activities of the group."

The material for this study was gathered over a period of three years. As the Rabbi of suburban Temple Emanuel of Newton, Massachusetts, and closely associated with that community since 1950, I have become increasingly aware of certain differences between urban and suburban Jewish community life and attitudes. It has seemed important to discover both the nature of these distinctions and their implications for Judaism and the Jewish way of life. Communication with and personal visits to numerous other suburbs during the years have pointed up the need for an organized study of Jews in suburbia—a study that would provide information and perhaps even insights helpful to all, Jews and non-Jews, who seek to learn more about the nature of suburbia.

Information for this study was obtained from Rabbis in eighty-nine suburban communities, numerous lay leaders of both religious and secular organizations and other local residents. In those suburbs where there was no rabbi, much information was provided by spiritual leaders in nearby towns and regional directors for both religious and secular Jewish organizations. The eighty-nine communities are:

CALIFORNIA
Alhambra
Altadena
Arcadia
Azusa
Burbank
Burlingame
Covina
El Monte
Encino
Hawthorne
Monrovia
Monterey Park
Piedmont
Redwood City
Rosemead
San Fernando
San Gabriel
San Marino
San Mateo
Santa Ana
Sierra Madre
Temple City
Whittier

CONNNECTICUT
Milford
West Hartford

ILLINOIS
Glencoe
Highland Park
Skokie

MARYLAND
Bethesda
Chevy Chase
Hagerstown
Kensington
Silver Spring
Wheaton

MASSACHUSETTS
Belmont
Marblehead
Natick
Newton
Norwood
Sharon
Swampscott

MICHIGAN
Oak Park

MINNESOTA
St. Louis Park

NEW JERSEY
Bridgeton
Cliffside Park
Closter
Englewood
Fair Lawn
Kearny
Linden
Livingston
Millburn
New Milford
Rutherford
South Orange
Teaneck

NEW YORK
Baldwin
Bay Shore
Colonial Heights
East Meadow
East Rockaway
Elmont
Franklin Square
Freeport
Glen Cove
Great Neck
Hewlett
Hicksville
Huntington
Jericho
Larchmont
Laurelton
Levittown
Lynbrook
Malverne
Mt. Kisco
Mt. Vernon
New Hyde Park
Nyack
Ozone Park
Rockville Center
Roosevelt
Roslyn
Sands Point
Valley Stream
Wantagh
Westbury
White Plains

OHIO
Euclid

This study, like *Jews in Transition* [6] which preceded it, employs primarily the "participant-observer" technique which, in my experience, provides the greatest depth of sociological understanding of situations as complex as Jewish suburban life. Unguarded statements, ideas and opinions that might not be expressed if direct questions were asked, often come to the surface in apparently casual conversations. So also do bits of gossip that tend to explain the motivation of those whose words are being recorded. As a resident of one of the suburbs included in this study, I have been able to gain insights and to understand values that might otherwise have been neglected or ignored. I have not knowingly betrayed confidences, but reactions from those among whom I have lived for nine years have proved most helpful in this effort to interpret the way of life of Jews in suburbia.

There may be some disagreement with Becker and Geer's [7] sweeping opinion: "The most complete form of the sociological datum, after all, is the form in which the participant-observer gathers it; an observation of some social event, the events which precede and follow it, and explanations of its meaning by participants and spectators, before, during and after its occurrence. Such a datum gives us more information about the event under study than data gathered by any other sociological method." It must be noted, nevertheless, that the participant-observer technique does provide us with much information which would otherwise seldom come to light. Though I have not relied upon any one method entirely, the participant-observer technique which helps us to observe the daily life of people and understand it more thoroughly has been an invaluable aid.[8]

As for other methods: questionnaires which were addressed to every tenth member of the congregations in the suburbs under observation yielded a random sampling of the ideas, opinions and way of life of 599 synagogue affiliates in twenty-eight separate suburbs [9] in all parts of America. (The questionnaire had been mailed to 2,500 persons.) Non-congregation members of these same suburbs were reached through both written and oral communication with many of the leaders of Jewish suburban organizations, as well as with the lay leaders in the adjacent central city. Personal visits to all sections of the country and interviews, wherever possible, with the community leaders have helped to round out the picture.

Still another questionnaire was addressed to eighty-five Rabbis who are presently serving suburban congregations in the United States. This elicited responses from eighty-one spiritual leaders in seventy-eight suburban communities.[10] The reactions of these Rabbis to their congregations and communities are of interest in themselves. They become even more important when we correlate their responses with those of their congregants or other townspeople as expressed in yet another questionnaire. It is pleasant to report that there appears to be considerable agreement between the laymen and their spiritual leaders in their interpretations of such important matters as religion, the family, Jewish leadership, the importance of class and caste in the suburb and the tensions and fears that result from taking up residence in suburbia.

Examination of many suburbs' historical documents; records obtained from the central cities' Jewish and non-Jewish agencies, planning boards and Chambers of Commerce; and the attitudes expressed by city managers, mayors, superintendents of schools, police department heads and librarians have helped piece the parts of suburbia's story together. Suburban newspapers, too, were examined for the light they would cast upon the image of the Jewish suburban community as interpreted by the editors. Meetings with ministers and other church officials in suburbia—including, in several cases, the leaders of the Church Federations and Ministers Association—visits to suburban shopping centers and casual conversations with storekeepers have added to my understanding of suburbia.

Statements made by Jews and non-Jews alike were jotted down —a phrase here, an idea there. These were later typed out fully and indexed for use in this study. Also recorded were personal histories of both new and old residents in suburbia, of those young and old in years, of the wealthy, the moderately well-off and those who were struggling to keep their economic heads above water. Anglo-Jewish publications, particularly weekly publications from the central city, were studied for clues to the ideas and behavior patterns of Jews in suburbia, as well as the attitudes of those Jews who represent the central city.

In the New England suburb of Newton, in which I reside, I have recorded, as faithfully and accurately as possible, all that I have seen and heard. In other suburban areas, the volunteer services of carefully chosen residents who could serve as qualified observers were gratefully received.

The tendency by such informants to protect their community from unfavorable comment is often marked. Aware of the need to guard against such understandable bias, I have, whenever uncertain about the complete accuracy of the information received, called upon other persons in other walks of life, members of a different class or group, for further information with the hope of eliminating the possibility of an incorrect evaluation.

Dollard [11] has pointed out that "comfortable people talk less and come forward less readily to the newcomer." How simple it is to record the complaints and antipathies of people who, often vehemently, state their dissatisfactions with their community and assume that the whole and accurate story has been told! An effort has been made, therefore, not only to balance conflicting statements, but also to weigh them properly so that they would be "in focus." Various informants were frequently used from the same suburb, because it seemed likely that the community culture might *not* be homogeneous and, further, because differences in knowledge and experience deserved to be noted. These persons were generally well informed, many of them being experts and professionals in various specialized areas of community work. In each community, interviews were arranged with local social scientists whose factual information was reliable. Every effort was made to guard against bias.

The estimates of Jewish populations in suburban communities, included in this study, were obtained from the following:

(1) Jewish Community Council and Jewish Federation directors in the central city, whose estimates were based upon direct contacts with the community in fund-raising efforts;

(2) Data recorded in the annual volumes of the *American Jewish Year Book*;

(3) Membership records of synagogues in suburbia;

(4) Articles in Anglo-Jewish publications in the area being studied;

(5) Directors and their assistants in national Jewish organizations having chapters or lodges in the suburb;

(6) Population studies already completed by local agencies for such communities and areas as St. Louis Park, Minnesota; the San Gabriel Valley; Lynn, Swampscott, Marblehead, Natick and Newton, Massachusetts; Skokie, Illinois; Greater Washington, including Montgomery County, Maryland.

(7) Federal census and local records available in the city or town halls of each suburb.

Would that the tools and techniques I have used were even more adequate. Certain phases of Jewish suburbia still remain unexamined. Yet the facts and impressions recorded in these pages are significant, primarily because the sources of information are so varied. The areas and types of suburbia whose residents are considered here offer important comparisons and contrasts, all of which may help us paint a comprehensive portrait in depth of the Jews in suburbia.

Even though I have used certain techniques of the sociologist and social anthropologist, I am not unmindful of the fact that I, a Conservative Rabbi for some thirty years, have not always been able to stand off at a distance and take a wholly objective and dispassionate view of all that I have observed and of which I have been a part. I look upon the Jewish community and its people with a certain set of beliefs and attitudes that are readily discernible in this study. I suspect that pure objectivity, if it could ever be really attained, would very likely result in a completely distorted view of Jews and Judaism, for the dimension of depth would in all likelihood be lacking. Inasmuch as suburbia consists of people, their ideas, aspirations and actions must be comprehended. It has seemed best to rely in considerable degree upon my years of close association with them rather than upon the use of the questionnaire and external observation alone.

During the past thirty years, I have served as the Rabbi of two congregations, one in the Midwest (Adath Jeshurun in Minneapolis,

Minnesota) for sixteen years, the other in New England (Temple Emanuel of Newton, Massachusetts) for ten years. During the years 1946-50, as Executive Director of the United Synagogue of America—the national organization of Conservative Jewish congregations in America—with headquarters in New York City, I was able to travel from one end of America to the other, to visit and come to know intimately more than 90 per cent of the Jewish communities, large and small, throughout the nation. It was during these years that suburbia had its greatest growth. In my official capacity, I "assisted" at the birth of many a suburban congregation, including Levittown, Long Island, which is included in this study. It was natural, too, that I write about St. Louis Park, Minnesota, because even during the years of my incumbency in Minneapolis— about whose Jewish community I have written in *Jews in Transition* —Jewish families were beginning to move to this suburb. I have known this community over many years and have observed its remarkable growth and development with admiration.

Newton, my home for the past decade, is another of the wonder-suburbs for which I have a warm regard. Although I have been intrigued by its record growth and particularly by the manner in which the Jewish community has established itself, I have, nevertheless, carefully noted the resultant stresses and strains here as within other communities, in the hope that the weaknesses may be strengthened and danger spots eliminated. To live with the people about whom I have written is to get to know and understand them intimately and well.

The major portion of this study is concerned with the families who are affiliated with the synagogues and temples. This is natural, I think, because approximately 60 per cent of America's Jews are known to be members of these religious institutions. They happen, too, to form the majority of members of the so-called secular Jewish organizations. It is my belief that over 90 per cent of all Jews belong to some Jewish organization. I believe, therefore, that the interests and attitudes and actions of all types and kinds of suburban Jews are accurately reflected in this study.

Jews in Suburbia focuses attention upon a religio-ethnic group which, through the centuries, has successfully maintained a distinctive way of life, even though it has been a minority people. May this account prove instructive, challenging and even inspiring to all who read it, whatever their religious or ethnic background.

ALBERT I. GORDON

April, 1959

Chapter 1   America on the Move

The universal Jewish migration to the suburbs is very recent. However, unless American cities are redeveloped at a faster rate than is currently apparent, the middle class may become almost exclusively suburban. Among Jews as well the suburban community may thus become the norm.[1]

The mobility of American families since World War II is nothing short of phenomenal. The statistics of each year indicate that we are well on the way to becoming a nation of nomads. In 1954, for example, 18.6 per cent of America's people changed their place of residence; in 1955, the figure was 20 per cent.

The most impressive trend is the move away from the central cities—those around which the suburbs are clustered—out to the suburbs themselves. Between 1948 and 1958, twelve million Americans moved to the suburbs. *More than forty-seven million people live in the suburbs today.*

Between 1940 and 1956, the population of the suburbs grew almost three times as fast as that of America's central cities.[2] Between 1950 and 1955, they grew almost seven times as fast. And detailed studies suggest that even this increase factor may be an understatement. For example:

———From 1950 to 1957, the population of Nassau County (New York), a conglomerate of suburban communities contiguous to New York City, increased by 75.2 per cent. In Suffolk County (New York), the increase was 90.6 per cent!

———In the suburbs of Boston, Mass.: the population of Newton has increased by 10 per cent in the past three years; that of Framingham, 40.1 per cent within the past seven years. Swampscott has grown by 12.5 per cent; Marblehead by 28.4 per cent; Natick by 31.6 per cent—all since 1950. In the same period, Sharon has demonstrated an unusual growth of 72.5 per cent!

——In 1940, Montgomery and Prince Georges Counties, adjacent to the city of Washington, D.C., had 173,000 residents. In 1958, the population has expanded to 600,000.

——New suburban towns such as Park Forest (Illinois) and Levittown (New York); little former crossroad towns like Skokie (Illinois); and the myriad of suburbs along the San Gabriel Valley (California) within a few minutes' drive of downtown Los Angeles —to mention but a few—have shot forward in population expansion. Park Forest has an estimated population (1958) of 25,000, against 8,138 residents in 1950. Levittown, which in 1946 was first laid out on potato fields, has today a population of over 55,000. Skokie had some 45,000 residents in 1958, whereas in 1950 there were but 14,832. And the growth of the towns along the San Gabriel Valley has been overwhelming. Just as the San Fernando Valley with 525,000 has quadrupled its population since 1950, the San Gabriel Valley, to the south of Los Angeles, has almost duplicated this record.[3]

America is on the move!

Despite its spectacular growth in recent years, suburbia is not an absolutely new development on the American scene. Large metropolitan centers of population, particularly along the Eastern seaboard, have known suburban communities for many decades. Philadelphia has numerous "main line" towns. New York City has such Westchester County cities, towns and villages as New Rochelle, Mount Vernon and White Plains, as well as such suburbs as Greenwich and Westport, extending into the southern portion of Connecticut. Boston has such lovely and staid residential communities as Swampscott and Marblehead to the north, Newton, Lexington, Natick and Wellesley to the west; and Sharon to the south of the core city. These and other communities have had the characteristics of suburbs long before modern suburbia became popular.

The suburb may be defined [4] as a formally structured community which is adjacent to and accessible to a larger central city. It is dependent upon the metropolis for most of the income upon which the town's people live. Such towns are far less dense in population, and many of them are of recent vintage, having been created and developed within two decades. Although the suburb is primarily residential in character, it provides the business and shopping areas required to meet the essential needs of its residents. These residential towns are often referred to as "housing" or "dormitory" suburbs. Whereas the big city's major interest is directed toward industry and commerce, that of suburban government centers about the home and the family.

The suburb, by its very nature, must be sufficiently close to the central city that the majority of men and women who depend upon the city for their livelihood may commute to and from it daily. That community which is independent of a big city cannot, by definition, be classified as a suburb. Each of the suburbs examined in this study is thus related to a metropolis in one or more ways.

The influence of the core city upon the suburb is marked, not only because of the distinguishing characteristics and personality of the big city, but because most of the men and women who today reside in the suburb were yesterday residents of the metropolis.

Because the suburb is primarily a community of homes, with industry and commerce incidental, city officials in suburbia direct their major efforts toward the maintenance and glorification of the home. The one factor above all others of interest to the suburban family is the home and its setting.

Suburban governments, therefore, pay greater attention to the aesthetic aspects of community living than seems to be true of central cities. The condition of trees that line the streets becomes the concern of an entire community. Foliage is trimmed, sprayed and protected because it is truly precious in the eyes of suburbanites. More playgrounds, youth programs and picnic areas are set aside per square mile in the suburbs than is generally true of large cities. Public golf courses become important adjuncts to suburban living.

As today's family is child-centered, so the modern suburb is definitely home-centered. Huge shopping centers which, Topsy-like, have been developed in or near the suburb, aim at making shopping a pleasant and leisurely experience for the whole family.

Mother, the children and the household become the focal point of interest to storekeepers in these shopping centers. A check of such shopping centers in all parts of the country revealed that for every business centered about the man and his clothing needs, there were eight shops catering exclusively to women or children. Stores catering to toddlers, tots and teen-agers predominate.

The suburban government remains unique because of its primary interest and concern for the home and the family. Its officials, readily accessible to the town's residents, help to give Mr. Average Citizen the feeling that his well-being and the happiness of his family are of primary concern to his elected officials.

The fact that suburban government is autonomous plays an important role in the way of life of the average suburbanite. The right of a community to set its own tax rate and to establish its own zoning restrictions, to determine the kind and quantity of housing, apartment buildings and factories which may be erected; the emphasis it may choose to place upon its public school and youth program, and the percentage of its taxes it proposes to make available for them; the nature of the shops and shopping centers that are permitted within the suburb—these ultimately establish the character of the suburb itself and serve to regulate the kind of people who will comprise its citizenship. That families move into certain suburbs and not into others is determined, among other things, by the kind of city government that prevails and the officials who are to be found in the area.

Another major factor gives to suburban autonomous government a significance and personal importance less often associated with central city government. The suburbanite tends to lose his anonymity in suburbia. He is known to his neighbors as an individual. He has a name and a personality. The local storekeepers, the policeman on the beat, his alderman, the editor of the local neighborhood paper, the principals of schools which his children attend and often the mayor, as well, are aware of him. They may even know him by name. The association between the individual and his local government (and those who represent it) is intimate. Problems affecting the individual, his family, his finances and the civic welfare are directly and speedily brought to the attention of an official who is in a position to be helpful.

On a recent radio program, Mayor Whitmore of Newton, when asked his opinion about the proposal to create a metropolitan government of greater Boston, disapproved of the idea. "A metropolitan government," he said, "would tend to create another bureaucracy *which would further remove the people* from the close and intimate association with local matters and decisions." [5]

Individuals from many suburban areas agree with this opinion:

"I feel no hesitancy in calling up the chief of the sanitation department to complain about laxity in garbage collection. When the snow is high and cars can't get through, a call to the city hall will bring a prompt response. When I go away for a few days and there is no one at home, I call the police department and ask them to keep an eye on my home. And, believe me, they do it. I have sat down with the mayor on any number of occasions to register my ideas about certain improvements in ordinances. Now, where else could I do these things if not in my suburb? I would never dream of calling the mayor of Chicago or any other really large city. We get personalized government in the suburbs. We matter to every single department head in city hall, and that's mighty important."

The "personalized" government becomes important in still another way. In a crucial situation, there is always someone able to communicate directly with the mayor, the chief of police, the superintendent of schools or other public officials in a matter of minutes.

"When a young boy was assaulted only because he was a Jew— and this was a verified fact—I was able to put in two phone calls to the chief of police and to our suburb's mayor. My personal complaint brought quick action from the officials and brought the offenders to quick justice. I had lived in a large city before. There were other occasions when an immediate response was necessary, but I never got it before."

In another situation—

"Mothers complained bitterly about the attitude of one school principal during the Christmas season. This educator insisted that all children, whatever their religion, must sing the Christmas carols in their classrooms whether they wanted to or not. The children were embarrassed, and the mothers became angry to the point that they threatened foolish action. When I was informed of the matter, I phoned the superintendent of schools and, quickly, a time was set for a meeting with him. The religious issues for the parental objections were explained to him. He expressed grateful appreciation for my effort to explain the problem to him, and he then discussed the problem with the school principal. This issue was resolved more quickly because people are treated as fellow citizens rather than as opponents of public officials."

Of America's 5,500,000 Jews, 3,700,000—two-thirds of the total—live in or adjacent to ten of America's largest cities.[6] A primary reason for the marked growth of suburban communities is that these erstwhile big-city dwellers have, in even larger proportion than their numbers, taken up residence in suburbia. There is every indication that this trend will continue at an even more accelerated pace.

Many cogent reasons for the growth of suburbia suggest themselves.

First and foremost, of course, are the effects of the marked increase in population which has characterized this nation for the last decade. And the increase is expected to continue. The Bureau of the Census estimates that the number of families in the United States will increase from forty-three million in 1956 to fifty-one million in 1960, and to about fifty-four and one-half million in 1975—a rise of 27 per cent in twenty years! Over eighty-three million people are projected for the suburbs by 1975, and there is general agreement that, as the population increases, America's suburbs will continue to grow in size, in number and in influence.

But the shortage of living-space was also an important factor. The depression years of the 1930's were followed closely by World War II. During that fifteen-year period, few, if any, new homes were built, and even fewer families could afford to purchase them, whatever their cost. Families "doubled up": sons or daughters who were recently married moved in with their parents until conditions improved.

Then, too, the uncertainties and insecurities of life during the war years made it less likely that these young married couples would establish more permanent homes. The requirements of military service and the high degree of mobility associated with the National Defense and Training Programs accustomed young people to "live out of a suitcase." Who could say where one was likely to be tomorrow?

At the end of World War II, the situation changed radically. Building materials were once again available, and a great building boom followed. The Federal government made money available to ex-G.I.'s to purchase homes through a long-term payment plan. Soldiers and their young families, anxious to move out of houses, streets and areas into which they had been crowded, could now move into the newest, if not always the most choice, areas adjacent to the big city—suburbia. Young people with very young children —many middle-class, self-employed businessmen, some professionals, many skilled workers and salesmen—made the move to the suburbs.

The builders of mass produced homes, such as those in Levittown, provided "low-cost housing." Prices were reasonable enough to satisfy young people who were determined to establish their own family life, independent of parents and in-laws.

Before and during the war years, the big cities had deteriorated to a considerable degree. Houses had become older, and they could not be adequately maintained. Hence older families, too, felt the urge to get away from the debilitation, the smoke, the crowded streets, the noise and the many other sources of irritation and concern.

Newer and faster means of transportation had also become available. Roads had been built that assured easy access to the outlying suburbs as well as to the city. It was simple to commute rapidly to and from the city daily. Automobiles were helping to reduce distances, and this led, as a consequence, to changing patterns of living.

The phenomenal rise in the birth rate following World War II has played an important role in the rise of suburbia. Various hypotheses have been advanced to explain the marked increase in the birth rate. Ryder[7] has observed:

One suggestion is that it is now fashionable to have a large family. This is either a tautology, which presents us not with an answer but merely with another question, or else it is a denial of the possibility of understanding this strategic area of human behavior. Another idea is that the insecurity of the outside world is impelling individuals to withdraw into the haven of fundamental values represented by the family institution. A further notion is that husbands with more time to spend at home are discovering—or rediscovering—within themselves an innate love of children. . . . There is one line of inquiry which has received much less attention than it deserves, perhaps because it is obvious. Whatever desires for children couples may have must compete with other desires for the scarce resources of the couple's income. If that income rises, as it has in the United States in the past two decades, then the "purchase" of children, like the acquisition of other consumer goods, may increase without altering the scale of values. People avoided having babies during the depression because they could not afford them; people are having babies now because they *can* afford them. Too, depression-era families were usually small. One or two children at most was all that parents could "afford." These children now grown to adulthood have been heard to vow, "When I get married, you can bet on it that I will try to have a large family of kids. None of this only boy or only girl in the family for me. You can't imagine what it means to feel so completely alone as the one child in the family or even not to have a brother or sister."

The desire of parents to provide their children and themselves with yards, parks, trees and a generally more natural and beautiful setting is not to be underestimated.

"I always dreamed of the day when I would be able to spend more time with my wife and kids out in our own backyard or having a cookout or a social away from the city. It seems right that we relax together in our sport clothes just taking things easy, but—and this is most important—taking things easy together."

In explaining the growth of suburbia, Riesman[8] offers the shrewd observation that "among such suburban dwellers and in general in our society, we are witnessing a tremendous but tacit revolt against industrialism." Suburban life, then, becomes not only escape but revolt from what is to many an intolerable way of life.

The belief that life can be lived with less personal strain and effort in suburbia, that family and children are important and that "it is better to be a big fish in a little pond than a little fish in a big pond" has helped to bring ever-increasing numbers of families out to the suburbs.

There are those, too, whose love of "growing things"—flowers, plants, trees and grass—could be satisfied best in a suburban setting. This sense of pleasure and personal satisfaction can hardly be over-estimated.

"I grow my own flowers. I care for our lawn, I trim the bushes and trees and perform the many chores in and around the house with real satisfaction. I call *this* living."

Suburban living is also status-giving in two very distinct ways. If one can afford to live in a well-established, upper-middle-class community, one automatically acquires prestige and a sense of importance. Prestige can also be acquired by assuming leadership in some activity or program within the suburb. To have a next-door neighbor or the folks down the block think well of one for leading some distinctive enterprise or activity is, to many, a sufficient recompense, even if the cause itself proves less rewarding.

In certain big cities, notably New York, Philadelphia, Buffalo, Chicago, Cleveland, Washington, D.C., Baltimore, Minneapolis and Los Angeles, there is yet another reason for moving to the suburbs.

In New York City, grave concern has been expressed over the years because of the infiltration of Negroes and Puerto Ricans into neighborhoods that had been all white. Because standards and habits are different and because people like to live among their own kind, New Yorkers have been in mass flight from Manhattan to the suburbs. A recent survey [9] shows that the number of non-white persons in the five boroughs of New York City increased by 320,-221, or 41.3 per cent, between 1950 and 1957, while the white population *decreased* 416,707, or 51.9 per cent, and Nassau County, the heart of suburbia, increased its white population 75.2 per cent.[10]

By 1970, almost half of Manhattan's population and 28 per cent of the entire five boroughs will be Negro and Puerto Rican, according to Dr. Harry L. Shapiro, Curator of the American Museum of Natural History. Such prediction only tends to hasten the exodus from this and other urban centers to the suburbs.[11]

In ward eleven in the city of Buffalo, Negroes formed 10 per cent of the total population in 1950. By 1956, the Negro population was estimated at 70 per cent. The same trend, to varying degrees, was also found in certain other wards in that city.

Cleveland was faced with a similar problem when the expanding Negro community moved into what had been an almost exclusively Jewish neighborhood (East 105th Street). Here as elsewhere, Jews and others who were faced by the "problem" sold their homes and moved to the several suburbs on the "Heights." About 85 per cent of Cleveland's Jews now live in the suburbs.

The non-white populations in the fourteen largest metropolitan areas in the United States have grown tremendously between 1940 and 1950. In the San Francisco-Oakland area, the increase was almost 200 per cent. During that decade, the non-white population increased 120 per cent in Los Angeles, 76 per cent in Cleveland, 110 per cent in Buffalo, 70 per cent in Boston, 80 per cent in Chicago, 100 per cent in Detroit, 55 per cent in Minneapolis-St. Paul, 65 per cent in New York, 50 per cent in Philadelphia, 50 per cent in Washington, D.C., 35 per cent in Baltimore, 40 per cent in St. Louis and 30 per cent in Pittsburgh.[12]

The same condition prevails today on the North Side of Minneapolis. This area, long the center of Jewish life in this midwestern city, has now become the center of the Negro community. The white exodus to suburban St. Louis Park was accelerated by the opportunity to move into newer homes in a status-giving area and yet be within a short distance from their businesses in Minneapolis. Synagogues, Jewish centers and Hebrew schools have so far remained on the North Side of the city, for many Jewish families still maintain their residence in this section.

It would be an injustice to many of those families who move to the suburbs seeking to escape the inroads of Negroes, Puerto Ricans and Mexicans, if their reasons were not recorded.

"My move to the suburbs has a great deal to do with the influx of the Puerto Ricans into our neighborhood. But it isn't because I am opposed to Puerto Ricans or Negroes or anyone else just because of the color of their skin or for any other such superficial reason. I had to move because I was worried about my children and their welfare. When my children are afraid to play out in Riverside Park because of these gangs of boys who pull knives and rob not only my children but all the others of their playthings, then it is time to do something about it. I don't know if the fault lies with the Police Department or with anyone else. If my children were molested by a gang of white boys, I would move. In fact, I'm ready to keep on moving until my children can live peacefully without the fear of being robbed or even stabbed by these vicious boys who sneak up on them in the park. My wife tells me that she's afraid to walk out onto the avenue at night. I read of gangs robbing people like myself every day in the year. I say again—I'm not concerned about skin color or economic status, but I am concerned about living in security and peace. I find that the city can no longer protect me adequately, so I moved to a little town that can. This suburb is determined to keep these ruffians out."

This attitude can be duplicated in every major city of the nation. The irony that some Jewish residents in suburbia are among those bent upon maintaining segregated neighborhoods in their new setting thus becomes understandable, even if one disagrees with their logic.

Families often move to suburbia when they find that the homes in which they have reared their children are now too large for their needs. Their married children have moved to the suburbs, and the desire to live close to their children and grandchildren is an additional incentive to move to the new area.

An understanding and wise leader of the Minneapolis Jewish community was asked: "Why do children who have grown up in Minneapolis and whose memories are so closely associated with it move to a suburb like St. Louis Park?"

He replied: "There is always the tendency to get away from one's childhood environment and to come back to it only after one has made good. When, in so many cases, there was simply no place

to which to move following return from army service and then
marriage, it was natural that these people would turn to the suburbs. It was either that or move out of town away from family.
It must be remembered, too, that not all young people were happy
as children on the North Side. Their childhood homes reminded
them of poverty and Depression years. They remember the heart-
aches resulting therefrom. It is natural, therefore, for them to want
to move into a new community where they could begin all over
again."

Suburban life is assumed to be free from the tensions, haste,
crowding and crime of the city. Its schools are assumed to be less
crowded and to provide superior educational programs. Parents
assume that their children will find more pleasant playmates coming from more controlled homes and families. What, then, could
be more desirable for families so anxious to improve their status?
Synagogues, temples, youth programs, Hebrew schools, Sunday
schools, fellowship groups, culture and even a neighborhood "Jewish
style" delicatessen—all help to make suburbia seem eminently desirable. For people who own their own homes, who "can afford more
of everything, including children and sunshine," [13] life in the suburbs is especially attractive.

Conversations with residents in older suburbs disclose that
among the early residents of the Jewish community were those who
deliberately set out to escape from the Jewish community and its
responsibilities by moving to a suburb. The solution was only
temporarily successful, of course, for as soon as other Jewish families
moved to the same suburb, the escapist was identified as a Jew.
He had but two choices: either to move once again, or to acknowledge his identity. A Jewish family might avoid identification for a
brief period; it could seldom do so for a prolonged time unless
parents ceased to be concerned about the Jewish education or
spiritual welfare of their children. It is one thing to wish to escape
from identification as a Jew; it is quite another to identify oneself
with another religious (non-Jewish) group. Escapism of this kind
became almost impossible in the suburb.

Though they seldom constitute more than a minority in any

suburb, Jews, in a manner characteristic of minorities, are a conspicuous group in suburbia. They are largely a middle-income
group, either professional men or self-employed, salaried employees
in white-collar jobs or skilled crafts. Jews have established themselves and are at home in suburban communities across the nation.
We speak of them as middle-class people.

Warner [14] has distinguished six social classes in his studies of
Yankee City. He divides the middle class into the "upper-middle
class" and the "lower-middle class." The former "is composed of
substantial businessmen and professional people. These are respected members of the community who often act as civic leaders.
They are 'solid' folk, but not society. They live in comfortable
homes and their average income is less than that of the two upper
classes."

The upper-middle class is differentiated from the "upper-upper
class" and the "lower-upper class" in certain respects. Upper-upper
class members claim an "aristocracy of birth and wealth." They
are the old families whose wealth has been inherited through several generations. They take pride in their ancestry. They tend to
be closely intermarried and hence are often related to each other.
Skilled in ritual behavior and etiquette, they are the social arbiters
of the community.

The lower-upper class also live in large, expensive houses in
exclusive residential sections. They are often the financiers, indus-
trialists and members of the higher professions. "But they are
crucially lacking in ancestry, for the lower-upper class members are
'parvenues.' They have a slightly higher average income than the
upper-upper class members . . . but their wealth was not sufficiently legitimated by a long tradition of upper-class behavior to
make them members of the upper-upper group."

The lower-middle class, by far the largest of these groups,
consists largely of small businessmen, clerical workers, other lower-
level white-collar workers and a few skilled workmen. Warner
describes these people as "being careful with their money, saving,
far-sighted, forever anxious about what their neighbors think and
continually concerned about respectability."

The upper-lower class consists of "honest workmen and the clean poor"; while the lower-lower class, composed of the semi-skilled and unskilled workers, is often thought by the other classes to be immoral and not respectable.

It is the middle class in which most of the Jews who reside in suburbia may be classified. The mass-produced suburbs built since 1946 consist in the main of lower-middle-class families. In the older suburbs of New England and the Midwest, an admixture of both upper- and lower-middle-class Jewish families may be found. In Westchester County and several of the old well-established suburban areas of Long Island, Jewish lower-upper families reside in great numbers.

The movement of Jews and other ethnic groups from one urban section to another is well known. This mobility has, in the main, resulted from an upgrading in economic status. The immigrant generation was huddled together in a community-within-a-community in that section of a city where rentals were lowest. They superseded earlier immigrant groups whose economic condition had improved sufficiently to enable them to move from these sections. This was characteristic of the Jews in the Eastern seaboard cities, such as New York, Boston, Philadelphia and Baltimore. Midwestern cities like Cleveland, Detroit, Cincinnati and Chicago, as well as the younger city of Minneapolis, also had their immigrant areas in which particular ethnic groups lived because (1) this was all they could afford; (2) they were thus among their own kind and could establish their synagogues, Hebrew schools, fraternal and philanthropic organizations along patterns they knew in the "old country"; and (3) better sections of the city were nearly always closed to them through prejudice against "foreigners." In Los Angeles, the earliest Jewish residents, though not all immigrants, established their own community in Boyle's Heights. This too became a ghetto area, self-sufficient and quite satisfactory for its ever-increasing numbers of Jewish residents.

As their economic conditions improved, whole Jewish communities moved to other and better areas within the big city. Rented homes gave way to private homes now owned by these first and second generation Jews. This process of transplantation within the metropolis took on the force of a tidal wave during and immediately following World War II. Yet each new section could be regarded as a ghetto—glorified perhaps, but still a ghetto.

As the Jewish communities grew, these Jewish sections divided, amoeba-like, into two or more sections. The more affluent families lived in one section and developed their own synagogues and schools, while those whose economic fortunes were less favorable moved to another. In Cleveland, for example, Jews who originally resided on the lower East Side moved either to the 105th Street area or to the Kinsman Avenue development. Each was, in fact, a separate Jewish community. In Minneapolis, Jews moved from the area of Sixth Avenue—Lyndale Avenue, North, to the Homewood area on the North Side or to the southwest side of the city. In Chicago, Jews developed three major areas—Douglas Boulevard, the South Side and the North Side. In Boston, they moved from the South, West or North End to Chelsea, Roxbury or Dorchester. In Los Angeles, many of the families from Boyle's Heights moved into other sections of Los Angeles or, if they could afford it, into another glorified ghetto area like that centering on Fairfax and Wilshire Boulevard.

In each instance, of course, some Jews remained in the old neighborhood. Synagogues, settlement houses, ladies groups, Free Loan Societies and similar organizations were maintained in the old area, where they constitute the core of a weakening segment of Jewish community life. Thus, though the central agencies, the fund-raising organizations and the community councils brought the Jewish community into a strong organizational unit, certain differences remained in economic status, national origin or cultural background between different segments of that community.

Since 1946, the reasons for the mobility of Jews into the suburbs appear to have changed. Though mobility must certainly be correlated positively with vastly improved economic status, this is no longer the only reason.

Riesman's [15] suggestion that there appears to be a "revolt against the city and industrialism" ought not to be minimized. Jews, like other Americans, have come to feel that the relaxed life is more desirable than the hurried, tumultuous existence so often associated with the big city.

The new Jewish suburbanites believe, too, that since we are all Americans, it is not good for Jews—or any other ethnic or religious group—to live together, forming their own community. They *fear* segregation, in contrast to their parents, who in many cases sought it. Although they discover, much to their surprise, that even in suburbia they are often surrounded by other Jewish families, they know that they have not openly sought segregation. All-Jewish neighborhoods frequently result from the withdrawal of non-Jews from the neighborhood.

As noted elsewhere,[16] these suburbanites do not immediately, upon moving into a suburb, organize a synagogue for public worship. Jews in many suburbs do not find it necessary to build a house of worship in their newly established community. Often these families retain their affiliation with the "old" synagogue or temple in the city from which they have recently moved.

St. Louis Park (Minnesota), which built its first temple only this year, provides an excellent example of this way of thinking. The Jews' most important reasons for building a synagogue at all were, I believe, the Jewish educational needs of their children and the surprise (and shock) of their non-Jewish neighbors, who had *expected* them to build at least a modest synagogue. These Jews are *not* irreligious. They live sufficiently close to the big city to be able to attend services in any synagogue or temple of their choice—and they have done so. These suburbanites identify themselves with the Jewish people completely and wholeheartedly. Few really seek to escape from Judaism, nor do they feel compelled to live within a wholly Jewish environment.

The uniqueness of present-day Jewish suburbanites, then, is associated with the fact that they, unlike their fathers' generation, feel "at home" and secure in their Americanism.

The American Jew is convinced that the virulent form of anti-Semitism that had for so many decades been natural to Russia, Poland, Rumania and Germany will not manifest itself here. He is well aware of the attempts of such organizations as the Ku Klux Klan, the Silver Shirts and America First to spread their poisonous philosophy into the bloodstream of the nation, yet he does not regard them as typical of America. He knows that America is different because its Constitution, with its emphasis upon the equality of all men before the law and its recognition of man's inalienable rights to life, liberty and the pursuit of happiness, is unique among the nations of the world. He is aware of the many minorities that comprise this nation and accepts the fact that each has contributed its manpower and talents toward the nation's growth and development.

The Jew is even less fearful of overt anti-Semitism today because he has noted that, since World War II, differences in religion are more than ever being accepted by all Americans as quite normal and even right for this nation. The Jew believes that this nation is sufficiently young for most of its citizens to remember that all Americans were immigrants and foreigners only a few generations ago. It matters little, therefore, if particular groups or even individuals speak and act as if they and they alone are Americans.

The generally improved economic status of the American people is credited with having brought about a marked reduction in anti-Jewish prejudice. The reasoning follows this course: "When times are good, people are usually pleased with themselves and with their neighbors. There is little to complain about. However, when depressions or recessions set in and jobs become scarce, people begin to worry, and soon they look for someone or something to blame. The Jew then becomes the scapegoat. It is in a time of economic scarcity and competition for work that anti-Semitism is greatest."

Whether or not this reasoning is wholly true, it is certainly evident to the Jew that when jobs are plentiful and wages are high, tensions and prejudices lessen. This latter condition has generally applied since the conclusion of World War II.

The mass annihilations that occurred during the war years were followed by the Nuremberg trials, in which war criminals who were guilty of incomparable barbarities and cruelties were publicly tried and even punished. These trials, which brought their deeds to the attention of the world, perhaps indirectly taught men to recoil from such bestiality. Anti-Semitism, which had so frequently expressed itself in those forms, was now less overtly expressed or acted upon. One who, as a result of his prejudices, performs acts of violence is generally regarded as uncivilized.

On the other hand, although anti-Jewishness is less frequently expressed in these violent forms, American Jews are well aware of a variety of other forms that this bias is presently taking. These I shall discuss in later chapters.

The Jew is not only a member of a religious minority, but also part of the *majority* of Americans known as the middle class. Jews identify and are themselves identified with this class in all matters except religion, where it is assumed that they will have a religious affiliation of their own. In fact, as Herberg[17] has pointed out, "to be a Protestant, a Catholic or a Jew are today the alternative ways of being an American."

There are few foreign-born Jews in America today; estimates indicate that 75 to 80 per cent are native-born. Evidence gathered in three widely separated American communities indicates that 83 per cent of the Jews in Washington, D.C., 78 per cent of those in Des Moines, Iowa, and 77 per cent of those in Canton, Ohio, are native-born. The studies for the first two communities were made in 1956; the latter figure was ascertained in 1955.[18] The proportion of foreign-born Jews becomes smaller with the passing of each decade. Identification of Jews as "foreigners" no longer really exists.

As for educational background, all evidence points to the high standard of American Jews in this respect. Forty-one per cent of the Jews in Washington have attended a college or post-graduate school, while 37 per cent of Des Moines' Jews had the benefit of similar higher education. Thirty-six per cent of the Jews in Canton, had attended a first-year college course as of 1955, compared with but 12 per cent of the general population. In Des Moines, twice as many Jews (38 per cent) attended college as the general population (19 per cent).[19]

Finally, Jewish youths today feel more secure than ever before

because they were members of the armed forces in World War II
and fought this nation's wars in all parts of the world with America's
other sons. Jew and non-Jew fought and lived side by side during
those sad years. As a consequence, these boys have come to know
each other better than ever before. Even if this rapport was not
generally continued after their military service, it did, at the very
least, help to create a healthy mutual respect, and this fact is certainly not to be regarded lightly.

America is the home of American Jews. They know that they
are secure in this land by right and *not* by sufferance. Economically,
socially, educationally and psychologically, the American Jew feels
that America is his land, and that he is as much American as is
anyone else. He does not become as upset and disturbed about
many things that two decades ago would have caused him no end
of anguish. Bad jokes about Jews or unprincipled attacks upon him
or his religion may cause him at times to smile, at other times, to
strike back directly and forcefully, through his own organizations
and in his own way. When he discovers that any minority of any
class, color, nationality or religion is under unwarranted attack, he
speaks out forthrightly, precisely because his image of America is
being distorted by others.

When the American Jew feels that he is being deprived of his
constitutional rights to live and work or to establish his house of
worship where he chooses, he does not hesitate to use every legal
means to correct the situation. He assumes that the relaxed, fashionable, status-giving life supposedly to be lived in suburbia is as much
his due as it is the privilege of any other American who can afford
it. In turn, the suburb is helping to produce marked changes in
the basic structures of the Jewish family and its educational, political, religious, cultural and social life.

Chapter 2   Saga of the Suburbs

The meaning of what was happening was that America was resettling itself, wherever it could, looking for open spaces and "grass for the children to walk on," and better schools and a garage for the car and a closer-knit community. . . . The whole process was a kind of development by sprawl.[1]

The many small towns that form a huge ring around the metropolis are spatially separated from the central city, but psychologically they are very much part of it. These suburbs are directly influenced by the metropolitan community and are dependent upon it as a source of goods, services and jobs. The character of the suburb—the kind of homes that are erected, the social and cultural composition of the suburb, and the interests of the people who inhabit it—is inescapably affected by the nature of the metropolis.

Let us look in detail at seven metropolitan areas and certain of their suburbs throughout the United States:

(1) Boston, Massachusetts, with the particular reference to the contiguous suburb of Newton;

(2) New York City and one of its most recently developed suburbs, Levittown, Long Island;

(3) Cleveland, Ohio, and its semi-industrial suburb, Euclid;

(4) Washington, D.C., with specific reference to the three major suburban communities—Silver Spring, Bethesda and Chevy Chase—located in adjacent Montgomery County, Maryland;

(5) Chicago, Illinois, to which so many of the male residents of the suburb, Skokie, commute daily;

(6) Minneapolis, Minnesota, from which over five thousand Jews have moved to suburban St. Louis Park; and

(7) Los Angeles, California, with its myriad of little suburban

communities, the newest of which are located in the San Gabriel Valley.

These areas and specific suburbs within them were chosen because they differ from each other in many ways—the location, size and age of the suburb; the characteristics of the general population within the area; the general economic and cultural levels of the residents; the status-giving quality associated with the suburb; and its general character as, in whole or in part, residential or industrial. These factors have in large measure influenced both the growth and development of these suburbs and the quality and character of Jewish communal life within them.

Beyond these seven areas, dozens of other suburban communities in which Jewish families live have also been examined in preparation for this study. I have drawn on information secured from their leadership, both religious and lay, wherever such material adds depth to our understanding of Jews in suburbia.

I. NEWTON, MASSACHUSETTS

The metropolis of the New England area is, of course, Boston. Known as the heart of New England, it is perhaps even better known as the "Hub of the Universe"—so rich are its historical, cultural, commercial and religious assets. With a tradition that dates back to the year 1630, Boston is the capital of the Commonwealth of Massachusetts and the oldest major city in the nation. Proud of its many contributions to the growth and development of the American democratic tradition, Boston is also one of the world's foremost educational centers: Harvard University, Massachusetts Institute of Technology, Radcliffe, Wellesley, Simmons, Tufts, Boston University, Northeastern University, Boston College and Brandeis University are located in Boston or in the suburban ring just outside the city.

The metropolitan Boston area comprises a population of 2,600,-000 in one hundred cities and suburbs—all within a twenty-five-mile radius of Beacon Hill. One and three-quarter million people are thus considered *both* Bostonians *and* residents of suburbs and cities adjacent to the Hub.

Pre-eminent as an industrial, commercial and research center, Boston is a universally recognized leader in the shoe industry and a manufacturer of myriad other products. It possesses a fine natural harbor, with international shipping facilities, deep-sea fisheries and commercial potentials. With these resources, the Boston area in its early years attracted hundreds of thousands of immigrants. Boston's past is represented by the proper Bostonians, who now constitute but a small segment of its varied population. The Irish comprise about three-fourths of the city's total population. The Jews number about 140,000. Italians, Poles, Negroes and other minority groups all live close together in this major city area.

Though there is no record of Jewish settlement in Boston before 1842, the first Jewish synagogue is known to have been established in that year. From those early days, Jews have been intimately associated with the cultural, economic and spiritual growth and development of the city.

Jews have lived in just about every section of the city. The West End, South End and North End of Boston became the first homes for thousands of the East European Jewish immigrants who, beginning with the 1890's, converted these areas into flourishing Jewish communities. The immigrants and their sons earned their livelihood as peddlers, merchants and small manufacturers in the shoe, garment and wool industries. As they prospered, many moved into other and better areas in or around Boston. Chelsea and Lynn became large centers of Jewish community life, as did Cambridge, directly across the Charles River. Jewish families moved into the Roxbury and Dorchester sections of Boston, and there established a community within a community in which Jews could live as Jews and Americans, with a sense of at-homeness in each culture.

The sons of immigrant fathers, now grown to manhood and often well-established in the world of commerce, improved their comfort and status by moving into these sections. Immediately after World War I, a few of the more adventurous and affluent moved on to the status-giving suburb of Brookline, where they established synagogues, Hebrew schools and social and cultural organizations that helped to enrich their lives.

Most of the breadwinners, wherever their homes, maintained their businesses in the city of Boston. There they shopped; and there they expressed their love of music, the theatre and forums, and their interest and philanthropic concern for the whole community. They remained Bostonians, no matter where they resided.

Fewer than a dozen Jewish families are known to have resided in the suburb of Newton in post-Civil War days. The number increased in limited degree by the early 1900's, and after 1930, as the Depression waned, the growth of Newton's Jewish community became noticeable.

Newton is the largest of Boston's numerous suburbs: its population of 89,000 (1958) has increased by 11 per cent since 1946. With its fourteen "villages" or divisions, Newton may be classified by some as a metropolis because of its size. It is basically a residential area, just eight miles from Boston, in which a large proportion of that city's business and professional men and their families live. Whether they use the railroad trains, the bus, street car service or their own automobiles, Newton's residents are primarily commuters.

Built on seven hills, Newton is almost completely surrounded by the Charles River. Replete with many excellent shopping centers, small businesses and branches of larger, in-town retail establishments, the city is justly famed for its beautiful homes and long avenues, for the natural beauty of its gardens, parks, hills, streams, shaded streets and rolling terrain and for its excellent school system —67 per cent of its high school graduates go on to college every fall. Newton now has twenty-six elementary schools, five junior high schools, one high school (another is under construction), a technical-vocational school and a junior college, with a total school enrollment of 16,863 pupils (1958).

Newton has a long, honorable history. As early as 1631, it was settled and fortified. In those days, it consisted of a tract of land with dwellings scattered here and there. During the Revolutionary War, the men of Newton joined in the fight for independence. They were among those who gained fame at Lexington and Concord and went on to share the hardships that the crude army led by George Washington endured.

Today, in the eyes of Boston's populace, Newton stands for prosperity and success. It signifies elegance and beauty: the residents call it "The Garden City." It is a community of vigorous people and good homes, located west of Boston and easily accessible to it by excellent roads. Ninety-three per cent of the total area is zoned for residences. There are an estimated forty thousand automobiles in Newton, or one car for every two people.

Newton's eighteen square miles are largely populated by native-born Americans; in fact, 87 per cent of Newton's population is native-born. Forty per cent of its population is Catholic; 36 per cent, Protestant; and 22 per cent, Jewish. The religious affiliation of the other two per cent is unknown.[2]

Newton attracts many new residents because of the reputed excellence of its public school system. It spends more money for education in proportion to its school population than do most other American cities: $327.50 per pupil for its primary and secondary schools, or a little more than 32¢ of every tax dollar. There is one teacher for every twenty-two pupils in average attendance; this compares with an average of one for every twenty-four in other cities of its size.

There are forty-seven churches and synagogues in Newton. (The first church was organized in 1633.) Here also is the Andover-Newton Theological School (Congregationalist-Baptist), organized in 1825, which today is recognized as one of the greatest theological seminaries in the liberal tradition.

Relations between clergymen of different faiths have been excellent. A friendly, neighborly and ofttimes brotherly attitude is clearly in evidence. The Rabbis of Newton are members of the Newton Ministers Association by invitation of the Protestant ministers; in fact, the Association recently changed its name to "The Newton Ministers and Rabbis Association." Catholic clerics, though cooperative, are not officially members of this organization, but relations between individual Catholic and Jewish clerics within the community are generally friendly.

For many years, Newton has enjoyed the reputation of being peopled by upper-middle-class and wealthy residents. Status could be acquired by taking up residence there. The Jewish community is generally regarded as "well-off," even though there are signs that many Jewish families can be classified no higher economically than lower-middle class.

Though we have no certain means of identifying the earliest Jewish residents of Newton, there is reason to believe that three of the families recorded in Newton's first directory in 1868 may have been Jews. Individual Jews and their families have surely lived in Newton since post-Civil War days. There is no evidence, however, that any *organized* Jewish life existed in Newton before 1898, when Benjamin Gilfix, who had recently landed in New York City as an immigrant from Kiev, Russia, moved to Newton after a brief sojourn in Boston. According to Philip Gilfix, son of Benjamin, the Gilfixes found two Jewish families already in residence in the old Nonantum district in Newton, the only area in which Benjamin Gilfix could obtain a license from the city to establish a scrap metal yard. There in the midst of Irish, French and Italian residents (mostly Irish), the Gilfix family established itself.

"I can remember vividly walking home on Friday nights from the synagogue after it was built in 1912, when the Irish youngsters would run after us Jews, throw stones, call us the most awful names you can think of, like 'Christ Killers,' 'damned Jews'; and we would defend ourselves. It was one fight after another. Strangely, despite these fights, the parents were usually friendly. The Jews were held in esteem by the city officials. When the synagogue, Congregation Agudus Achim Anshei Sfard, was built on Adams Street, Hon. John W. Weeks, who was the Secretary of War, contributed to its support. From the time that my father came to Newton, we observed our traditional practices and prayed at home. That was in accordance with Jewish tradition.

"Most of the early Jews in Newton whom we knew were in the same business—or they had tailor shops or retail groceries. The

Fried family had a retail department store of general merchandise. There was Alexander Fox, who had a drug store, established, I think, in 1902. The Perlmutter family were in the drygoods business. We were all in the Nonantum area. We knew of a Jewish tailor, Jacob Brookman, who lived in Auburndale. He had lived there since 1900. Mr. Sam Schwartz, a hardware merchant, was also an early settler in Newton.

"As our economic status improved, we got nicer things for our homes and lived better, but all in all, it was a good Jewish life always.

"There never was any real association between the Jewish and non-Jewish communities. We lived pretty much isolated from each other. Our relations were, in the main, through business or not at all. They knew we were here. They knew we were honest people. But that is really all they knew about us.

"The Jews in Nonantum lived within one-half mile of each other. We were visited by 'meshulachim' [representatives of various Jewish academies of learning who came to Jewish communities throughout America for the primary purpose of collecting funds for their support]. We families each contributed to them whatever we could. Most frequently, they stopped at my parents' home over the Sabbath. We were happy to provide them with room and board and, in return, only asked that they make a 'few remarks' about the portion of the Torah [Bible] that was read in the synagogue on the Sabbath or report on Jewish life generally. We were so anxious to hear a word of Torah.

"Jews began moving into Newton in small numbers after World War I, and in ever-increasing numbers since then. Around 1918, I remember that we Jews used to say that there were 170 Jewish people in Newton. It is difficult to realize that today there are as many as twenty thousand Jews in Newton."

In the 1920's, additional Jewish families moved into Newton but not into the older Nonantum area. Rather, they purchased homes in the more residential villages known as Newton and Newton Centre. Here their children were reared in the atmosphere of a staid New England town, while their businesses flourished in the metropolis. The religious affiliations of these new residents remained with synagogues and temples in Boston.

People were not satisfied that their children's religious education was adequate under these conditions. Distance and school schedules made it exceedingly difficult for them to attend religious school classes in Boston with any regularity. With this fact primarily in mind, a second congregation was organized in Newton in 1935. It affiliated with the Conservative movement in American Judaism (the older Agudas Achim congregation was orthodox) and was officially named Temple Emanuel.

Since 1946, the Jewish community in Newton has doubled in size. Its greatest growth began in 1950; and for two years, 1954 and 1955, the Jewish population grew by approximately 2,500 annually. As of January 1, 1958, it numbered 6,028 Jewish families, or 21,700 persons.[3]

Before 1950, most of Newton's Jewish residents came from the town of Chelsea, north of Boston. Since then, however, the largest number have come from others of the cluster of towns and villages in and around Boston, as well as from the heart of the city itself.

From July 1, 1954, through December 31, 1955, a total of 353 Jewish families coming from the environs of Boston and other areas established their homes in Newton. Brookline, the status-giving suburb immediately adjacent to Boston, provided 102 families. Thirty-eight families moved from Dorchester, a rapidly deteriorating neighborhood of Boston. Brighton, another area bordering on Boston, provided twenty-nine families. Roxbury contributed twenty-seven.[4]

On the other hand, since 1946 the Roxbury and Dorchester areas—two of the earliest Jewish communities—have lost great numbers of their Jewish families. In 1945, there were 15,500 Jews in Roxbury: by 1955, these had dwindled to 8,574. The decline in this area within the past two years may best be described as a flight. In Dorchester, there were 32,161 Jews in 1945; by 1955, the number had been reduced to 29,698.[5] Here, too, vast numbers of Jews in the past several years have moved to new residences in the many suburbs around Boston, including Newton.

Thirty-one per cent (1,321) of the total number of homes purchased in Newton in 1955 and 35 per cent (1,096) of those purchased in 1956 were bought by Jewish families. Of these, the largest segment were in the $20,000-$30,000 [6] class (177 homes in 1955 and 161 in 1956). In the $30,000-$40,000 classification, Jewish families purchased fifty-four homes in 1955 and sixty-one in 1956.

Of the 161 homes in the $10,000-$20,000 category purchased in 1955, 81.2 per cent of the price was covered by a mortgage. In 1956, of 126 houses in the same cost bracket, 72 per cent of the cost price was covered by a mortgage. In the two years together, homes in the $20,000-$30,000 classification were 60 per cent mortgaged.

The figures are significant since it is frequently assumed that only the wealthy moved into Newton, with the implication that these new residents can well afford their new homes. This appears to be true with respect to the majority of those new residents whose mortgages are placed at 60 per cent (for various reasons, it is more economical to carry this size mortgage than to invest a large sum of money in a home).

Mortgages of 72 per cent to 82 per cent in the lower cost bracket indicate, however, that many a newcomer to Newton is not as affluent as he is reputed to be. Heavy mortgage payments, the high cost of home maintenance and costs involved in rearing a growing family may place him under great financial pressures.

Though Newton looks forward to continued growth, there is reason to believe that the rate of growth will decrease. Land is becoming less available and zoning requirements more rigorous. The school population has rocketed a staggering 40 per cent since 1947, and additional school buildings are being erected because crowding is evident. The attraction of Newton's noted school system is thus considerably reduced—especially for Jewish parents, with their characteristic desire to provide the best possible education for their children.

Meanwhile, in even newer suburban community developments, such as Weston, Natick, Framingham, Sharon, Belmont, Lexington and Arlington, to name but a few in the immediate vicinity, the cost of homes appears to be less than in Newton. These communities seem likely to reduce the number of new residents moving to Newton.

We shall return to Newton in succeeding chapters to discuss other phases of this large suburb, particularly its relationship to its Jewish residents.

II. LEVITTOWN, NEW YORK

More Jews live in New York City than in any other city or country—including Israel—in the whole world!

In 1654 the first Sephardic Jews arrived in what was then known as New Amsterdam and, after a heart-breaking experience with Governor Peter Stuyvesant, gained the right to take up residence there. For the next three centuries Jews have poured into the world's largest city in ever-increasing numbers. Today, 2,018,-000 Jews reside in its five boroughs—approximately one-quarter of New York's total population.

New York City's position as the business and cultural center of America is undisputed. The contributions which Jews have made to its growth in all fields of endeavor—financial, cultural, social, educational, political and spiritual—are recorded on the pages of this nation's history.

The early Jewish immigrants lived for years on the lower East Side of Manhattan, where they established a community of interest despite inadequate housing conditions, economic impoverishment and an often hostile environment. Though mostly unskilled workers, obliged to eke out a livelihood under conditions that bordered on the primitive, this people did not ignore or forget its rich religious and cultural heritage. It established Hebrew schools (Yeshivos) for the study of Hebraic lore, homes for the aged and the indigent, and an Education Alliance in which young and old could socialize and become Americanized. Despite their narrow setting, New York's East Side Jews brought positive influences to bear on all phases of the life of the great metropolis. Its sons and daughters enriched the culture of America by their gifts of song, drama, art, poetry and music, even as they contributed to the economic and political growth of New York.

The ever-expanding Jewish population flowed over into Harlem, the Bronx and Brooklyn, and as soon as it was financially possible, settled Jewish families moved from the East Side to these other areas. The more affluent moved up to Riverside Drive and Washington Heights. Some who could afford it even chose to move out into Westchester County, with its many model suburban communities.

During the 1920's, with the general improvement of financial conditions, the lot of Jews also improved. Many Jewish families, now middle class, considered themselves happy because they could afford the good things of life, both material and cultural. More and more sons and daughters were given the opportunity to receive college and university education. Former skilled or semi-skilled workers in the garment and other industries were becoming employers and opening their own factories. It was a thrilling experience for these erstwhile foreigners to acquire status within one generation.

The economic holocaust which hit the nation beginning in October, 1929, played havoc with these Jewish entrepreneurs as it did with all businessmen. Retrenchment was the order of the day. Through the next decade, which, at its close, found this nation on the brink of war with Nazi Germany, conditions were difficult indeed. When America finally engaged in World War II, Jewish families, like all other American families, were disrupted when sons entered the armed services. On the local scene, the effort to keep family together occupied the parents' attention. Newly acquired daughters-in-law and grandchildren were often housed in apartments and homes already filled beyond their normal capacity.

G.I.'s returning to civilian life at the conclusion of the war were determined to establish their own families in homes of their own. The Federal government helped to make this possible by providing loans to encourage enterprising builders to erect new housing facilities as quickly as possible.

At this critical moment in American history, new and even exciting suburban towns were conceived and established, particularly on Long Island. Areas that had formerly been regarded as "exclusive" were now swiftly taken over for mass-produced housing. To these new suburbs flocked thousands of young families, including, of course, the young Jews who had lived hitherto in the three most crowded areas of New York City—Manhattan, the Bronx and Brooklyn. Among these modern suburbs is the noted suburb of Levittown, product of the imagination of William J. Levitt, home builder extraordinary.

The acute housing shortage and the availability of veterans' loans led to the idea that, by the use of mass production methods, vast quantities of homes could be erected and either rented or sold at a moderate price to veterans only. Casting about for land on which to undertake this program, William Levitt and his sons secured four thousand acres of potato land located near and governed by the town of Hempstead (Nassau County), about twenty-five miles from New York City. There, in September, 1947, the town to which they gave their name came into being. During the first year, 2,000 Cape Cod houses were erected and rented to veterans only. In 1948, 4,000 more such houses were built. Thereafter, the Levitts built ranch houses. From 1947 through 1951, they built 17,447 single-family homes on the flat, former potato field.

The new residents of Levittown were all servicemen who had but recently been discharged from the service. Most couples had been married only a year or two. A few had one child and were expecting their second. The Levittown homes were designed for their price range. The first Cape Cod houses sold for $6,900; the first ranch houses for $9,500. The rental charged for the first three hundred Cape Cod houses was $65.00 a month.

These mass-produced homes proved to be little short of revolutionary. Although the homes were all of the same basic design with but minor variations, the builders encouraged the new owners to change and alter houses as they saw fit. Many families did alter them, even adding new rooms, and numerous contractors specialized in such alterations.

Six "village greens" were established, plus twenty-five play fields, twelve ball fields, nine community swimming pools and a community hall. School building sites were fixed, and the Levitts provided church sites gratuitously for organized church and synagogue groups.

Levittown has made history because: (1) It was a mass-produced town, planned and designed by private builders and built with the aid of Federal funds. (2) Its growth was phenomenal. In 1945, there were only 721 people in the 7.3-square-mile area known as Levittown. Today it has a population of 82,000, living in 21,000 privately owned homes. (3) Its residents are primarily young, former servicemen, their wives and young children. Their two major interests are homes and children. (4) Though more than half of Levittown's population is less than seventeen years old, there is no evidence of juvenile delinquency. A well-organized and well-executed youth program is actively supported by the community through its churches, synagogues and schools, and its park and playground programs. Some eighteen hundred boys took part in the town's Little League baseball program in 1957. (5) Levittown has undertaken a unique educational program for both children and parents. The interest in adult education runs high, with one hundred eighty different courses offered for adults. In 1956, there were one hundred special-interest organizations in the community. And Levittown's adults like to read. "Forty-four thousand books in Levittown's library have a circulation three times the national average." [7]

Before 1946, Nassau County was predominantly composed of Protestants. In 1957, 45 per cent of Levittown's population was Catholic, 40 per cent was Protestant and 13 per cent was Jewish.[8] Studies made by Professor Herbert Rosenbaum of Hofstra College indicate that since World War II, 60 per cent of the new families moving into Nassau County (of which Levittown is but one community) are Catholic, 20 per cent are Protestant and the remaining 20 per cent are Jewish. There are few Negroes or other non-whites in Nassau County suburbs.

Jewish community leaders estimate that most of the Jewish heads of households are employed by others, that they are in the main white-collar businessmen and that practically all men commute daily to New York City. It is believed that these people earn, in general, between $7,500-$8,500 annually (July, 1957, estimate). Their homes, including alterations, are said to be in the $12,000 class, with 75 per cent of the cost in the form of a mortgage. These Jewish families, according to the town's rabbinic leaders, have three or more children.

Levittown's economic life is shaped and molded—as are the contiguous suburbs of Hicksville, Manorhaven, Farmingdale and Greenlawn—by the four large plants of the Republic Aviation Corporation located nearby. Many of Levittown's new residents depend upon this company or others in the vicinity for their livelihood.

Levittown has been identified in the public mind as "a creature of industrialism." [9] This, the first mass-produced, uniform-design suburb in Nassau County, provides ample rewards for research as well as for sympathetic understanding. We shall examine it in much closer detail in Chapter 4.

III. EUCLID, OHIO

Cleveland, Ohio, is America's seventh largest city and one of the nation's biggest steel-producing and ore-handling centers. It ranks tenth in metropolitan area size, with a total population of almost one and one-half million. Located on the shore of Lake Erie, Cleveland is one of the world's greatest industrial and manufacturing centers, providing many and varied opportunities for economic development.

The history of Cleveland's Jewish community dates back to 1837, when the first Jew settled there. Because of the city's industrial importance, Cleveland has attracted many Jewish settlers through the years. Its spectacular growth as a Jewish community of first magnitude really began in 1881, when Russian Jewish refugees took up residence there. The Jewish community in the Cleveland metropolitan area now totals 85,000 persons.

Largely engaged in manufacturing and retail businesses, Jews have established themselves in every phase of the city's life. From the first, while they were concentrated on Cleveland's lower East Side—and continuing through the years—the Jews have maintained their own religious, cultural, social and philanthropic institutions on so high a plane that the larger community has regarded them with respect and even admiration. And Cleveland's Jews are civic-minded: they have participated in all efforts tending to improve the life of the total community. The growing affluence of the Jewish community following World War I led first to the development of the East 105th Street and the Kinsman areas, so that they became almost all-Jewish neighborhoods. As has already been noted, the influx of Negro workers and their families from the South hastened the movement of Jewish families to the Heights,[10] where, in the early twenties, they took up residence in considerable number in four truly beautiful suburban communities: Shaker Heights, University Heights, Cleveland Heights and East Cleveland. Of these, Shaker Heights has the highest average family "buying income," $16,215 a year. University Heights, Cleveland Heights and East Cleveland follow in that order. The annual income of residents of another suburb, Euclid, is $8,355. In these five suburbs about 85 per cent of all of Cleveland's Jews reside.

This study will focus especially on Euclid because that city is in a sense isolated from the rest of the community. It also contains gigantic factories and plants, as contrasted with the Heights suburbs, which are all residential in character. Euclid is generally regarded comparatively as a "workingman's suburb."

Euclid is located on the shore of Lake Erie, just east of the metropolis and only a fifteen-minute drive from Cleveland's Public Square. The freeway, a superhighway which runs parallel to the lakeshore, has cut the driving time to the city markedly. (This road, which runs through Euclid, continues east and joins the New York Thruway, leading on to New York and New England.) Euclid's

accessibility to Cleveland might lead one to assume that it has
no character of its own—that it is, in fact, just another of Cleveland's numerous dormitory suburbs. But this is not quite so. It is,
in certain ways, different from other suburbs which surround the
metropolitan area. It exhibits a degree of psychological separation
paralleling its physical separation.[11]

This suburb is indeed different, for it is both a residential and
an industrial city. An increasing number of major industries are
located in Euclid; these employ many skilled and semi-skilled workers who need not be commuters in order to earn a livelihood. Euclid
is also different in that it has little or no relationship with those
other Cleveland suburbs located on the Heights, southeast of
Cleveland.

The Jews who live on the Heights regard themselves as an integral part of the Cleveland Jewish community. Most of the
workers and leaders of the Jewish Community Federation of
Greater Cleveland and of practically all the other metropolitan
Jewish organizations reside there. Social welfare services offered by
the Jewish community are integrated into the Heights area. In
contrast, the Jews of Euclid appear to be inclined toward greater
autonomy. They do not turn to the Jewish Community Federation
as readily, and their organized Jewish life appears to center about
their own temple-center, with its religious, cultural and social program for young and old. Whatever assistance or expert counsel is
required by the temple-center is gladly provided by Cleveland's
Jewish Community Federation.

Whereas Jews move easily from one Heights suburb to another,
there is little mobility of families from the Heights to Euclid. The
majority of the new Jewish residents in Euclid are newly married
couples looking for an inexpensive apartment or a modest home.
There are many apartment buildings in the area for young couples,
particularly newlyweds.

Though they appear to be contented in Euclid and associate
themselves with the temple-center, B'nai B'rith, Jewish War Veterans, the temple Sisterhood or Brotherhood, Hadassah or Pioneer
Women, many families move to the Heights as soon as their finan-

cial situation improves. At present, there is some movement by Jewish families from Euclid to other small communities further east, among them Willowick, Willowby and Painesville, where real estate is less expensive. Painesville, just twenty miles east of Euclid, has begun to organize its own Jewish community. Euclid's more permanent residents are those who either have a business of their own in or very near the town or are employed in one of the local manufacturing plants.

Sixty thousand people reside in Euclid. The Jewish community numbers about 650 families, or 2,400 persons. Many of the heads of these households are World War II veterans.[12]

A housing project—the Briardale Community Project—built during the war and supported by the Federal government in order to provide low rental housing, attracted many veterans to Euclid at the close of the war. Among them were Jewish veterans and their wives, who took up residence in this and other private housing projects which were being completed in Euclid. The comparative low cost of housing was their chief inducement. Most homes were sold at an original purchase price of less than $10,000. Today, of course, their value has doubled.

Most of Euclid's Jewish families have formerly lived in the East 105th Street section of Cleveland or on the East Side generally. There are some, too, from the Kinsman area in the southeastern part of the city.

These young people are proud of their homes. Their own skill and ingenuity make possible numerous home improvements. Many of the men are skilled mechanics who utilize their knowledge by adding rooms to their homes or otherwise improving their property.

Although their homes are small and often heavily mortgaged, Euclid's Jewish families use them wisely and enjoy them fully. These people, who cannot afford luxuries or lavish entertaining, enjoy friendly socials, get-togethers and parties in their homes. Their synagogue is highly important to them. Two hundred and eighty families, or 43 per cent of the 650 families in Euclid, have affiliated with it according to its own report as of July, 1957. These members participate actively in temple life in all its phases.

Life is pleasant, even as it is earnest, for the residents of Euclid. Though comparatively few in number, its Jewish families have established themselves as respected citizens whose identification with their people and their synagogue is marked.

IV. MONTGOMERY COUNTY, MARYLAND

The capital of the United States, situated on the Potomac River, is something more than a beautiful city. Within the sixty-one square miles of the "District" live 870,000 people.[13] Within the metropolitan area of which Washington is the center, almost two million persons reside, 260,000 of whom are employed by the Federal government.[14] Well over one-half of the total population in the metropolitan area is dependent for its livelihood upon some position with the United States government. The remainder derive their livelihood through trade or professional dealings with government employees.

Despite its size and grandeur, the city could hardly provide adequate housing for so many families. The population—which includes those permanently established in Washington as merchants, tradesmen or professional persons, as well as the thousands of "transients" who must live within commuting distance of the capital— has overflowed, in the main, into the Maryland counties of Montgomery and Prince Georges, which lie adjacent to the District. Still other families have moved further out, many to the suburbs of the adjoining state of Virginia.

Movement into the suburbs results not only from the marked increase in population, but also from the great increase in the proportion of Negroes in the District. It is estimated that almost one-half of Washington's population is Negro. In the face of this influx, the middle-class whites have moved to the suburbs, while Negroes, to whom housing in the suburbs has been "unavailable," have moved into the heart of the city of Washington.

Federal workers are faced with very special problems of social adjustment. They are often newcomers to the community, and many regard themselves as transients, living temporarily in the environs of Washington but likely to be transferred to other posts at any time or even to learn that their jobs have been terminated. In other cases, because of the nature of the work in which the husband or wife is engaged, social contacts and friendships are frequently discouraged.

Jews have resided in Washington since at least 1849. They have established themselves as respected citizens, whose contributions to the cultural and spiritual life of the community have been notable. For years they maintained an integrated Jewish community in the very center of the city. Until post-World War II days, this remained the heart of the District's Jewish community.

Living in the very nexus in which the nation's major political decisions are made, Jews naturally took a marked interest in legislation associated with the nation's political and diplomatic affairs. These are well-educated people, in the main. "Nine out of ten persons, aged 25 or over . . . have had some high school training, and over half, at least a year of college. Almost a quarter of the total had some college work [15] beyond the four year undergraduate course." Over a half of Montgomery County's Jewish adults have done graduate work in some college or university.[16]

Of special interest is the fact that almost a third of the Jews in the Washington area are government employees. About one-half of these are professionally trained social scientists, men and women who possess special technological skills and scientific training.

We focus our attention upon the Jews who reside in Montgomery County not only because they live in suburban communities, but also because these Federal employees, so many of whom have unusual skills and abilities, have come to this area from every state in the Union.

Montgomery County is contiguous to Washington, and is considered part of the metropolitan area. It is often spoken of as the capital's dormitory. Certain facts concerning the Jews who reside in

Montgomery County will help us to understand them and the suburban communities in which they live:

Eleven and three-tenths per cent—or 27,000 persons—of the county's total population is Jewish. Over 80 per cent of the Jews in the entire Washington area are native-born, and the same proportion appears to hold true for the Jewish population of Montgomery County. One-third of the Jewish population have moved into the Washington metropolitan area since 1945.[17]

Fifty-two and three-tenths per cent of the Jewish population of Montgomery County have had seventeen years or more of schooling.[18] Over half of the adults, in other words, have gone beyond a four-year college or university course to receive higher degrees and specialized training in some advanced field.

Thirty-nine per cent of the Jews of Montgomery County are under fifteen years of age; 18.4 per cent are twenty-five to thirty-four; and 31.5 per cent are thirty-five to fifty-four. Only 3.4 per cent of the county's Jewish population is fifty-five or over.[19]

There are four Conservative congregations, one Reform temple and no Orthodox synagogues in Montgomery County. Forty-six and one-tenth per cent of all Jewish families in this county are affiliated with a synagogue. Specifically, 31.7 per cent belong to a Conservative congregation, 4.2 per cent to a Reform temple, 5.4 per cent to an Orthodox metropolitan congregation and 4.8 per cent claim some "other" congregational affiliation.

The median Jewish family income in Montgomery County ranges from $7,000 to $10,000. Almost one-fifth of all the families have an income of less than $7,000.

The status-giving suburb in Montgomery County is Chevy Chase. It possesses some of the finest homes in the area and is famed for the many top-flight Federal employees in key governmental positions who reside there. Its prestige is sufficiently high that high-middle-class homes can be located immediately adjacent to the homes of Negroes in what is regarded as a "depressed area" without loss of status. There are, in fact, no really poor whites in this area. There is little opposition to integration of Negroes and whites;

a program of gradual integration is presently being carried out with considerable success.

Chevy Chase and Bethesda, two of the finest and most affluent suburban communities, just minutes away from the city of Washington, had between them no more than 150 Jewish families in 1946.

The story of the origin of the first temple in Montgomery County varies in minor degree from the pattern we have already described.

In 1946, the number of Jewish residents in the county was 1,875, or 550 families. Late in that year, philanthropic Mr. Sam Eig offered land for Jewish community purposes, provided that it was used to benefit *all* the Jewish families in the area. The Montgomery County Lodge B'nai B'rith and a small group of Jews from Bethesda and Chevy Chase who were interested in improving the Jewish education of their children decided that here was a project worthy of their best efforts.

These families envisioned a Kehillah-type (community) central Jewish organization through which all interests of the Jewish community would be channeled, in keeping with the ideas of Professor Mordecai M. Kaplan.[20] Believing that a central organization could meet all Jewish needs, they organized the Montgomery County Jewish Community and planned to erect a building to house their activities in Chevy Chase.

Within the several years that followed, 350 Jewish families in the fast-growing area signified their intention of joining this center-school-synagogue institution. Their goal was to develop a center-oriented program as well as a good religious school for their children. High Holy Day services, to meet this special need, were also arranged. The building program was completed in February, 1950, and the new center building was then occupied.

The Montgomery County Jewish Community (MCJC) provided a manifold program of activities—educational, religious and social. It was warmly received by the fast-increasing number of Jewish families who moved into the county.

By 1958, there were 500 member-families in the MCJC. They

include, however, a few residents from three nearby communities in the county, Silver Spring, Bethesda and Kensington. Chevy Chase, the deluxe "bedroom community" outside of Washington, has a Jewish population of about 4,000, or about 1,100 families. About 45 per cent of the Jews in Chevy Chase are thus affiliated with the MCJC, which is affiliated in turn with the Conservative Religious Movement.

A major portion of the MCJC's program is devoted to a program of youth activities. Allowing for duplications, about 1,200 different young people are enrolled in its club and other activities, which include parties, dances and group social programs.

Three hundred fifty pupils, or 67 per cent of the total number, are enrolled in the Sunday school (1958), with 170 pupils enrolled in its three-afternoons-a-week Hebrew school.

Another of the fine suburban communities in the county is Bethesda. Its homes—newer than those in Chevy Chase—range in price from $19,000 to $30,000; in one neighborhood, the homes are priced at $40,000 and more. People own their own homes; there are few apartments or homes for rent. Bethesda is definitely upper-middle class.

During the war years, Jewish families in comparatively small numbers took up residence in Bethesda, as well as in Chevy Chase. In 1942, there was organized a Bethesda-Chevy Chase Cultural Group through which Jewish families kept in contact with each other. As its name implies, this group was primarily interested in cultural pursuits without specific religious interest. Strangely, it was this same group which later organized the MCJC in Chevy Chase.

In 1951, thirteen families decided that they wanted to be identified with something more than a "center" type of Jewish organization. As a result, Congregation Beth El was established in Bethesda.

Beth El is a young and growing congregation—to serve the religious, educational and cultural interests of Jewish families in the Montgomery County area. It is a Conservative congregation. Members of Beth El seek an interpretation of Judaism—a way of life—helpful to our country, our present-day society and ourselves.

We aim to impart to our children through education and happy participation an invulnerable pride in the Jewish heritage.

These words, quoted from a congregational brochure, suggest goals and objectives of the congregation, which in 1958 consisted of 224 member-families, 40 per cent of whom live *outside* of Bethesda (but in Montgomery County). These family heads ranged in age from twenty-five to sixty-five. Most, however, were between thirty-five and forty-five years old.

Of special interest is the fact that about 75 per cent of the heads of families affiliated with Beth El, or 175 persons, are Federal employees. Many hold responsible positions with various departments of the government. Although their knowledge of Judaism may not be deep, their interest in and concern for Jewish survival is high.

Transfers of government employees from one position to another result in an annual loss of 10 per cent of the congregation's membership. This has so far been more than offset by the additional Jewish families who have moved into Bethesda and affiliated with Beth El.

The congregation pays close attention to the needs of its young people. In its education program, two hundred ninety-seven children are enrolled in the Sunday school, and ninety children are pupils in the more intensive Hebrew school program, which meets two afternoons a week for a total of three and one-half hours. A lively and entertaining program for the youth of the congregation is provided; among the activities are two United Synagogue teen-age groups of about sixty boys and girls, sports, outings, ballroom dances, forums and meetings with other Jewish youth groups.

The congregational program provides opportunities for worship, discussion, cultural stimulation and fellowship for young and old. It is a synagogue-center in which community participation is sought and, in considerable measure, gained. The completion of a new congregational building promises to make Beth El one of the most effective synagogue-centers in all of Montgomery County.

A third community, Silver Spring, is Maryland's second largest "city." Its population is 131,000, of whom 27,000 are Jewish.

Located northwest of and immediately adjacent to Washington, this suburb is unique in several respects.

Fifty-seven per cent of Silver Spring's population is employed by the Federal or District of Columbia government. The proximity of this suburb to Washington, as well as to the various commissions and research agencies in and around the District, makes Silver Spring an ideal place of residence. Scientists and other high-ranking professional men and women make Silver Spring one of America's highest rated communities in the number of years of schooling which its residents have enjoyed.

This suburb, with its colorful, well-kept gardens and land-scaped lawns, is minutes away from the center of Washington. Its four excellent shopping districts; its homes, which range in price from $19,000 to $25,000 and even higher; its 3,000 rental garden-type apartment dwellings; its excellent public school system and many churches make Silver Spring a fine suburb in which to live. It is indeed a "family town."

Rapidly expanding, Silver Spring borders on several other communities which were completely independent and separate from the others less than a decade ago. Today, such suburbs as Wheaton, Kensington, Takoma Park and Langley Park are, to all intents and purposes, really part of the Silver Spring suburban area.

Wheaton, which is primarily a private home development contiguous to Silver Spring, has homes which range in price from $16,000 to $19,000. There are also a few apartment houses in this area. A Conservative Jewish congregation, Har Tzeon, is located in Wheaton.

In Kensington, an incorporated area surrounded by Silver Spring, homes range in cost from $19,000 to $40,000. Temple Emanuel (Reform) had a membership of 400 families (as of January, 1958), with 625 children enrolled in its Sunday and Hebrew schools. According to its Rabbi, the Temple's program is "purely religious." It has no center activities program.

Jewish families in Takoma Park—which is also contiguous to Silver Spring and, except in name, part of it—reside mainly in apartment houses.

Silver Spring and Wheaton together have the largest number of Jewish residents in all of Montgomery County. Though the concentration of Jews in Silver Spring is higher than in any other area in the county, there are no all-Jewish streets or neighborhoods. There appears to be little group feeling, especially on the part of teen-agers. Jewish families reside over a wide geographical area.

Six hundred twenty-one Jewish families are members of Silver Spring's largest congregation, Temple Israel (Conservative). The heads of about half these families are government employees who commute to and from the District daily. The others are merchants and white-collar workers, with a considerable number of professional men, doctors, lawyers, dentists, engineers and others who, though not directly employed by the Federal government, are engaged in some work in which the government may be directly interested. These people average thirty-five years in age. They are young, capable and independent in their thinking. Talking with them, one feels that these Jewish families are "at home" with themselves. The degree of "self-acceptance" as Jews is certainly high: few appear to desire to escape from Jewishness. These families voluntarily seek Jewish identification for themselves and their young children, whom they enroll in Hebrew and Sunday school when they reach school age.

In September, 1951, one Jewish mother in the area known as Langley Park became especially concerned about her young son's Hebrew training. Nine other families cooperated with her to engage a Hebrew teacher. Classes were conducted in a basement room of an apartment building. Soon other Jewish families became interested, and before long a Hebrew school was well established.

In 1952, these parents decided to formalize their organization by establishing the Langley Hebrew Congregation and Center, a home which shows their awareness of the need for something more than a Hebrew school or even a house of worship. By 1953, there were 200 family-members in this congregation. Recently the congregation adopted a new name, Temple Israel.

Temple Israel has continued to grow in size and influence. It provides a broad and stimulating program of Jewish education; 206

youngsters are pupils in the Hebrew school, and thirty-five others
are enrolled in the Sunday school. "Center" activities are being
expanded, and religious services are being provided for ever-increasing numbers of Jewish families.

Housed in a fine structure which has already grown too small
for its full program, Temple Israel promises to become the most
influential congregation in the county, because it impinges so
directly upon the lives of so many Jewish families in the county's
largest Jewish district.

Montgomery County's Jews enjoy life in suburbia not only
for the physical comforts and relaxed living associated with it, but
also because it has drawn them closer to their fellow Jews and the
synagogue. We shall examine the sources of strength and weakness
in this context in later chapters.

V. SKOKIE, ILLINOIS

Two hundred and eight-two thousand Jews live in Chicago,
America's second largest metropolis. Five and one-half million people reside in the area of which Chicago is the center. Resting on
the shores of Lake Michigan and sprawling out to the north, west
and south, Chicago is the main junction point between East and
West and second only to New York City as America's great market
place. Merchants come from all parts of America to purchase the
many kinds of goods that are processed or manufactured there.

Jewish settlers first came to Chicago in 1837 and have continued to pour into the city and its environs, engaging in business in
all its forms, establishing great hospitals and cultural centers. Ger-
man Jews, the earliest arrivals, and the Russian Jews who followed
in the 1880's have contributed generously to all phases of the community's growth and development. Large Jewish settlements are
located both on the North and South Sides of the city. The latter,
the older of the two areas, has housed several of the world's famous
houses of worship. Kehillat Anshe Ma-ariv, the city's first Jewish
congregation, was established in 1847 and Sinai Congregation (Re-

form) was organized in 1858. Reform, Orthodox and Conservative Judaism are strong and vital in Chicago.

The greatest movement of Jews to the suburbs ringing the city began immediately after World War II. Thousands of families have moved to suburban communities north and west of Chicago. One of these suburbs whose growth has been phenomenal is located in Niles Township, northwest of the city, and bears the unusual name of Skokie.

The area known as Niles Township was largely settled by immigrants from Germany and Luxembourg before the turn of the century. Before 1940, however, this was nothing more than a farmer's country-store community. As late as 1920 Skokie consisted of but 763 persons. Plans were made many years ago to develop this area into a suburban community, but the economic crash of 1929 destroyed all hopes for such a future. Depressions have a way of defeating man's best-laid plans. Thus Skokie and all of Niles Township remained a sleepy, undeveloped area a short distance from the great metropolis of the Midwest—Chicago.

The great building boom of the years immediately following World War II changed the future of this area just as it affected so many other communities. Skokie was transformed from a little town into a lively suburb. By 1950, Niles Township (which includes the suburbs of Lincolnwood, Niles, Morton Grove and Skokie) had a combined population of 25,183. Of these, 14,832 persons lived in Skokie.

It is interesting to note that during the decade 1940-1950, the percentage of increase of population of Skokie as compared with other well known communities in the state of Illinois, was nothing short of phenomenal. The city of Chicago itself, in that decade, increased in population by 6.6 per cent; Highland Park's population increased by 16.1 per cent. Evanston increased by 12.6 per cent, whereas Skokie's population grew by 106.8 per cent.[21]

Niles Township grew for reasons with which we are already familiar. Its towns, particularly Skokie, were easily within commuting distance to Chicago and hence made this area especially desirable. Homes could be mass produced here inexpensively. One could be a suburbanite and still remain a Chicagoan.

Residents came from all of the older, crowded areas of Chicago. The sons and daughters of mid-town and West Side Chicago residents found Skokie attractive and even exciting. It became doubly so when Jewish building contractors undertook less expensive, mass housing developments in Niles and Morton Grove, in addition to the more expensive homes project that had been inaugurated in Skokie and Lincolnwood. The area became especially attractive when large industrial plants were established in Niles Township, thus providing job opportunities for many of the townspeople.

From October, 1953 to October, 1954, the new Jewish residents constituted 39 per cent of the total number of persons who moved into Skokie in that period of time. From January through December, 1956, 66 per cent of the new residents in the community were Jewish. . . . The population of Skokie in 1957 was listed as 44,000 with 14,000 or 33 per cent of the total population recorded as Jewish. It is estimated that by 1960, the Jewish population of Skokie will be 25,000.[22]

Lincolnwood, the next largest village in Niles Township, has 3,000 Jewish residents, or 30 per cent of its 9,500 population. It is expected that by 1960, there will be 4,600 Jews in this village.

Morton Grove, with a population of 15,000, has an estimated Jewish population of 2,300 (1957), while Niles has 1,700 Jews out of a total population of 14,000.

A recent evaluation of this area by the Jewish Community Centers Association of Chicago indicates that, of the four villages in the Niles Township, Skokie and Lincolnwood have higher educational, occupational and economic levels, with Skokie "the most desirable."[23] Skokie's residents are young people whose median age is 31.4 years; 12.5 per cent of its population are under five.

The majority of Skokie's middle-class Jews have moved from Chicago's West Side, formerly the heart of Jewish community life in Chicago and home of many of the old Orthodox congregations.

The Hebrew Theological Seminary, for the training of Orthodox Rabbis, as well as the famous Jewish Peoples' Institute, with its exciting center program for young and old, were all well established on the old West Side. The Lawndale section, a highly desirable area for Jewish residents for many decades, became outmoded partly because of the encroachment of the Negro community. Many Jews, whenever it was financially possible for them to do so, moved to newer sections.

Skokie proved to be one of several popular new areas of settlement. Most of the area's Jewish residents are concentrated in the northeastern section of Skokie, "interspersed generally throughout Lincolnwood and concentrated in the mass housing developments in Morton Grove and Niles." The Hebrew Theological Seminary is presently building its new school buildings in Skokie. There is said to be some feeling in the area that the establishment of the Theological College will tend to bring a more Orthodox element into the community, but my conversations with a number of its Jewish residents do not support this notion. I found a great pride in the fact that "so illustrious a seminary has come to Skokie."

Although the Jewish community has grown so rapidly and Jews no longer feel isolated in Skokie and environs, they are also satisfied because their children attend public schools in which the majority of students are not Jews. Parents are pleased because, even though they wish to live near their fellow Jews, they have no desire to live in any area that may be mistaken for a ghetto, gilded or otherwise.

The increasing Jewish population has made it possible for the community synagogues to establish many interest groups for all age levels. There is now little reason—from a social point of view, at least—for families to continue any form of affiliation with the Chicago Jewish community. It should be noted, however, that the vast majority of Jewish males commute daily to their businesses in Chicago.

The Jews in Niles Township are said to have annual incomes which range from $7,000 to $9,000. They own homes priced from $18,000 to $25,000, with fairly substantial mortgages. Rabbis and lay leaders in the community agree that "the newer residents are finding themselves heavily encumbered financially." The median income for all of Skokie's residents (1956) was $5,563.[24]

Jewish life with its many institutions and organizations appears to be flourishing. New synagogue buildings are devoted not only to services on the Sabbath and other Holy Days, but to Hebrew and Sunday schools and youth programs that have already made these facilities inadequate for the needs of the community. One of the two Conservative congregations, the Niles Township Jewish Congregation, is better known as a "Reconstructionist" synagogue. Its religious philosophy and program are based upon the writings of Dr. Mordecai M. Kaplan and his numerous disciples. This congregation offers a full program of Reconstructionist education and activity, in addition to conducting services and a Hebrew school.

In addition to the youth activities programs that are conducted in the four synagogues, adults find themselves occupied with problems associated with the rapidly expanding Jewish community and its building needs. There are also Parent-Teacher Associations within the public and Hebrew schools, fund-raising projects for the synagogue and general civic and philanthropic causes where Jews work together with the non-Jews. Local units of the League of Women Voters and the Independent Voters of Illinois have a high percentage of Jewish members. The Human Relations Council of Niles Township, recently established by some hundred major organizations of the three major faiths, has begun to provide an outlet for the interest of many citizens. Jews of this area also assist in raising funds for the Combined Jewish Appeal (which supports local, national and overseas Jewish causes) and the Bonds for Israel effort.

Skokie's residents report that this suburb is a good and a happy place in which to live the relaxed life associated with suburbia.

VI. ST. LOUIS PARK, MINNESOTA

The largest city in Minnesota in both area and population is Minneapolis—the City of Lakes. With a population of well over one-half million, of whom 20,000 are Jews, the city is acknowledged to be one of the most beautiful in America. Its residential areas, beautiful lakes and rich foliage are a perpetual delight to its residents. Minneapolis has not one but a dozen choice districts in which to establish a home. With all its natural beauty, the city is also an important industrial center in the Midwest. It is famed too for its symphony orchestra, its great university, its art centers and museums, all of which have helped to make Minneapolis the finest cultural center between Chicago and the West Coast.

In the midst of a predominantly Lutheran community, whose ancestors emanated from the Scandinavian countries, Jews have established themselves and their religious values in the community formerly known as "the capital of anti-Semitism." Minneapolis has taken stock of itself and is in the process of wiping the slate clean of any such stigma. Jewish families, therefore, now have more reason than ever before to feel at home there.

The Jews of Minneapolis who are largely merchants and manufacturers, live in three widely separated sections of the city: the South Side, the early home of many Rumanian Jews; the North Side, home of the early Russian wave of immigration that began in the 1880's; and the West Side, generally recognized as the more fashionable end of the city.

The inroads of the Negro population into the North Side has further influenced many Jews to establish themselves in the only major suburb, directly west of Minneapolis, St. Louis Park. Contiguous to Minneapolis and only ten minutes' drive from the city by excellent highways, St. Louis Park is a city of 38,200 people (January 1, 1957). With 11,000 living units, it is, in truth, a beautiful city of homes.

The area which was to be known as St. Louis Park was surveyed and subdivided in 1854, four years before Minnesota was admitted to the Union as a state. Originally called Elmwood, the area had been known as quiet farming and residential country. In 1886, it was incorporated as a village. Industries moved into the general vicinity of St. Louis Park as early as 1890, but depressions and cycles of decline prevented their growth.

The remarkable growth of St. Louis Park from simple beginnings to its present suburban status began when new roads and
improved public utilities were introduced into the area during the
depression of the 1930's. Because it adjoins the city of Minneapolis
on the west, St. Louis Park became an especially desirable place in
which to live. This prized suburb is now the fourth largest city in
Minnesota.

The "Park," as it is affectionately known, has a home-rule
charter of the council-manager type. From an economic point of
view, the area is overwhelmingly middle-class. As of 1956, 25 per
cent of its citizens earned $7,000 and over annually, while 42 per
cent earned $4,000-$7,000. The average family income is slightly
higher than in Minneapolis.

The Jewish population of St. Louis Park is 5,389, about 28 per
cent of the greater Minneapolis Jewish community. Thirty-two per
cent of all the Jewish children in greater Minneapolis live in St.
Louis Park. Of these, 81 per cent are age twelve or younger.[25]

The Park offers many advantages to its residents. It is new.
Homes range in price from less than $10,000 to $50,000 and over.
Twenty-nine per cent of all available land is residential, consisting
almost entirely of single-family dwellings. The most westerly point
of St. Louis Park is less than twenty minutes from the center of
Minneapolis. The Park is equidistant from Lake Minnetonka, the
largest and most beautiful of the city's lakes, and the downtown
Loop. The shopping centers in the Park are easily accessible.

St. Louis Park provides about 33 per cent of the members of
the several Jewish golf clubs in the environs of Minneapolis. In
July, 1957, of the 355 members who belonged to Oak Ridge, 132
resided in St. Louis Park. Out of a total of 329 members of Brook-
view, whose membership is almost exclusively Jewish, 178 lived in
the Park.

There are three street alphabets in St. Louis Park. Basswood,
the area closest to the city, is a colony of costly and beautiful homes.
As one proceeds in a westerly direction, the homes appear obviously
mass produced and less distinctive. With their recently landscaped
fronts and their young trees providing little shade against the hot

rays of the sun, the new homes are also decorated with children's bicycles, tricycles, fire engines, wagons and other toys. These remind us that this suburb is a city not only of homes but of young children as well. The high proportion of youngsters is most marked.

St. Louis Park's educational system, noted for its excellence, provides yet another reason for the rapid growth of this community. Concern for the education of their children marks the Jewish parent today as it has in the past. Other factors being constant, Jewish families are attracted to those communities that provide the best school facilities.

Most of St. Louis Park's Jewish residents have moved from the old South Side, once the very heart of the Jewish community. Seventy-two per cent of the Park's 1,500 Jewish families are still affiliated with a synagogue or temple in greater Minneapolis.

A limited number of Jews (2.3 per cent) live in such near-the-city suburbs as Anoka, Crystal, Robbinsdale, Brooklyn Center and Golden Valley. Fewer than 2 per cent of the Jewish population of greater Minneapolis live in the suburb of Hopkins (313 people), while 2 per cent live in Richfield and Bloomington, Edina and Minnetonka. The Jews on Minneapolis's West Side have not moved in any marked degree to any suburb. They are already very close to beautiful lakes; they own their own homes; and when their children get married, they may move nearby into an available small apartment. Besides, it takes only ten minutes to reach the Loop from this part of town.

St. Louis Park is different from most suburban communities in which a good number of Jewish families reside in that the number of Jewish organizations for Park residents is comparatively small. The most active of the local Jewish groups is B'nai B'rith.

St. Louis Park, though an independent suburb, is, in the minds of many of its residents, nothing more than a new *neighborhood* of Minneapolis. Families remain part of the already organized Jewish community: they contribute to the Minneapolis Federation for Jewish Service, belong to temples, synagogues, social and fraternal organizations, attend the theatres, visit the libraries and conduct their businesses in Minneapolis.

Though the new B'nai Abraham Synagogue-Center was recently organized in the Park and has erected a new building for its 300 members, the temples of Minneapolis have continued to grow. This Conservative temple, transplanted from the South Side of Minneapolis (where it was an Orthodox congregation), will meet many of the needs of the Park's Jewish families. However, not all of its families are likely to give up their membership in the older temples in Minneapolis.

The continued and marked growth of the Jewish population in St. Louis Park appears doubtful because land at moderate cost is no longer readily available. At least, this is the considered judgment of certain leaders of Minneapolis' Jewish community.

VII. SAN GABRIEL VALLEY, CALIFORNIA

The growth of Los Angeles, the core city of a great metropolitan area, can only be described in a word that is non-scientific—colossal. Two and one-half million people now reside in an area which in 1940 housed one and one-half million. Based on growth of population alone, Los Angeles is understandably the most discussed and even exciting area in the nation today. It is indeed many cities rolled into one.

The explosive growth of this western area (only 150 years ago, Los Angeles County was the hunting grounds of the Indians and the cattle range of a handful of Californians) startles and intrigues us. Since 1781, when the Spanish government granted land for what was to become the City of Los Angeles, the population has grown in such proportions as to stagger the imagination. Los Angeles County, with its forty-six incorporated cities and dozens of un-incorporated towns and villages, attracts almost 150,000 new settlers each year. These newcomers, who move from all sections of America to this land of fable and fiction, hope to find the warmth, sunshine and leisurely manner of living which they crave. Thus Los Angeles has ceased to be a small city and has become gigantic in both size and complexity.

Jews have lived in Los Angeles since 1849. Their number has increased rapidly each year so that by 1958 there were said to be 390,000 Jews in the metropolitan area—an increase of 21 per cent since 1951. This Jewish community is the second largest in the nation. The vast majority of Jews, about 200,000, live either in the City of Los Angeles, Beverly Hills, West Los Angeles, Pacific Palisades, Santa Monica, Hollywood and other "name" areas in or around the metropolis. About 81,000 live in suburban communities in the famous San Fernando Valley.

The majority of Los Angeles' Jews arrived after World War II. The Jewish population is now leveling off, according to a recent survey; fewer than 200 Jewish families are moving to greater Los Angeles each month. The child population (14 and under) is now 114,000, an increase of more than 60 per cent in the past decade. The aged population has increased too—from 22,000 to 29,000 within the same period.

The growth of Los Angeles has resulted in a natural decentralization of the community. Each neighborhood now has its own shopping area, and it is said that many residents never go downtown. Light industry, too, has decentralized by moving into new tracts of land near the suburban areas. Colleges and junior colleges are being located in or near these suburbs.

We shall be specially concerned in this study with the suburban communities that are springing up southeast of Los Angeles, yet which are very much a part of the central city. These are the suburbs of the San Gabriel Valley, with a total Jewish population of 15,000.[26]

The suburbs along the Valley are different in many ways from other suburban communities in the Midwest or East. They are growing so rapidly that one town fades into the next without either community being quite aware of what has happened. Citrus groves give way overnight to new, moderately priced homes. It is not unusual for the residents in these new suburbs to be uncertain of the name of the town in which they live. They know that they are in Los Angeles County, and can probably name the sub-division, but they may not know even the names of the town officials who are to be their representatives. The suburbanite pays his taxes to the county; his policeman is the sheriff of Los Angeles County; his public utilities are provided through Los Angeles County facilities. Hence, even though the suburb has a name, a shopping area and school facilities of its own, the new resident has little common purpose with others in the area. He belongs primarily to his street and family, rather than to a suburb. No wonder that Los Angeles has been described as "an untold number of suburbs in search of a city"!

The mushrooming of these suburbs can hardly be appreciated without statistics. For example, the suburb of West Covina, which had a population of 1,072 in 1940, had grown to 41,000 by 1957. Other suburbs in the San Gabriel Valley have had equally startling growth. Montebello and Monterey Park, each with 8,000 persons in 1940, now have about 30,000 persons apiece. Whittier grew from 16,000 in 1940 to 33,000 by 1957; and Arcadia from 16,000 to 37,000 in the same period. Monrovia more than doubled in size in those seventeen years (from 12,000 to 26,000). San Marino now has over 13,000 residents, as compared with 8,000 in 1940. In that same year Azusa had but 5,000 residents; today there are 18,000. So it has been in each of these suburban communities.

The Jews of these suburbs generally regard themselves as residents of Los Angeles. With businesses usually located in the central city, they tend to regard the suburb in which they reside as a neighborhood rather than an organized community. Angelinos speak of the suburbs along the San Gabriel Valley as "the barefoot and pregnant area." The phrase is self-explanatory.

Young Jewish couples tend to move to the San Gabriel Valley because homes are comparatively low in cost (except for the West Covina area, where prices range from $40,000 to $50,000). Suburbs like Anaheim and Fullerton are acquiring an increasing number of young Jewish families. Like residents of Levittown on the East Coast, many of the young married couples who move into these less expensive suburbs look forward to their first opportunity to move into even newer, more fashionable and expensive suburbs. Other

families, however, choose to live in the suburbs of the San Gabriel
Valley because of its proximity to the heart of the business district
in Los Angeles via the freeway.

Life in these San Gabriel suburbs is simple and leisurely.
Cook-outs and barbecues in one's own back yard are popular family
activities. Beautiful lawns, rich foliage, many fruit trees and a mul-
titude of flowers all help to make the Valley a desirable home setting. The Jewish population of this northeastern area, which includes the San Gabriel Valley, has increased by 95 per cent since
1950.

The Jews of the San Gabriel Valley have, in many instances,
established both synagogues in which to worship and schools in
which their children may receive knowledge of their rich Hebraic
heritage. In certain of these communities, center activities and programs have been developed which appear to meet the needs of the
suburbs' Jewish residents.

Whatever their place of residence, across the length and
breadth of America, suburbanites seem to agree—life is good in
suburbia!

Chapter 3   The Jewish Family

*The American Jewish family acculturates with the domi-
nant American middle class family, and at the same time
seeks to retain family patterns which are distinctly Jewish.
In this dual process, it reflects the accommodations the
urban middle class family is making to current middle class
social changes and deviations from a family pattern that
is peculiarly Jewish.*[1]

The family is recognized as the foundation upon which our
society has been built. It has been and still remains the basic unit
of our civilization. It is more than ordinarily important to the Jewish people because through it the bonds of cohesion to that people
and its distinctive way of life were assured.

Family life, which has helped us all to learn to say "we" rather
than "I," has made possible the continuity of the Jews' religious
tradition. The faith and values of Judaism—the moral and social
values that are incorporated in the Torah—have been communicated
to each succeeding generation of Jews primarily through the family.
This religious experience transmitted through a protective and
friendly environment has added a certain quality to the Jewish
family and home that has won universal respect and admiration.

The Jewish home was traditionally regarded as the "Mikdash
Me'at," the miniature sanctuary. The Jewish husband and wife
were its priest and priestess. The spiritual and moral qualities of
the love of God and Torah, the desire to do His will, to "do justly,
to love mercy and to walk humbly," were taught directly and by
example in the home.

According to Jewish tradition, the father was the head of the
family. It was he who had the responsibility of rearing his children
in the fear of God and the knowledge of His law. He was the
towering personality who protected and disciplined the members of

his household. In biblical days he was spoken of as the patriarch, or father of the extended family. His wife, as his helpmate, was the teacher and moral guide of the family. Her duties and responsibilities were directly associated with the home. In biblical times, she counseled and guided her husband and instructed her children. She was the matriarch, the mother whose influence and authority were obviously great. The husband was the "king," his wife the "queen." The two were intended to complement each other, according to the Hebrew sages.

We have but to read that striking section from chapter 31 of the Book of Proverbs (verses 10-31) to recognize that the "woman of valor" was the good wife. She was more than a self-effacing mother. "She considereth a field and buyeth it" and otherwise conducted herself so as to leave no doubt that, though she could attend well to her household, she was indeed a strong personality in her own right. Her activities, although confined in the main to the home and the rearing of her children, assured her of the right to be regarded as an equal with her husband. The accepted division of responsibilities and duties between husband and wife cast no shadow upon the importance of the woman's role within the family.

Historically, the entire responsibility for the support as well as the care of the family often rested on her shoulders. Jewish women, through the centuries, often carried on the business or earned the family's livelihood in order that the husband might devote himself to the intensive study of the Torah. Her influence with respect to her children and her husband was extraordinary. She took an active part in training her sons up to the age of five, at which time the father assumed the instructor's role. She guided and prepared the daughters for their wifely role all through their maturing years.

This reminder of the traditional role and position of the Jewish husband and wife may help us better understand the changes in degree and nuance in these roles that have occurred on the American scene.

Although immigrant American Jewish families have been termed "patriarchal," insofar as the relation of the father to his children was concerned, much of the responsibility of rearing the children and concern for their moral training was, perforce, placed upon the mother. There was a far greater degree of equality between husband and wife than is generally assumed. The men had their special duties, including the obligations to earn a livelihood and to train, influence and discipline their children in moral and social values and, above all else, in the reverence and love of God. The mother was the homemaker, but it was she whose personal piety and example within the home was expected to influence her children, while winning their love and veneration.

These roles changed in certain particulars when the immigrant fathers became peddlers "out in the country," remaining away from home and family all through the week and returning only for the Sabbath. The responsibility for the conduct of the home and the religious and moral training of the children rested, of necessity, upon the mother. Seldom, however, did she discipline her children, for that was regarded as the special duty of the father. When he returned to his family, infractions of family and religious practice were reported to him, and he meted out punishment. Although absent from the home for long periods, he was, nevertheless, paterfamilias, the disciplinary and moral head of the household. *His* standard of piety, morality and ethics became the standard for the entire family. No one thought of usurping his traditional standard-bearer role.

Although family structure in the American community is now generally regarded as symmetrical insofar as the relationship of husband to wife is concerned, this "equality" is more apparent than real. My observation of three decades, and particularly this intensive study of suburban Jewish family life, leads to the conclusion that the wife, by virtue of her increased duties and responsibilities within the family, has become the modern matriarch of Jewish suburbia. Her ideas, opinions and values clearly dominate.[2]

There is a high degree of truth in the witticism that "all major decisions are made by the husband while all the minor ones are made by the wife." The major decisions, of course, deal with such matters as war and peace, sputnik and satellites. The minor issues include rearing the children and choosing their schools, the particular synagogue with which to affiliate, the neighborhood into which to move and the kind of home to buy.

The Jewish woman has acquired her new position of executive leadership by default. Her husband, nice person though he may be, has become so completely engrossed in business affairs that he generally gives little attention to spiritual and cultural matters that involve his home and family. The husband's failure has led inevitably to the wife's new status.

The Jewish husband's position within the family has changed so markedly because his involvements with business affairs appear, in fact, to leave him little time for his family—at least, so he believes. He feels that it is his primary responsibility to provide for the economic welfare of his family. Often, as he assumes more responsibility in business, this becomes an obsession with him, to the extent that he leaves the rearing of his children, in all its phases, to his wife. To fill this vacuum, she has been obliged to step into the breach and set standards for her family. That is why, it appears to me, a new "matriarchate" is developing!

"What are you going to do when a business depends upon my being there to watch it every moment? I can't be home with the children and worry about keeping my business solvent and taking good care of the family. So I just *have* to leave the management of the family to my wife."

Women not only drive the cars, do the shopping, transport the children to and from school and take them to keep dentist and other appointments; they also keep the checking account in balance, pay the bills and make the many other decisions which Jewish husbands were more likely to make in past generations.

"My husband seldom sees the children during the week. He has to rush off to the office early in the morning. When he gets home, the children have usually had their dinner and are already doing their homework. Of course, he speaks with them and jokes with them. He even gets a quick report on how they are doing in school and with their music lessons. But he really doesn't know them very well. I wish he would spend more time at home with them."

Absence of the commuting, suburban father from the home leads to numerous problems that are not easily solved. In certain suburban communities, leaders report an increase in disciplinary problems, particularly among teen-age boys. Educators in suburbia complain that, except for occasional attendance at PTA meetings, fathers "do not give their sons enough time to really get to know them" and, as a consequence, cannot guide them in their choice of companions. I have noted, too, that children's moral codes and ethical standards require example and support, and that these often suffer because teen-agers fail to receive active and direct guidance from their fathers.

The authority associated with the father's role in the family is often lacking. The youth who may be rebelling against a mother's overprotectiveness finds himself without his father's guidance when he needs it most. It is not difficult for even the best of young people to find themselves in poor or bad company without realizing what has happened to them until they get into difficulties.

"Mother makes all the family decisions in our home. I really don't talk to Dad about my problems in school or about my friends, because I know that it is really Mother who knows what is going on with us kids. Oh, I don't mean to ignore my father. He's a fine man, all right. But I turn to him when I need more spending money, new clothes and for things like that. He looks at my report card and says whether he is pleased or disappointed. I try to please him. I know that he would do anything he can for me and all of us, but if things have to be done in our family, it's Mother who will do them. She really runs the family."

Few of suburbia's Jewish husbands earn their livelihood in suburbia. Each morning they are obliged to commute to the big city, where they conduct their business affairs. They tend to regard their suburban home as little more than a dormitory. In my experience, suburban husbands are seldom very well acquainted with the streets in their own suburbs. Suburban wives have commented that it would be difficult for husbands to find their way if obliged to leave the beaten path from their offices to their homes.

Thus, mothers have the responsibility not only for managing

the home, choosing schools and actually rearing and guiding the children, but also for making the choice of religious, congregational, organizational and social affiliations. Whether the home will include Jewish ritual and ceremony; the extent of religious worship on the Sabbath and festivals; whether the children will be expected to observe the traditional ritual, and to what degree—these matters, regarded a generation ago as the direct responsibility of the Jewish husband, are now increasingly the responsibility of the wife.

"I am the one who decided which temple to join. My husband doesn't really care very much about such things one way or another. I felt that I didn't want to belong to a temple where they use much Hebrew in the service, because I don't know Hebrew—except for a few blessings I picked up years ago. I don't see why I should send my children to an intensive Hebrew school when neither my husband nor I are planning to go to Israel and my children are just too busy with other things to do."

"When I was a child, my Judaism meant a great deal to me. I liked the very aroma of the home just before the Sabbath—the way my mother prepared everything. When I came home from school on Friday afternoon, the house was spick and span for the Sabbath. I remember the way in which we all scrubbed up for the Sabbath. And, as I look back on it, it was all very beautiful. But it's a very different world today. I'm busy till quite late on Friday. My wife sets a Sabbath table but all the preparation for the Sabbath has gone out of it. Maybe these are excuses, but the Sabbath isn't like it used to be. I've gotten used to it this way and just let it go at that. I just haven't the time to argue about it."

"I've never been able to understand my husband. His family was Orthodox, yet he doesn't 'keep' anything unless I insist that he should. I'm the one who said that he would simply *have* to get home earlier on Friday evening in order that we could have a family Sabbath meal. I light the Sabbath candles and try my best to make the Sabbath Eve beautiful. My husband had to be talked into making Kiddush over the wine—and then he did it only because the children asked him to."

The Jewish suburban wife not only guides the home, her children and her husband, but also plays a prominent role herself in the synagogue and temple of her choice. Through her temple

Sisterhood or Women's League, study classes and meetings, the Jewish woman, in large degree, shapes the religious pattern of her congregation. In my opinion, this does not necessarily connote a healthy condition within the synagogue, because the Hebrew education of Jewish women, generally speaking, is not yet sufficiently high to assure the continuity of religious life and its values on an elevated spiritual plane. Although her genuine interest and concern for her people and her faith are certain, Judaism requires that its lay leaders also possess specific and even detailed knowledge of the basic texts and rituals of Judaism. The Jewish woman is unfortunately not prepared as yet for this kind of leadership.

The opportunities for meaningful and purposeful activity within suburbia are numerous. The importance and relevance of well-thought-out and useful synagogual programs is often better understood by the woman than by her husband, because she really lives in the suburb every single day. She knows the interests and needs of her own children, and of her neighbors' children as well, at first hand. She knows the strength and the weakness of the public school, the PTA and many other community organizations. She is, therefore, in an excellent position to guide and subtly direct both temple and public school programming. What she may lack in Jewish knowledge is, for this area of activity, compensated for by her realism, devotion and concern. Whereas her commuter husband often has a rather blurred picture of his community, his temple and even his family's needs, the Jewish woman plays her ever-widening role with sympathetic understanding.

I believe that no synagogue in America could function well these days if it were not for the women who help to blueprint the program, agitate for its adoption and support it with their devoted efforts.

Alone so much of the day, the woman finds that her housekeeping and other chores are not enough to occupy her fully. She works not only for her synagogue and temple, but for a variety of organizations and "causes" that need many workers. Hence, Jewish suburbia has a veritable network of organizations, often even larger than those of the central city. She may be a member of Hadassah, the Women's Zionist Organization, Pioneer Women, Mizrachi, Women's Auxiliary of a hospital, O.R.T., or the Women's Division of Brandeis University, Federations or Jewish philanthropies. She joins the League of Women Voters, the PTA (usually more than one) and the Garden Club, and often helps the Cub Scouts and the Brownies, too. She campaigns for the March of Dimes, Community Fund, Salvation Army, Muscular Dystrophy and/or any other organization that requires support. She is indeed the modern prototype of the "woman of valor."

As if this were not quite enough to tax her energies, there are reports (Newton, Silver Spring, Skokie, San Gabriel Valley) that she sometimes engages in outside work which provides additional family income.

"About a year prior to the Bar Mitzvah of her son, she takes on a job in order to provide the financial means for meeting the expenses involved in Bar Mitzvah receptions or perhaps to pay for the new finished basement of her home. Many of these working mothers have small children. Part of the money they earn is used to pay for the services of a sitter or a helper who takes charge of the home while the mother is at work."

The average size of Jewish families in suburbia appears to be larger than that of urban Jewish families. Few demographic studies of suburban communities have thus far been made, but a recently completed survey of the greater Minneapolis Jewish population, in which the suburb St. Louis Park was the subject of detailed study,[3] reveals that in this suburb there are 3.48 persons per Jewish family. In Marblehead and Swampscott, fashionable North Shore suburbs of Boston, a recent study [4] indicates that there are 3.6 Jewish persons per family. The household size of Jewish families in Montgomery County is 3.65,[5] while the size of the average Jewish household in Natick (Mass.) is 3.94 persons.[6] These figures compare with 3.4 persons per family for the United States as a whole. Earlier marriages (in the late teens and early twenties) and a marked increase in the birth rate are characteristic of suburbia's Jewish residents.

Estimates of family size obtained from executives of metropolitan Jewish federations and councils in the areas included in this study bear out these surveys. The average household size of Jewish suburban families may be recorded as 3.6.

Jewish parents, whose concern for the child has been a source of general admiration through the ages, are today in the forefront of this child-centered world. Each of the suburban communities we have studied provides supporting evidence. Whatever the age or reputed class of the suburb—be it Newton or Natick, Massachusetts; Highland Park or Skokie, Illinois; Euclid Heights or Euclid, Ohio; Burbank or Temple City, California—the fact of child-centeredness remains the same.

"I moved out here for the sake of the kids. I want them to have the best that I can afford—the best schools, the nicest friends, the most beautiful clothes that my money can buy. Nothing is too good for my kids."

And parents, father and mother alike, are quite serious about it. The financial burdens that Jewish parents in suburbia gladly bear for what they regard as the best interests of their children is often astonishing (and sometimes disturbing) to persons who are aware of the sacrifices these entail.

Some parents, zealous beyond reason for their children's happiness, tend to mislead them by the very excessiveness of their generosity.

"I'm not a miser, yet my children tell me, quite emphatically, that I really am. They insist that their school friends receive far greater allowances and spending money from their parents than I give to them. Just imagine, the other day, my twelve-year-old youngster came home from school and asked me in which 'tax bracket' I was. When I inquired what it was all about, it developed that her school friends were talking about their parents' earnings, not in terms of dollar income, but actually in terms of tax brackets. This apparently was a sign of distinction and gave different status to the child whose parents were in a higher tax bracket."

The over-permissiveness of some Jewish parents results from their desire to keep their children happy at all costs.

"Parents are not inclined to make decisions for their children as they should. No, I don't mean that parents ought to handle their adolescents as if they were dumb cattle, to be steered as the parents please. I *do* mean that a child needs to be told what is right and what is wrong. And such decisions are not made on the basis of what the majority of other children or their parents do either. Children play off one set of parents against another, and because we do not wish to be 'bad' parents, we let our children do things that are often wrong. They are not disciplined enough or at all. We have responsibilities as parents which many of us, out of fear of being thought 'old-fashioned' or 'strict,' fail to accept."

In certain of the wealthier status-giving suburbs, I have seen material things—possessions, clothes, cars—become an obsession. What you have matters more than what you are. Rabbis in such communities often complain about the warped ideas of certain of their congregants in this respect.

"My daughter is sixteen years old, but she is sufficiently fussy about going out so that she will not accept a date from any boys who drive a banged-up jalopy. It has to be a first-class automobile or—no date."

Yet, most Jewish families in suburbia object to such over-indulgence and over-concern, and express their disgust and contempt for such misguided parents.

"Their ideas of love for their children are enough to make one sick at heart. Give them everything they want—even some things the children haven't even thought of—just to make them 'happy.' And what happens? Such kids grow up to be spoiled brats—expecting the world to treat them with special favor. Maybe they can get away with it, but I don't like it."

"When I see taxis pulling up at the elementary school discharging Mama's darlings just because it is snowing a bit, I really get angry. How do they expect these kids to grow up into self-reliant people after such treatment?"

"We Jewish parents spend too much of our time worrying about or assisting our children. We do for them many of the tasks they should do themselves. I know some who are self-reliant, fine in every way. But too many are growing up who expect everything to be done for them. They are getting everything of the best on a silver platter."

Youth activity programs in suburban communities are tremendously important for many reasons, especially for the security of children, particularly teen-agers, who are often disturbed by the move to the suburbs. Giving up friends and associates and establishing new relationships frequently proves to be a trying experience for young people. In the few cases in which the incidence of juvenile delinquency has increased among Jews, it is often associated with this kind of insecurity—resulting from the move into a new neighborhood and the consequent need for making new friends. Police officers in Newton and St. Louis Park have suggested that it is their experience that youngsters are likely to "get into bad company" at this early stage of their residence in the suburb.

The temple-center, the Jewish community center or the Young Men's Hebrew Association, one or several of which are established in nearly all suburban communities, have already proved their worth as deterrents to juvenile delinquency. The friendships established through these well-organized youth programs help Jewish young people not only to establish themselves in the strange suburban setting, but also to be guided gently but firmly by capable, professionally trained youth workers at a critical period in their lives. A Rabbi in a suburban temple-center cites the following experience:

"We have a very good youth activities program associated with our temple. I prevailed upon the board of the congregation to put trained group workers in charge of our program, which is intended to meet the needs and interests of the many young boys and girls who live in this suburb. We have opened our program to all young people, regardless of whether their parents are affiliated with our temple-center. This plan has proved its worth in a variety of ways, but two special instances come to mind that prove the point.

"A policeman called our attention to the fact that a group of teen-age boys were wandering aimlessly about the neighborhood. They were noisy youngsters. There was even some question about whether they were responsible for some of the damage done to cars around the temple, street lights smashed and other instances of vandalism. No one had yet been able to say with certainty that these boys were really responsible for these acts. Yet they were cause for our concern. One day we spoke to a member of this group as he loitered near the temple and invited him and his friends to organize a friendship club as part of our temple program. At first, suspicious of our motives, there was some hesitation by the group. Before many weeks had elapsed, however, they moved into our temple-center, organized a club and have been meeting under our guidance and supervision. They play on our teams, arrange parties and dances, do a bit of charitable work and feel perfectly at home with us as we do with them. What is more, the vandalism in the neighborhood has stopped—and we are all relieved.

"In another case, a mother who had just a month before moved into the area with her family came to express her unhappiness and concern because her young teen-age daughter was getting into bad company. We helped this girl by getting her to join one of our social groups, where she soon found better friends. We believe that we are really helping many young people to establish themselves in their new community, and we are happy for that."

In the Newton area, the newly established B-B-N Jewish Community Center (which serves Brighton and Brookline as well as Newton) has already shown how an organized community effort can help to curb and control incipient delinquencies. Referrals of Jewish delinquents and pre-delinquent boys have already been made by the Newton public school system to the detached worker employed by the community center for this purpose. Efforts to help known delinquents, individually or through their clubs, are meeting with favorable response.

Thus synagogues and centers in this area and, in fact, in practically all suburban communities are contributing their resources and talents in an effort to reduce delinquency to a minimum.

Even if well-organized youth programs were not deterrents to delinquency, they would be of inestimable value in helping the child to establish solid friendships and relationships in a socially approved setting. A police officer comments:

"Jewish children are not generally a source of delinquency. We of the —— Police Department believe that Jewish parents keep their children busy and off the streets. The fact that many of them go to their afternoon Hebrew school or club programs in their temple and Jewish centers is certainly not to be ignored."

Two new *rites de passage* as yet unrecognized as such have been introduced into the lives of young people in our generation. Both affect their attitudes and lives in marked degree. In addition to circumcision rites and puberty rites (confirmation, the Bar or Bas Mitzvah ceremonies), there has recently been added the rite of securing a license to drive an automobile. In Massachusetts, for example, where a license may be obtained by any youth sixteen years of age who passes a standard test, the months preceding the test are tensely important, for the youth believes that by passing the driver's test, he becomes an adult. No longer must a young man depend upon his parent or older brother or sister to get him places. He may "date" on his own. He acquires a higher status, too, in the eyes of his youthful friends, and his parents recognize this new status as a sign of maturity.

Teen-age youths, in most suburban communities, are offered special driver's courses through their high schools. Parents are generally pleased with this program. Even though a comparatively small number of young people have their own cars, many are permitted to drive their parent's car to and from high schools and on dates. There is no indication that Jewish young people take undue advantage of their newly acquired status. Police records in the many suburban areas under observation do *not* point to a general increase in delinquency as the result of an increase in youthful drivers, even though they indicate that infractions associated with speeding and double parking have increased among young people.

Another rite which has a direct effect upon our youth is of so recent a vintage that its actual psychological effect has not yet been determined. Yet, it seems clear that at the age of eighteen, a youth's status changes once again: he is now officially old enough to be registered by his Selective Service Board, and he is subject to the draft. Conversations with youths who have recently registered and received their draft cards have convinced me that this change in status ought rightly to be included among the new American *rites de passage,* so marked is its effect!

Jewish parents have long ago ceased to fret about the draft and its moral effect upon their sons, even though, characteristically, it often temporarily weakens close family ties. They have discovered that their sons usually return home from the service with even greater determination to be an integral part of the family.

Jewish suburbia, at present, is generally little concerned with youthful draftees. The children of most of the new suburbanites are not old enough to register, and by far the largest proportion of Jewish male suburbanites are familiar with the armed forces from their own service during World War II or the Korean war.

In Newton, many parents utilize the summer period to further their youngsters' Hebrew knowledge and religious experience by sending them to the excellent Jewish-motivated camps sponsored by the New England Zionist District, by high-minded philanthropic Jewish community leaders and by the Jewish Welfare Board. Other parents may send their children to private, costly camps. Still other children attend day-camps or Scout camps within the area. The local Jewish center [7] had a day-camp enrollment of about seventy-five children from Newton out of a total registration of 350. For the stay-at-homes, the City of Newton provides supervised play-ground and swimming facilities.

The temples in Euclid, Levittown, Chevy Chase and Silver Spring sponsor stay-at-home summer day-camp programs. In Euclid, a few children attend Cleveland's Camp Wise for a brief period; they are called for daily and guided through a carefully selected program of outdoor play and indoor games under professional group workers. The Jewish community of Euclid offers no special summer program for teen-agers because there are, in fact, so few Jewish teen-agers in the suburb.

"Out in Temple City [California], our Jewish children don't seem to need Jewish clubs particularly. We do have a B'nai B'rith youth organization. We have some seventy of our youth, from seventh grade through high school, who meet in the temple every Wednesday night. There is a craft program. We have movies and other fun activities for our youth."

Communities like Sharon, Swampscott and Marblehead, in the Boston area, are regarded as ideal summer communities, with lakes and the ocean close by. Sharon's all-year-round youth program, under professional direction, is regarded as excellent.

St. Louis Park is close to parks, numerous lakes and golf courses. In addition, Temple B'nai Abraham in the Park sponsors a stay-at-home camp. Temple Israel (Reform) and the Conservative congregation, Adath Jeshurun, both in Minneapolis, which together have a membership of 489 St. Louis Park families, provide summer play programs for children.

West Coast suburban communities appear to have fewer organized summer play camp programs for Jewish children. There are, however, several excellent summer camps for children in Southern California, known as Brandeis and Ramah camps. Other Ramah (Hebrew-speaking) camps are located in Wisconsin, Pennsylvania and Connecticut. Children from eastern communities attend the latter two, while a number of Jewish children from the Midwest (Chicago, Minneapolis, St. Paul, Kansas City and their suburbs) spend their summers at the Wisconsin camp.

Summer camp programs are popular with the Jewish families of suburbia. Fifty-two per cent of the respondents to our questionnaire send their children to such camps.

"Yes, I know how much it costs to send my two children to camp, but my wife and I consider it a good investment. What would the children do around the house all summer? They could get into more mischief than anything else. This way, they receive expert instruction in sports and, in addition, they study Hebrew. Each year, they come back all aglow with new knowledge and valuable experience. I work hard for my money, but I think that my children really profit by their camp experience. It is good for them."

Twelve hundred young people are enrolled in the Montgomery County Jewish Community program in Chevy Chase. The number of children in the youth programs in Bethesda and Silver Spring runs into the hundreds. Temple Emanuel of Newton, with a full-time professional director of youth activities and a large staff of group workers, has 900 children enrolled in its program. Temple Shalom of Newton (Reform) has two youth groups, the SPOTS, the Senior Pioneers of Temple Shalom, and the JOTS, the Juniors of Temple Shalom. These junior organizations provide cultural and social programs for their membership. (The youth programs of the three more recently established congregations in this suburb have not yet organized such programs.) About one hundred fifty children of junior high and senior high school age use the facilities of the B-B-N Jewish Community Center for socials, club programs, parties and athletic purposes. Midwinter vacation programs have also proved popular.

In Niles Township, despite limitations of facilities and transportation problems, the Jewish youth is very well served. At Congregation B'nai Emunah in Skokie, approximately 200 youths of junior and senior high school age meet each week under the guidance of a part-time youth director. The Niles Township Jewish congregation's program for teen-agers and young adults, under part-time direction, meets a definite need. Temple Judaea's youth program, in Skokie, also guided by a part-time youth director, serves the children of its own members and of any resident of the community.

Everywhere in suburbia concern for youth is marked, and temples and synagogues appear to be providing important leadership. Metropolitan centers and Jewish federations provide some guidance for suburban communities, but the need for professionally-trained group workers for most of the suburban youth programs is apparent.

Except for the suburbs around Boston, Jewish children do not generally attend private boarding or day schools. Even in the Boston area the number of Jewish children registered in these schools appears to be small—certainly far less than the proportion of Jews to the general population. We have no way of ascertaining whether this is due to a policy of the schools to keep the number of Jewish pupils at a minimum, or to an attitude of Jewish parents with respect to such schools.

Parents who do register their children in private schools believe that their reasons are sound.

"I'm concerned with my son getting into a good, first-rate college. It seems more likely that he can do that if his record in a small school is such that the headmaster can recommend him."

"My boy needs the attention and guidance he can get only in a small school. The high school has gotten so large. No one knows anybody any more. My son can very easily get lost in the large school. Here, in private school, he can be studied and guided. If he has any good qualities, they will surely be brought out."

Jewish children in suburbia, despite the concern and attention given to them by their parents, are not spoiled. I have found them to be, generally, obedient and reliable students who perform their school and home duties in creditable fashion. There are exceptions, to be sure, yet Jewish parents appear to expect good work and good behavior from their children and usually get it.

I can attest also that the home is the center of the social life of Jews in suburbia and that it represents security for an obviously insecure generation. Though homes are not always large, they provide the setting for visits, chats, gossip, informal dinners, picnics and study or discussion groups. Families generally use their homes wisely. A look at specific suburbs reveals that:

"In the suburb of Euclid, people cannot afford luxurious living. They make that quite clear. Yet they do entertain their friends frequently, and home parties are the usual thing."

Social life in St. Louis Park is not especially marked by "partying." However, families who live near Lake Minnetonka, outside St. Louis Park, do a considerable amount of socializing and visiting. Dinner parties and teas at the nearby golf club are popular.

The New England suburban home is used for socializing and family gatherings. There are many groups, cliques and sets within each community, however, and each group establishes its own standards. Some families conduct every social function at a country club, while others enjoy intimate home parties, garden parties and weenie-roasts with neighbors and relatives.

The lush beauty of the San Gabriel Valley makes the informal party centering about the home truly delightful. Socials are arranged around the family unit, and home visiting is natural to this entire area.

The temple community hall or vestry has become the center for most of the larger Jewish gatherings, receptions and parties in suburbia. This is true even in suburbs where predominantly Jewish golf clubs are located. Families in ever-increasing numbers bring their receptions, wedding parties and Bar Mitzvah celebrations into the temple meeting house, and the newer synagogue structures usually provide excellent arrangements for these major social needs.

Jewish families like to assemble on religious festivals and holy days in order to enjoy the occasion as a family unit. Indeed, the Passover Seder traditionally enjoined upon the Jew *must* center around the family table, where the story of the Exodus from Egypt is recounted and the implications of the ideal of human freedom are discussed. Father, mother and children join with other members of the family, not only to relive the experiences of that far-off day, but to enjoy the repast that follows the reading of the Passover narrative. The Jewish New Year, the Day of Atonement and other religiously significant days on the Hebrew calendar are directly associated with the family: family gatherings help the Jew to identify himself with traditional religious values.

Parents and children, grandparents, uncles, aunts and cousins—indeed, all those who comprise the extended family—frequently assemble on the Sabbath Eve and other joyful occasions because they "like to be together." Young married couples often speak with satisfaction of visiting their parents' home with their young children —especially on Sabbaths and festivals, when children may note the rich symbolism and ceremonial associated with these occasions. Grandparents speak of their delight when grandchildren who attend Hebrew or Sunday school classes are able to join in reciting the Hebrew prayers and to observe the ritual of the day.

Sixty-one per cent of our suburban respondents and their children visit with their parents and other relatives at least as frequently as they did when all resided near each other in the central city. The majority of those who report that their visits with parents and relatives are now less frequent attribute this reduction to the increased distance between their homes. And yet there is a startling uniformity in *all* the responses: however difficult it may be to travel longer distances, they are seldom absent from the parents' homes on the traditional Festival and Holy Days. As long as this Jewish emphasis upon the family continues, I believe, Jews in suburbia will manifest the same positive values that have characterized them in the past.

The sudden disappearance of the use of the Yiddish language in the suburbs is often noted by observers in all parts of the country. Not only are there no longer many readers of Yiddish newspapers, but Yiddish terms and expressions which children acquired through their parents are rapidly fading from the vocabulary of the suburban Jews. Jewish children who live in the suburbs seldom understand even the most commonly used Yiddish words or phrases. This cultural loss should not be minimized, for it represents, if not the loss of a cultural arm, at least the severing of a nerve essential to the normal use of that arm.

Grandparents to whom Yiddish is a language of discourse, even though they may understand and speak English, are another channel through which Jewish culture may be retained for another generation.

"I sometimes wish that my children could really understand my parents. My folks are quite old-fashioned. They live over in Dorchester. They speak Yiddish mostly and only a little English. They talk to the children in English. The children like them, I know, but I'm sure that they don't really understand them. They don't know what they went through, how hard they worked to give my sisters, my brother and me a chance to get ahead. But I guess there's always a division between generations, and maybe we have no right to expect it to be different. Maybe that's why I try to see to it that we are all one happy family here in my home."

Communities in which few old folks or grandparents reside are, in a sense, abnormal. The knowledge, experience, wisdom and the very presence of this older generation could surely mellow and deepen the lives of the younger suburbanites. For this reason, it seems to me, the synagogue and the Jewish center in suburbia must provide greater opportunities for fellowship, recreation, cultural exchange and worship for these golden-agers, whose lives may, in turn, enrich the total Jewish community.

The degree of socializing in *new* suburbs is far greater than in the older pre-World War II suburbs. New suburbs usually are peopled by young couples with young children. These young people have much in common, including their dreams about tomorrow, and those who move to new communities often enjoy the informal sociability of the suburb at the outset. However, it is not long before they tire of it and speak of socializing as a waste of time and a bore.

When, for example, Levittown's first residents moved into the new suburb, visiting between neighbors was quite common. Today, some twelve years later, the situation has changed considerably. The community has grown rapidly and, as with other large suburbs, friendship groups are smaller. Furthermore, the original families have grown older and are less inclined to socialize.

"In 1947, when the community was young and everyone knew everybody else, you could expect that some couple would be dropping over at any old time just to talk. But that's over with now. We are all older. We have our children and our increasing obligations, and our husbands are still trying to become economically independent. So, we just don't visit like we used to."

The homeowner in suburbia often discovers he has less leisure time than he anticipated, for home ownership implies that he will care for the home, trim and water the lawns and bushes, put up screens, take in and out summer porch furniture and answer the numerous other responsibilities and emergencies that are sure to arise. These frequently absorb all his leisure time.

The suburbanite soon discovers, too, that commuting is seldom a joy.

"I get home tired after battling traffic all the way. Then after dinner, there is usually a PTA meeting to go to or an adult educational program to keep me moving."

Evenings can be spent in rehearsals for the town symphony or chorus, in which the residents of Sharon take great pride, or they may be used for adult education classes, Levittown's most popular civic enterprise. Whatever the special interest, the commuter is certain to find far more things to do than he really wishes.

Young Jews in suburbia evince very nearly the same concern for intellectual pursuits as did earlier generations. Knowledge, education and what Jews call "Torah" or "Learning" are still of paramount importance. In the newer suburban communities, few children have reached college age, yet parents already talk about their children's future in terms of higher education. In the older, well-established suburbs, it is generally expected that their children will go on to college. Well over 80 per cent of the Jewish children who graduated from Newton High School in 1958, for example, are attending colleges or universities. This pattern is generally characteristic of Jewish suburbia throughout the nation.

Even those parents who are financially burdened take it for granted that higher education for their children is absolutely essential.

"If God blessed me with a good son and he has the wish to study for a higher degree, I am grateful. Anything that I can do to help him, I will do."

Interest in a college education, though often directed toward a specific profession, is much more often concerned with study of English literature, world affairs, languages, social sciences and the humanities. Jewish youths, in ever-increasing numbers, are turning to the study of the physical sciences. Though parents are heard to sigh and even to express concern at the costly graduate years, one seldom hears outright complaint. Learning for its own sake is still highly prized.

The Jewish religious tradition with respect to learning thus remains manifest all through Jewish suburbia. Encouragement of children to achieve good school records begins at a very early age and continues through the college years. What some regard as over-concern on the part of many Jewish parents, these parents consider a natural and perfectly correct course to follow.

"How can you let a child grow up without care and supervision? If I want to have a really good lawn, I have to watch it every day. I have to water it and otherwise care for it and protect it. Ultimately, I may have the kind of lawn I want. If I ever neglect it, I'll get quack grass or weeds. The same is true of children. They have got to be worked with every single day, corrected, encouraged, goaded and congratulated in order to make them do their best. I have got to know what my son is capable of doing and then help him to do it. That's my job as a parent. If he turns out to be a real person with some sensitivities and concern for others, some knowledge and some skills, I'll really have good reason to thank God."

Despite this great interest in learning and schooling, Jewish husbands do not read very much. The women, however, read the "best sellers," particularly those with Jewish themes, and belong to book clubs and lending libraries. Study classes sponsored by temples and by organizations like Hadassah, the Women's Zionist Organization and the Council of Jewish Women attract thousands of female Jewish suburbanites throughout the country. Interest in the State of Israel and the desire for Jewish identification manifest themselves, too, in numerous elementary and intermediate Hebrew classes that have become exceedingly popular.

Rabbis and Hebrew educators report the zeal of these young Jewish suburbanite matrons as they turn to serious study of the Hebrew language, Jewish history, Jewish ritual and ceremonies, the Bible and even theology. Home-study classes, too, have become popular. In these classes, husbands and wives usually study a fixed textbook; the courses are usually conducted by the Rabbi or some other Jewish educator. The many classes sponsored by Hadassah are usually led by one of the more learned Jewish women in the community.

Something quite remarkable is happening to the Jewish woman in the suburbs and, through her, to her husband. Never in all the years of my rabbinical career have I seen such concern for factual knowledge about Judaism and the Jews. Mothers seem anxious to know as much about Judaism as do their young daughters, who are attending Hebrew schools in greater numbers than ever before. They have all been much impressed by the State of Israel and its accomplishments. Whatever it is that impels them, I must pay my tribute to them. It is they, even more than their husbands, who are re-establishing today's Jews as "the People of the Book."

The number of books of Jewish interest in homes, aside from the children's Sunday or Hebrew school textbooks, is still pitifully small. A prayer book, a Bible, sometimes a few precious Hebrew volumes out of a deceased father's sacred library, and several of the current best sellers are the only books of Hebraic interest to be found in many of these homes. However, this marks a vast improvement over the situation as it existed a decade ago. Here, too, increasing strength is indicated.

Popular weekly magazines such as *Time, Newsweek, The Saturday Evening Post,* even *Harper's* and *The Atlantic Monthly* are usually read avidly. The daily newspaper is a "must" for most Jewish homes. Interest in radio and TV reports on world affairs is extremely high, demonstrating an obvious concern for the state of the nation and the world. Though Jews seem less ready to attend public lectures, forums and debates than was true a decade ago (a characteristic of non-Jews as well these days), they seem ever ready to discuss political events and their meaning in the privacy of their homes.

Most Jewish upper-middle-class families read the Anglo-Jewish weekly newspaper published in the central city. Through its columns, they keep informed about all that occurs of Jewish interest within the metropolitan area, nationally and internationally. They also keep in constant touch with all the social news—the births, Bar and Bas Mitzvahs, marriages, deaths, organizational and club news and the latest news about the State of Israel. The syndicated articles and columns published in these newspapers provide them current information and opinions on many weighty and important Jewish themes.

Many suburban Jews are interested in and thoroughly enjoy the theatre, ballet, the opera, museums—indeed, all forms of art. Husbands jokingly remark that their wives are responsible for their attendance at these functions, and yet they *do* attend and even appear to enjoy them.

Many men attend "do it yourself" classes in home repair, where they work at such hobbies as furniture refinishing and woodworking, while their wives often attend garden clubs and flower arrangement classes.

Suburbanites often associate the community in which they live with a general class and a fixed social status. For example, "old-timers" in Newton are under the impression that only rich or moderately well-off families reside in Newton.

"It costs so much more to live in Newton than it does in Roxbury or Dorchester that it is impossible that any Jew in his right mind would move here unless he has money."

Actually, I have observed that this assumption is not borne out by the facts, for in Newton, as in numerous other old suburbs, there reside *two* classes of Jewish families—those who moved into the suburb in the 1930's, and the newer suburbanites who appeared beginning in 1946. The former group is generally well established financially, whereas the second group includes many families who look forward to a better financial status for themselves in the years ahead. These are lower-middle-class families who aspire to be included among the upper-middle class. The earliest residents in these suburbs have long since ceased to belong to PTA's because their children are already grown up. They do, however, contribute liberally to the support of the Community Fund, Red Cross, synagogues and temples.

The newer group struggles desperately to meet mortgage payments and provide its children with every "advantage" mothers and fathers may conjure up.

"There are a goodly number of families who, though they live in this suburb, can hardly afford to pay tuition fees for their children in Hebrew schools. They are usually taken care of by the temple. Their children are taught without cost. The identity of these families is kept secret. But I have noticed that the number of such families has increased markedly in the past five years."

Unlike the former class, these families do not belong to exclusive golf clubs, health clubs, or town and country (dining) clubs.

Rather, their emphasis in this phase of their lives is upon family parties and gatherings, temple socials, skating and skiing parties, picnics, outdoor parties with children. The two groups often serve on the boards of the same organizations. Seldom, however, does the older group understand the younger, and the younger group does not have a high regard for the older. As a consequence, cliques, classes and castes tend to exist in the older suburban communities.

St. Louis Park, for example, has several different "classes" based upon economic factors. To live in Basswood is generally recognized as an indication of membership in a more exclusive group than those families who live in other areas of the Park.

Skokie, too, has its castes and classes based upon economic differences, as evidenced by the place of residence. Yet the relationship between these groups in this new suburb is said to be good.

There are no sharp class divisions in Euclid, precisely because the majority of the residents are in the same economic class. Three or four very wealthy men now reside or have resided in Euclid, and their gifts to the Euclid Jewish community have been munificent. They are, as a consequence, greatly respected for their beneficences.

Though there is said to be very little of the "caste and class" spirit among the Jews of Levittown, certain cliques or divisions that depend upon economic level have been noted. People who can afford the same quality of material comforts, who have the same kinds of homes, cars and attire, usually associate with each other. Still, distinction between the people is not rigidly marked.

Mobility *within* suburbia is surprisingly high. One would expect that the expense involved in moving to the suburbs—the purchase of a home and its furnishings, as well as numerous unexpected expenses—would deter further mobility for years to come. Yet that is certainly not the case.

Jewish families move from one area to another within the same suburb or between suburbs. In Chevy Chase, for example, it is estimated that 10 per cent of the homeowners move annually to other areas within Montgomery County, usually to such places as Kensington, Rollingwood or other sub-sections of Chevy Chase and

Bethesda. In Silver Spring, the mobility rate for the Jewish community is equally high.

"We gain 200 members annually in our temple and lose 50 annually, because they either move into a newer section of the country or out of the area."

During 1956, 31 per cent of all the families in St. Louis Park moved from one section of the Park to another.[8] Euclid leaders report that mobility rates are high there, too. At the first sign of improved economic status, many Jewish families move out of Euclid and take up residence on the Heights in one of a series of "class" suburban communities. Homes are larger, and—most important for the former residents of Euclid—teen-age Jewish children have other teen-agers with whom to join in fellowship. The opportunities for "Jewish atmosphere" are obviously much greater on the Heights than elsewhere.

From Levittown, also, come reports of high mobility. Here, too, the reason is clear. Levittown is regarded by many Jewish residents as a "stepping stone" to other and more glamorous, prestige-giving suburbs. These qualities are usually associated with communities in which homes cost, on the average, more than one's own. To live in a suburb with a "better post-office address" is the desire of many of the town's residents, for whom Levittown is a rung on a ladder— not the lowest, to be sure, but certainly not the highest. To reach to the top of the ladder is the great goal.

There are a good number of Jews who are now living in Plainview or East Meadow who we believe would be living in Levittown if they didn't really want status more than anything else. Because they simply cannot get status with a Levittown post-office address, they stay in these other suburbs.

This holds true in numerous suburbs around the country. The price of homes determines the degree of prestige associated with the suburb, and vice versa. Thus "Wellesley is regarded as a 'better' suburb than Natick, and Newton is a 'better' suburb than Framingham or Sharon."

Thirty-six per cent of all Jews moving into Newton in 1956 had formerly lived in the suburb of Brookline, while 307 Jewish families moved from one location to another *within* Newton. In 1957, more Jewish families moved into Newton from Brookline than from any other environ of Boston.[9]

In the very new suburbs along the San Gabriel Valley, 10 per cent of the families move annually. In some suburbs, the turn-over is even greater, for reasons which have already been suggested. Although little thought is generally given to the implications of this mobility, there is reason to believe that its consequences may be marked.

It is my belief that, if our suburban communities continue to change internally as they have since 1950, Jewish communities will hardly be in a position to erect expensive houses of worship, Hebrew or Sunday school buildings and youth and community centers. Not only will it be impossible to establish impressive structures—which in themselves help to provide a sense of security—but Jewish residents will inevitably feel that they are a rootless community. They will not feel "at home" or at ease within any given area. To regard the suburb in which one lives as a *temporary* home is to destroy the sense of permanence that all families need.

It has been suggested that our communities are in ferment and that the settling-down process will soon commence. If stability in human relations is desirable, then surely it is not too much to hope that the present high rate of mobility will be considerably reduced. Jewish family relations, which to date have remained excellent, may not be able to survive another decade of extreme mobility without showing signs of great stress and strain.

The family is still the nuclear institution of the Jewish people in suburbia. I believe that it will continue its time-honored role if, among other important considerations, it is able to sink its roots deep into the life and soil of a community and remain fixed there for at least one generation. No matter how beautiful the houses, no matter how excellent the synagogues, temples and community centers—these are no substitutes for sound and healthy family life. Relations between husband and wife, between parent and child, remain happiest and healthiest when stability for all the members of the family is assured.

I believe that the suburb has strengthened Jewish family life. Even though the parental roles are somewhat different from what they were a generation ago, the home remains the central institution in Jewish life, and the children are the center of attention and concern for their parents. Whatever the present weakness and defects of suburban life, it is my belief that they may be more than counterbalanced by a more closely-knit Jewish family life in the suburban home.

Chapter 4   The Synagogue—Center
of Jewish Life

If "secular" means "worldly" and "religious" means "spiritual" there is as much that is worldly in the Synagogue as there is what is spiritual in the Community Center.[1]

The synagogue is suburbia's nuclear and most important Jewish institution. More Jewish men and women are identified with it than with any other organized body within the community. It continues, as it has through the ages, to fulfill its threefold function as a House of Prayer, House of Study and House of Assembly. Although there has been a marked change of emphasis in our day, with the House-of-Assembly aspect receiving more attention, the synagogue remains the central institution in Jewish surburban life. It meets the social and cultural needs of its adherents even as it provides the opportunity for prayer and study. Jewish families require the synagogue in suburbia because by affiliation with it they voluntarily identify themselves with a people and its way of life.

It has been estimated[2] that 60 per cent of the entire American Jewish community were affiliated with synagogues in 1956-57. The national average affiliation with churches for all Americans in this same year was estimated as 62 per cent by the National Council of Churches.[3] Examination of the synagogue affiliations of Jewish families in the seventy-eight suburbs included in this study suggests that the percentage of membership matches that of the nation as a whole.[4]

Membership in synagogues and temples in suburbia varies, as may be expected, according to the age of the suburb, the number of very young families who reside there, the suburb's proximity to the central city, and the central city's tradition of synagogue affiliation. I have noted, too, that affiliation may depend upon the status-giving nature of the suburb: in communities in which low-cost housing predominates, Jewish families tend to affiliate with the synagogue when their children are old enough to attend Hebrew or Sunday school. Synagogue membership appears also to be correlated to family income; primary financial obligations consist of mortgage payments, direct support of the family and the maintenance of the family car, which can no longer be regarded as a luxury. If affiliation with the church is the generally accepted pattern of the suburb, we may expect Jewish families to become associated with the synagogue relatively quickly. Finally, it has been noted that membership rises rapidly in a crisis situation. A noticeable increase in intolerance and organized prejudice within the suburb, for example, causes Jews to seek the protection and security of the synagogue.

Jews have traditionally regarded their synagogues as the proper place for fellowship, as well as for prayer and study. The synagogue was, in fact, the center of Jewish life in all ages. The dichotomy that exists in other religions between the "religious" and the "worldly" is less in evidence in Judaism.

Like the home, known as the "Little Sanctuary," the synagogue was never regarded as too religious to be used for purposes of both study and fellowship.

The "Shtetl," or small-town community of eastern Europe, which has often been described as the normative pattern of Jewish living, always regarded the synagogue in this manner.

The structure of the community is, in fact, the structure of the synagogue. This is not because the secular order is carried into the synagogue, but because it would be impossible to separate the religious from the secular—they are fused into one whole. Every act of the weekday world falls within the jurisdiction of Divine law and nothing is too trifling to be considered in relation to the Law.[5]

Though the emphases in Jewish life, expressed through the synagogue, have changed and continue to change under new and different conditions, it remains true that for most Jews religion is not a separate compartment in life. A religion separated from daily life would be a self-contradiction.

Changes in emphasis within the synagogue were never unusual

because they resulted directly from the changing conditions under which the people lived. American synagogues in this decade of the twentieth century differ from those transplanted from the East European communities in the 1890's because the needs of Jews are different. As Schneider [6] points out, this century has produced a revolution not only in industry and commerce, but in the folkways, ideals and interests of the American people, as a direct result of the motion picture, the automobile, radio, television, the phonograph, aviation and numerous other inventions.

The threat to traditional religious habits has been recognized by both the synagogue and the Christian church. The challenge of modern knowledge concerning the universe, and the questions raised by science and the scientific method about the traditional way of life, have been revolutionary. The thought and action patterns of Jews and Christians who have lived within the framework of organized religion have inevitably changed.

Though undeniably affected by these major forces and inventions, the synagogue was able to accept the new conditions and even come to terms with them because it had never divorced itself from the world.

During the last decades, the work of the American religious bodies has become so specialized, organized and practical that the very life of religion seems to be shifting from worship to "service" and from altar to office . . . whether all these activities are religious or not is, after all, an academic dispute for no one can tell precisely where business leaves off and religion begins, or at what point politics becomes "the strategy of the Kingdom."[7]

My conversations with liberal Protestant clergymen in many suburban communities attest that although suburbanites tend to take religion much more seriously than residents of central cities, they no longer believe that church attendance is so important. A liberal position in matters of theology and liberal attitudes toward the Bible are generally acknowledged by suburban Protestant clergymen. The number of fundamentalist churches in these suburbs is limited (as is the number of Orthodox synagogues). And there is today obviously less concern over matters of creed. Although clergymen do not neglect theology, their sermons indicate that problems of ethical living occupy their major attention.

One Protestant suburban clergyman has described his congregants as "religiously complacent."

"They just don't get worked up over many things in the church. They seem to feel the need to live in good relations with their non-Christian neighbors, are often disturbed and 'upset' about the trend of Catholic movement into suburbs much more than they are about Jews because they believe that Catholics take control of cities politically wherever possible. They come to their minister much more frequently with personal problems. Counseling has become a major part of the clergyman's responsibilities. In suburbia, we must serve our own church people, watch out for their many spiritual and cultural needs, try to establish good church programs for the youngsters. But our major concern is with the Christians in our community. We try to be for them the center of a religious community."

The status and problems of the present-day suburban Protestant church are similar to those of the suburban synagogues. Each, functioning within the framework of its own distinctive religious tradition, is increasingly emphasizing the neighborhood, the community, the ethical, moral and social values associated with religion, and the needs of living people. Theological and denominational differences are seemingly less important. The rapid growth of the ecumenical movement in the church today offers support for this thesis.

Jews, too, differ less and less among themselves on matters of theology and ritual observance. The latter, as we shall see, is recognized not as an end in itself, but as a means to attain the good society or to become a more spiritual people. Denominationalism, though it appears to be strong, seems to me, in reality, less a factor in the lives of the Jewish suburbanites than their strong national organizations and some of their Rabbis would make it appear. Some Jewish families, for example, affiliate with several synagogues and temples—Conservative, Reform and Orthodox—within the same community. In many other cases, members of the same family join synagogues of officially divergent points of view.

In the suburb, too, the Rabbi is much more of a pastor, coun- selor and guide to moral and ethical living than is generally true in urban centers. The Rabbi, or "Rav," was traditionally the learned and pious Jew. It was his duty to decide ritual matters and to judge disputes between Jewish members of the community. On the Satur- day before the Passover Festival and on Yom Kippur, the Day of Atonement, he delivered learned discourses before the congrega- tion. His primary duty, however, was to study the Torah: his au- thority within the Jewish community rested on his learning. From the Middle Ages through World War I, especially in Eastern Euro- pean Jewish communities, this may be said to have been the primary function and duty of the Rabbi.

The role of the Rabbi has changed drastically in America. It was necessary for the spiritual leader to concern himself with cul- tural, personal, educational and philanthropic, as well as purely ritualistic matters, if the unity and strength of the small Jewish community were to be assured. He became the preacher, the edu- cator, the youth worker and the counselor, especially concerned with human relations and with the problems that resulted from misunder- standing, prejudice and intolerance.

In suburbia, mobility and transiency have also created problems of adjustment. Children who have just moved into a suburb must be made to feel "at home" where all is strange and different. Finan- cial problems arise within these families, unexpected economic obli- gations which suddenly require attention and concern. Marital problems are ever present, not only because there are so many re- cently married couples, but also because the social patterns of sub- urban life create opportunities for "triangles." That divorce rates are not higher is due to the increased use of counselors; the concern of religious leaders, psychologists and psychiatrists; and, of course, the number of young children, who help hold families together.

"I devote a good deal of my time to counseling work. Young people come to me for help when they do not get along. I may not always be able to help them, but I do know where to refer them, so that they may receive the guidance of skilled and trained technicians. I keep an eye on them even when I turn them over to a psychologist or psychiatrist. And, all the while, I read as much as I can on the subject of counseling."

Rabbis in suburbia find that they are able to help many new-comers overcome the feeling of loneliness in their new environment by encouraging families to become acquainted with each other, making innumerable phone calls and pastoral visits. Such matters in a metropolitan congregation would more than likely be ignored; in suburbia they become important.

The Rabbi in suburbia usually finds himself the spiritual leader of a comparatively youthful congregation. Throughout the nation, the lay leaders and board members of most suburban congregations were young men when the congregation was organized. Although these leaders express and interpret the ideas and values of the membership, they turn sometimes (though not frequently enough) to the Rabbi for guidance in matters pertaining to Jewish congrega-tional life.

I have found that these young people often lack experience in synagogual work. They have fuzzy memories about the synagogues with which they and their parents were affiliated during their child-hood years. They believe that Jewish children ought to be educated, but seldom have any real ideas about the nature of that education. They talk about democratic operation of synagogues, but often mean that their voices alone should be heard. What is perhaps most dis-concerting is that, lacking Jewish knowledge themselves, they are completely unaware of what they do not know. Under these cir-cumstances, they turn to the youthful Rabbis asking for guidance, but in reality seeking support for their own ideas. This, I feel, constitutes one of the major difficulties with suburban congrega-tions.

In most suburban Jewish communities, particularly those whose growth has been greatest since 1946, Jewish leadership is generally in the hands of young men and women, rarely over forty years old. Such suburbs as Levittown, Skokie, Park Forest, Fair Lawn (New Jersey) and most of the communities in the San Gabriel Valley are guided by such young laymen, whose good intentions, energy and devotion may not always compensate for their lack of knowledge or experience. I suspect that the role of the Rabbi in suburban synagogues would be even more difficult than it is, were it not for the fact that these lay leaders are aware that the Christian community looks upon the Rabbi as the religious and hence primary leader of the Jews. Since it is religion which gives the Jew his distinctiveness, the Rabbi's position is thus clearly reinforced by the non-Jewish community.

Lerner [8] has pointed out that the five great goals in American civilization which make for happiness are success, prestige, money, power and security. These, plus love and sex, are supposed to spell happiness.

As I have come to know the leadership in many suburban congregations, I have been obliged to record the fact that the attainment of material success is often equated with the possession of knowledge, wisdom, a positive and healthy philosophy for living and all other values which men generally hold in high esteem. A position of leadership can, unfortunately, be acquired in many communities by a sizable contribution to the synagogue or to some other worthy cause. Prestige and status are often acquired in this manner.

There are of course many persons who possess worldly goods, yet recognize that spiritual values—including humility—are of equal if not surpassing importance in the life of man. Many leaders are well aware of the truth of the Biblical dictum, *Man does not live by bread alone,*[9] but they often find it difficult to remain in positions of leadership in the current "struggle for power" between the "aristocracy of wealth" and the "aristocracy of learning."

"Too many of our leaders have no humility whatsoever. They believe that position and honors and distinction are rightfully theirs just because they are good salesmen who know 'techniques' rather than any other thing. It is people of this kind, sometimes people without decent moral standards, whom we place in positions of leadership."

Synagogual officers and board members whose economic positions are about the same level tend to be more friendly, peaceful and cooperative than those from different economic levels.

I have seen disharmony, often contentiousness, occur in those suburban communities which had Jewish residents before the end of World War II. Here problems result when older residents, who have helped to establish a Jewish community pattern, build a synagogue structure or otherwise distinguish themselves, find themselves engulfed by the "youngsters" on congregational boards. Mark Twain is said to have remarked, "When I was fourteen, I was disturbed at how little my father knew. When I was twenty-one, I was surprised to discover how much he had learned in seven years." Most of the young men are viewed by their elders as "about fourteen years old." That they do indeed have a lot to learn does not minimize the fact that their elders have much to unlearn.

The increasing number of young, capable, intelligent men who approach their synagogues with humility and sincerity of purpose has been noted by spiritual leaders throughout the country. What remains is for these dedicated few to be given an opportunity to serve their people and their God.

Complaints are often heard also about those lay leaders who approach their temple as if it were a plant, a business or an industry.

"I have been active in the congregation for three years. I have lived here, on the West Coast, for four years. I became active in the temple as an officer because once, at a meeting, I expressed the belief that things needed to be done in a more business-like manner. My interest in seeing to it that the temple's financial affairs are run as a business has prompted me to continue my work. I have an interest, too, in community welfare. That is why I work so hard for the temple."

All too often, these men believe that "everything, including religion, can be bought." When they discover to their surprise that this is not so, they part company with the temple.

"The leaders in any given suburban Jewish community change every few years. They get fed up with people, inactivity, lethargy and even with Judaism. They believe that the reason the Rabbi doesn't succeed in 'getting his program across' is because he doesn't present it properly. He doesn't use modern publicity methods (poor neb!) and the leader knows how! After all, his method may sell dresses or beer or hosiery, why then shouldn't it work with a temple? So he takes on the task of 'selling' Judaism. And he tries—oh, how he tries! And yet—it just doesn't work. People are not standing in line to purchase 'salvation' from God through the temple.

"Poor Mr. Leader! He knows advertising methods. He can invent slogans and catch phrases, but he just doesn't know Judaism—its ideas and ideals. He just has no depth. He is just a shallow, well-meaning fellow who happens to be Jewish, pretending to be a 'leader'!"

Despite the frustrations of so many of suburban Rabbis and the ofttimes inadequate lay leadership of synagogues and temples—both conditions appear to exist in suburban Protestant churches as well—the synagogue remains the strongest and most important Jewish institution in suburbia.

Suburban Jewish community life has placed a double responsibility upon its spiritual leader. Despite the numerous problems associated with "growing pains," he must often direct his congregation along paths that are new, not only to them but to himself. At the same time, he must serve as the symbol of an age-old tradition and faith, both for his congregants and for the larger community. His duties are varied and often even incongruous.

The Rabbi must know something about synagogue architecture (the new temple must be built!), school room construction (First-class construction with second-class costs!), how to carry out a successful program of youth activities (After all, we are building for our children!) and fund-raising techniques ("Rabbi, we need an organizer—a go-getter who knows as much about motivational research as the Madison Avenue admen."). The Rabbi is also expected to win the new Jewish families in suburbia for the temple. And, of course, he should be the congregation's "ambassador of good will." ("After all, I don't need a synagogue to pray in. I want the Christian community to think well of Jews, and the Rabbi is certainly the best representative we have.") The Rabbi ought also to lead study classes, preach sermons, conduct the services in the temple, officiate at weddings and funerals and, if possible, teach a Sunday or Hebrew school class.

In practice, he meets these varied duties and responsibilities rather well. Not only do seventy-seven Rabbis serving sixty-eight suburban Jewish communities state that the Rabbi is the recognized Jewish leader in suburbia, but congregational lay leaders and Jewish Community Council leaders in all sections of the country concur in this opinion. Discussions that I have had with Christian clergymen serving the same communities provide further assurance: the Rabbi is the person to whom they turn as the most representative Jew in the community. The larger community's civic leaders, educators, ministers and other lay leaders and organizational heads turn to and consult with the Rabbi first in practically all situations involving the total Jewish community. He is the spokesman for all Jews— those affiliated with a synagogue and, even though they may not wish it, those who have no synagogual ties.

The temple has gained its pre-eminence in suburbia less as a religious institution than as usually the first organized body to provide a physical structure in which Jews can meet as Jews within the community. The temple meets more of the real needs of Jews, religiously, socially and educationally, than any other Jewish institution. The lay leaders of temples and synagogues, well aware of these facts, usually ask all persons and families who seek any service through the temple to become formally affiliated with it. But this is not always possible, for there are always those whose financial position is such that they cannot afford such membership. I am not aware of a single instance anywhere in the country in which families or children have been deprived of any service or need because of the parents' inability to pay.

Rabbis are frequently called upon by the unaffiliated for family counseling, for situations resulting from illness and, most often, for religious ministrations. To the religious leader, the matter of affiliation is, under these circumstances, of little importance.

"We feel that the synagogue ought to be supported by all the Jewish families in town. Of course, if they can't afford it, they will be served without cost. That's what we're here for. But, we feel that we must protect ourselves against the 'free-riders' who expect others to pay for what they get."

The synagogue is the center of the life of the Jewish people because, in a sense, it provides for the formal Jewish education of the children. It teaches the history, custom and ceremonies of Jewish life, the organizational structure of the Jewish community, the Hebrew language and the Bible. It also helps Jews "feel" Jewish even when there is very little religious symbolism within the home. Busy, commuting fathers, who see their young children less often than they would like, cannot adequately fulfill their duties as teachers of the tradition. They turn to the synagogue, its Rabbi, its religious school and its youth activities program for assistance. The center of gravity in Jewish religious life in our day has thus largely shifted from the home to the synagogue.

It would be reasonable to assume that most Rabbis of suburban congregations are happy in their work, yet many express marked degrees of heartache and frustration.

"Suburban congregations were supposed to be homogeneous. But that just isn't true. Because my temple is the only one in this suburb, and because Jewish families are moving into town in such great numbers, I am getting not a congregation but a conglomeration of people from many different kinds of synagogues, representing many traditions and points of view. As a consequence, I can hardly express an opinion or present an idea without getting an harangue from these many self-styled 'authorities' whose Judaism has no breadth and no depth. They imagine that the practices and ideas of the little synagogue they once attended is all there is to Judaism. They act as if their parents or grandparents constitute the sole authorities in Jewish life."

Heterogeneity, a characteristic of new suburban communities, and a myopic approach to Judaism are but two of the causes for the Rabbis' unhappiness. Another disconcerted spiritual leader comments:

"Frankly, I accepted my present suburban congregation because I was looking for a small congregation where I would come to know my congregants intimately and, as a consequence, be friend and counselor as well as teacher. But I find that I reckoned without due consideration to the likelihood that my quiet suburban community would grow and grow and grow. It has reached such proportions that I can hardly serve all my congregants adequately. I cannot get to know them as I had originally planned. I cannot share their joys or sorrows as I had thought would be possible. The congregation has grown too large—and there seems to be nothing that I can do about it. I cannot suggest that people join other congregations because there are no other congregations. There are no other Hebrew schools. People are not too ready to invest in more buildings, more schools, more temples. My congregants seem to be pleased, but I feel very badly frustrated."

Yet not all Rabbis are unhappy about suburbia. To most, the challenge represented by these new communities and the opportunity to mold their young families into a meaningful and positive Jewish pattern are both challenging and exciting.

"Recently I heard of one of my congregants who built a beautiful new home. It has a large living room. But there isn't a book in the room—let alone a Jewish book. This is most upsetting for me. To think that we Jews were spoken of as 'The People of the Book'! It so happens that this family has two children who are attending our Hebrew school. They're good pupils, and they give me reason for some hope. Frankly, I believe that *they* can be cultivated. They will be more cultured people, better Jews by far, than their parents. And the parents will even learn from their children! But all this will take patience and so much time. So, even though my heart is often very heavy with anguish, I feel that my effort in the field of education is worth while. Tomorrow will be better."

The nuclear position of the synagogue in suburbia is best understood if we note that nearly all of the observed community synagogues began as Jewish centers rather than as religious institutions.

Young married couples, recently settled in a suburb, look first for fellowship and friendship. They decide that they "ought to have some kind of a Jewish club, maybe even a Jewish center, like a Young Men's and Young Women's Hebrew Association." Enthusiastically they set out to establish the center, only to discover that soon the religious educational needs of their very young children will have to be met. And "how can that be done without a Rabbi or a teacher?" After much cogitation and self-examination, they agree that they really need an institution that will provide for their children's religious needs, as well as for their own social and fellowship interests. They conclude that a religious institution can provide for social as well as education needs. Hence, they expand their original concept to include a synagogue. Now they have blue-printed a synagogue-center—an all-inclusive organization which will serve the needs of these young families.

There remains another problem to be resolved. What *kind* of a synagogue or temple ought it to be—Orthodox, Reform or Conservative? Debate and argument follow, and the decision is arrived at by a vote of all participating members.

In most cases since 1946, the first synagogue in a new suburban community is Conservative. In 1949, for example, 392 congregations were affiliated with the Union of American Hebrew Congregations (Reform). These grew to 530 by 1956, an increase of 138 Reform temples. During the same period, the United Synagogue of America (Conservative) grew from 365 to 599 congregational affiliates, an increase of 234 congregations.[10] Conversations with the leaders of the Conservative group indicate that the major growth in affiliation occurred in the suburbs.

This appears to indicate that the choice of denomination is often a compromise between extreme points of view. Seldom have I found a strong ideological belief which impels suburban congregations to organize as Conservative, Orthodox or Reform. Often the matter is decided by this strange kind of compromise "in the interest of the total Jewish community":

"We asked our organizers what kind of synagogue they wanted. Some thought it ought to be Reform; others wanted an Orthodox synagogue, and a great number wanted the Conservative. We figured that the Conservative was 'middle of the road' and would not offend any group in the community. So we called it a Conservative congregation."

The choice is usually between Conservative and Reform; seldom, if ever, is an Orthodox synagogue the first synagogue in any suburb. The Conservative temple is established first, followed in a year or two by a Reform temple, if the size of the Jewish community warrants. It, too, is usually a temple-center.

The temple-center endeavors to meet all the needs of the Jewish community, young and old alike. It is, in fact, *the* center of the Jewish community, providing educational, cultural, social and recreational programs as well as religious services. Even when the name "center" is not included in the title, these duties are usually incorporated in the synagogual programs. Thus, the newly-established synagogues on Long Island are in almost all cases synagogue-centers; this is also true of the synagogue established in St. Louis Park.

The temples of Skokie, the San Gabriel Valley, and Newton, Sharon, Swampscott and Natick have organized youth programs, and most receive professional guidance in group work.

"The community needs a place for our children and we adults need some place to carry on our social lives. What better place can there be than our synagogue?"

The nature of the growth and development of the suburban Jewish community center is best illustrated by material gathered from a brochure published by the Israel Community Center of Levittown:

WHAT IS THE ISRAEL COMMUNITY CENTER?

The Israel Community Center is what its name implies—a Synagogue Center, combining the functions of a Synagogue with those of a Community Center. It invites into its ranks all Jews from Levittown and vicinity who seek to affirm their Judaism rather than to escape it. Our members look upon the Center, not merely in terms of "seats for the observance of three holy days," but rather do they and their families look to the Center for "all-year-round Congregational activity," social as well as cultural and religious. This they receive in full measure.

ACCENT ON YOUTH

Our Congregation is a young one. This is true in a double sense: first, the ICC came into being only a few years ago (founded in 1948); and second, its membership consists of young people.

RETHINKING AND RETURNING

Most of our people have had little previous contact with synagogue life, having hitherto regarded the synagogue as the province of their elders. Many have not seen the inside of a "shule" since their Bar Mitzvah. Now, however, they feel that it is time that they "grow up" and they have consequently acquired a renewed interest in synagogue activity. The responsibilities of parenthood have led many to rethink their position with regard to the Jewish heritage which they now seek to maintain in order to be able to transmit it to their children. In Levittown, this "return to Judaism" is facilitated for them through the existence of a synagogue consisting of like-minded young Jewish parents.

THE CENTER OF THINGS

The Israel Community Center is the hub of all cultural, religious, social and recreational life in the Jewish community of Levittown and its surrounding area. Our Temple is distinguished for the dignified simplicity of its architectural style which blends with that of the homes that make up Levittown. It is centrally located in the heart of Levittown and serves as the rallying point and meeting place for the Jewish organizations of the community.

CONSERVATIVE JUDAISM

Our Congregation is a Conservative Congregation. This means that we are dedicated to the advancement of Traditional Judaism by revitalizing the tradition and making it more inspiring and more meaningful to the modern American Jew. Our Rabbi is a graduate of the Jewish Theological Seminary of America which is the fountainhead of Conservative Judaism. Our Congregation is affiliated with the United Synagogue of America which embraces all Conservative congregations in the country.

Another phase of the fascinating story of the origin and development of Levittown's Israel Community Center is best told by the young people who were its early leaders:[11]

HOW A GROUP OF VETERANS FORMED THE ISRAEL COMMUNITY CENTER OF LEVITTOWN

This is a story about a group of veterans, an abandoned hangar, a cocker spaniel, two finished attics, a sacred Sefer Torah, irksome problems and ingenious solutions. And, above all, the infectious spirit of youth. But let's start at the beginning.

The story goes back a few months to May, 1948, when a few of the fellows in Levittown, Long Island, the largest all-veteran community in the country, put their heads together and decided there was a void in the neat picture of their spanking new community. They rolled up their sleeves, began knocking on doors, and a Levittown synagogue and community center began to take shape.

Then, in rapid succession, came a meeting with Rabbi Karp, who was then director of the Metropolitan New York Region of the United Synagogue; a public meeting at which the members voted overwhelmingly to become a Conservative congregation, and decided to call themselves Israel Community Center in honor of another organization which was already exhibiting a plucky beginning; a whirlwind membership campaign spearheaded by Harry Kasden; and vigorous preparations for the congregation's first big services on the High Holy Days.

If there were any lingering doubts that the young men and women of Levittown, many of whom, it must be confessed, had not seen the inside of a synagogue for many years, knew where they were going, it was dispelled by the time the High Holy Days rolled around. Unable to find an adequate place to house the services, the congregation was obliged to rent a cavernous, grease-stained airplane hangar which hadn't been used for years. Unperturbed, the committee went to work and got a local paint company to donate 800 gallons of white paint, and a local paint contractor to donate the services of his painter. Meanwhile, the men built the Ark, the women sewed the altar cloth, local funeral parlors supplied the chairs, the United Synagogue loaned the siddurim, etc., etc. In the end, 600 people attended the services and most of them were so impressed that they joined the congregation right after the holidays.

With services behind them, the congregation had the problem of paying for the hangar it rented for a month. The solution: a bazaar. On October 29 and 30, the hangar was teeming again. Donations for the affair had ranged from a television set and fur coat to a pedigreed cocker spaniel. More than 1600 people packed around the booths at one time and the congregation not only got out of the red, but put a tidy piece of change into the congregational coffers as well.

The membership was snow-balling, community enthusiasm was red hot when a new problem arose: what about religious education for the kids between now and the time the synagogue-center is built? This problem too, the congregation disposed of in its unusual but effective manner. The men got their hammers and saws out and finished off the attics of two of the homes and equipped them with school chairs and school equipment. Now every Sunday morning, 24 youngsters between the ages of 4 and 6 report to "Sunday School" to receive religious training.

The unique religious school has had its problems. One night, while a couple of men were standing on ladders sawing and pounding an attic into a classroom, one man lost his balance and fell hip deep through the plaster-board ceiling. The owner of the house, who was frantically walking the floor with his howling infant, looked up in time to see two legs dangling foolishly through holes in his ceiling. It is rumored that he was sorely tempted to call the whole thing off.

Since May, this fledgling congregation *has grown to 400 members*. It now holds regular Friday evening services, has an active Sisterhood, publishes a monthly bulletin, has created a building fund, laid plans for an adult study group, and, above all else, it has infused its members with such a sense of community excitement that the members themselves find it hard to believe.

Rabbi Harry Katchen, Director of the Metropolitan New York Region, who has advised and assisted the congregation for the past few months, announces that a fitting climax to Israel's spectacular development will be the formal presentation to the congregation by Theodore R. Racoosin, Chairman of the United Synagogue Committee on Expansion, the Sefer Torah which was the first Sefer Torah to be returned to Germany after liberation by American troops and is a very treasured one.

Meanwhile the Jewish community of Levittown continues to flourish. Says chunky, enthusiastic Lou Goldberg, President of the Congregation, shaking his head in wonderment: "I still can't believe it. Do you realize that 90% of these people haven't been in a synagogue since they were Bar Mitzvah? And look at them now, working like beavers. I guess it's just that there's a lot we don't know, and we want to know—we're hungry for Jewish learning and Jewish life."

The Levittown story, as an example of synagogue-center development, may be even better understood by meeting Louis Goldberg, ex-G.I., who became the first president of the new congregation. When he and his wife moved into Levittown in October, 1947, they were one of the original 300 families in the new town. The Goldbergs had come from the Bronx. Nearly all of those first Jewish residents had either lived in New York City or come from out of state. Only ex-G.I.'s could rent homes in Levittown.

Louis Goldberg's parents had strong Jewish loyalties and interests. Mrs. Goldberg's father had been a Yeshiva Bochur (student of the Talmud) as a youth in Europe. Lou had no strong Jewish loyalties or interests at that time. He had been a student at Long Island University for two and one-half years and was then drafted into the army. Following his period of service, he returned to New York and married his sweetheart from Brooklyn, whose Jewish background was like his own. Six months after their marriage, the Goldbergs moved to Levittown; he commuted to New York City, where he was employed.

Concerning the beginnings of the Israel Community Center, Louis Goldberg told the following story:

"It was May 14, 1948. A few of us (six couples) sitting in my living room on that night heard the radio broadcast that Israel had declared itself a nation. We were all excited about that. The men in the room were all ex-G.I.'s. We suddenly decided that we just *had* to organize a synagogue and center in Levittown and that we *must* call it Israel Synagogue Center in honor of the new State of Israel. There must have been about five hundred Jewish families in Levittown. At that time, the Levitts had about 2,000 homes here. I felt that if people in Israel could stand up as they were doing and saying 'We are Jews and we're going to create something worth while,' then I, too, wanted to stand up and really belong to the Jewish people.

"In the spring of 1949, Mr. Levitt gave the Congregation the land upon which to erect a synagogue. He also provided land for other church groups. With the assistance of a local builder, the Congregation undertook the erection of a building whose cost was $35,000. On April 10, 1949, we received a Scroll of the Torah as a gift from the United Synagogue of America and were underway."

The Israel Community Center has 450 member-families. Enrollment in weekday Hebrew classes was 306 in 1956 and 273 in 1957. In 1956, eighty-nine additional children attended its Sunday school (one day a week). In 1957 enrollment in this school was seventy-eight.

The second congregation to be established in the Levittown

area was a Reform temple. Congregation Beth Avodah was established in October, 1950, in the suburb Westbury, just "next door" to Levittown. It has a membership of 350 families, its own temple building and a Sunday school with an enrollment of 657 pupils in 1956 and 508 in 1957.

These two congregations together total 800 families, or only 28 per cent of the total Jewish community. In addition to Hebrew and Sunday schools, they provide a program of youth activities, Boy Scouts, Young Adults, Brotherhoods, Sisterhoods, a summer daycamp and an adult education program.

The Levittown Workman's Circle School, with its emphasis upon Yiddish culture, was organized in 1957 with an enrollment of 103. This school, which operates one day a week, evidently drew children from the other two schools. In 1958, it added two days to the schedule of one class, presumably expecting to develop into a three-day-a-week school.

Reports from these congregations indicate that the average attendance at Friday Eve (Sabbath) Service at the Reform temple is 125 persons, with no Sabbath morning adult service. Attendance at the Friday Eve Service in the Conservative temple is approximately seventy-five, with a Sabbath morning service attendance of about thirty-five persons, when there is no special occasion such as a Bar Mitzvah ceremony. The Conservative congregation maintains a daily Minyan or worship service attended daily by twenty to thirty men.

Though the number of families affiliated with synagogues in the community is small—less than one-half of the national average —both Rabbis report that "there appears to be a greater respect and concern for religion than there used to be. Something is happening."

Why do so many of Levittown's Jewish families not belong to a synagogue or temple? I asked this question of many different Jewish persons in many walks of life, including the several Rabbis. Their answers suggest the following conclusions:

(1) Young people do not usually belong to a synagogue unless they require a special service from the temple or the Rabbi. This

may mean a Hebrew or Sunday school for their children or, most often, preparation and training of a son for Bar Mitzvah. In this community, it is not unusual for parents to drop their temple memberships after the formal Bar Mitzvah ceremonies.

(2) Many of the people in the community cannot afford to be dues-paying members of synagogues. At least, so they say. They identify themselves with Jewish life through membership in B'nai B'rith, Hadassah, Jewish War Veterans and similar organizations which cost far less, while identification is still assured.

(3) The degree of mobility of Jewish families on Long Island is high. Families remain in their community only until they can "afford something better." They expect to move "any day" and do not consider themselves stable members of the community. Many such families spend their years moving from one town to another, expecting—even hoping—that they will become settled members of a community "tomorrow."

(4) Many families really don't know what to expect or want from synagogual affiliation. They have seldom had any experience with congregational affiliation, for many of these young people's parents never "belonged" either. Synagogual affiliation has no more meaning for them than affiliation with any secular organization. And besides, it is more expensive.

Suburban synagogual activity has performed a positive service for the Jewish people of this Long Island community. They look for and find some form of Jewish identification, whether they belong to a synagogue or not. They acknowledge thereby the fact that they are Jews. They take this fact for granted. What is more, they relate themselves to other Jews in the community through social contact and other organizational affiliations. They may not worship, but they want their children to know that they are Jews.

The story of the origin of the Levittown's Israel Community Center could be duplicated, with minor modifications, almost everywhere in our newer suburban communities.

In St. Louis Park, the effort to establish a synagogue-center has been recorded as follows:

Some wished for the establishment of a Jewish center—defined as a place at which Jewish residents could gather, and have social affairs, at which various organizations could meet, a place which would be a symbol of Jewish residence and permanence in the Park. Some wished for a synagogue. . . . there was a considerable overlapping between people who were concerned about a center and people who were concerned about a congregation. There were some who said that either one would be satisfactory, that both were not necessary. . . . there were many people who felt that the most urgent and immediate need was for the development of nursery schools. . . . there were a number of people who were resistant to the development of any sectarian program as they felt that this would create divisions within the Park that did not now exist. Some felt that attendance of their children at religious school was sufficient, in terms of Jewish background and that their leisure time was better spent in the various non-sectarian programs—as a means of integrating with the total community.[12]

In the spring of 1952, a mass meeting of Jewish residents of the Park was called to consider the community's Jewish needs. The meeting, attended by about 125 family representatives, resulted in the organization of the Park Jewish Civic Association. (The B'nai B'rith Lodge in St. Louis Park was primarily responsible for this effort.) In May, 1956, a home in St. Louis Park was converted into a chapel, classrooms and offices. By 1956, 294 families had affiliated with the Association.

As noted elsewhere,[13] B'nai Abraham Congregation of St. Louis Park, for many years located on the South Side of Minneapolis as an Orthodox congregation, has now officially become a Conservative synagogue. When the Rabbi was asked why his congregation, which had been Orthodox since its organization in 1888, decided to change, he answered: "Simply because there are no Orthodox Jews in St. Louis Park today."

The Congregation's reason for undertaking to erect a new modern temple building is suggested by the brochure,[14] published prior to its fund-raising campaign.

HOW IMPORTANT ARE OUR CHILDREN?

Are not all our dreams and hopes centered around our children? In them we see our future and the fulfillment of everything dear to us.

Don't wait until the moment when they will come home to us

saying: It is your fault that I did not make the right friends. It is your fault that I have to spend time in places that you don't like. It is your fault that my adolescent years were guided by the wrong people. It is your fault that my love and loyalty can be shaken by the lightest wind.

Let's not wait for this moment—too much is at stake. Join in a sincere effort to build a Community Center where our children will meet the right friends in dignity, be guided by the right leaders, and grow up to be good Americans and Jews.

We intend to build a functional building, suitable for all our needs—a building to house a gymnasium for our children to gain athletic skills, lasting friendships and to use their leisure hours to the best advantage. A center that will provide a meeting place for all groups, young and old: B'nai B'rith Youth and Adult Groups, Scout Groups and kindred organizations.

Your confidence in this endeavor is the insurance of the future of our children.

HOW IMPORTANT ARE OUR CHILDREN. . . .

Nowhere in this fund-raising appeal is Judaism mentioned as a religion or as a way of life with its center in religious idealism. The worship of God and the ritual of Jewish life, while obviously taken for granted, find no place in this publication intended for broad appeal. In mimeographed material prepared by the congregation's Rabbi, however, "proper religious training" is discussed, as is the interfaith factor that "Jewish youngsters are asked by their Gentile friends, 'where is your Temple?' "

In old, pre-World War II suburban communities such as Newton, the Jews were primarily concerned with establishing a house of worship. Though the synagogue was always an important meeting place for young and old, the home was the primary social center or house of assembly. All community functions except the very largest were arranged in the home.

An early settler[15] in Newton reminisces about the community's first synagogue:

"The Synagogue which we named Agudas Achim Anshei Sfard was built in 1912. Our family had moved to Newton in 1896 and found a small group of Jewish families already established.

"At first, we conducted High Holy Day services in our home. Later the several family heads arranged to hold such services in a hall on Washington Street near Walnut Street. We conducted services on the Sabbath either at my parents' home or at another home in the Nonantum section where we all lived.

"That synagogue building was most important to us. We actually built a large part of the building ourselves. We were carpenters, masons and just about everything required for this purpose. It was especially important to our families because we lived an intensely Jewish religious life. We had no Hebrew school, but we did acquire a teacher now and then when some itinerant teacher would come into the community. He would teach us how to read Hebrew and how to pray in Hebrew. He always translated everything into Yiddish, not English. Though we children always spoke English to each other, we spoke Yiddish at home.

"Most of the Jewish families in Newton were quite observant. They were very careful about the Sabbath and the Dietary Laws. Not all Jews really kept the Sabbath because some were in the retail business in Newton and just couldn't keep it."

The synagogue-center of World War II days, with its numerous "activities" and youth programs, would hardly have been comprehended—let alone accepted—by Jews of an earlier day.

Newton's second congregation, Temple Emanuel (Conservative), was organized in 1935, when there were only 490 Jewish families in the suburb. Temple Emanuel is in fact a temple-center: it provides for the educational, spiritual and social fellowship of its affiliated families, who numbered 1,360 in 1958. It is also Newton's largest temple. One thousand and sixty children attend its religious schools, and 900 young people participate in its youth activities program. In addition to its Rabbi, assistant Rabbi and cantor, the congregation has a trained director of Jewish education, a director of youth activities with a staff of youth and group workers, and an executive director who assists in the management of the temple's business affairs.

The religious school program has changed its emphasis over a period of years. In 1950, 300 children were enrolled in a one-day-a-week Sunday school program, while 188 participated in a Hebrew school meeting a maximum of three afternoons a week. By 1958, enrollment had more than doubled: 927 children were attending

Hebrew school three afternoons a week—or four afternoons, in certain intensive classes—while 133 children were attending Sunday school. The Sunday school, in turn, ran only through grade two; students who wished to continue their religious education were required to attend the Hebrew school three days a week.

This temple also sponsors a well-attended series of Jewish education classes for adults with a collective enrollment of 250. In its Golden Age Club, with eighty-five members, the parents of congregational members and other "golden-agers" within the community find both companionship and an opportunity to serve Boston's Beth Israel Hospital and other worthy causes.

The temple has also a Sisterhood, Brotherhood and PTA. Its Couples Club attracts 225 young couples, who are drawn closer to the temple and its religious and cultural programs. Sabbath services are well attended both on Friday evenings and on Sabbath mornings.

The explosive growth of Temple Emanuel, beginning in 1949, made a building program highly necessary. Before a new structure could be completed in 1952, Andover-Newton Theological School (the oldest Congregational-Baptist Seminary in America and located in Newton) graciously offered its facilities to the congregation for school use. The offer was promptly and gratefully accepted.

Newton's first Reform temple was organized in April, 1950, by a small group of young men who had recently returned from World War II. By May of that year, 225 families had joined the congregation, which they named Temple Shalom (peace).

Because the congregation had no meeting house of its own, the First Church of Newton (Unitarian) and the Second Congregational Church of West Newton shared their sanctuaries, classrooms and other facilities with the new temple. Schools and services were conducted in these churches until, in May, 1956, a modern temple and religious school building, "contemporary in design, though traditionally Jewish in content" [16] was dedicated.

Temple Shalom's membership in 1957 included 551 families, with 842 pupils in the Sunday and Hebrew schools. The congregation is served by a Rabbi and a part-time youth director, as well as a trained director of religious education.

In 1952, another Conservative congregation, Temple Reyim, which had organized originally as a Jewish center, established itself in West Newton. Its program, too, includes "center" activities for its youth. A beautiful new temple building assures the future growth of this congregation from its present membership of 350 families. Here, too, Rabbinical and group workers have combined to provide a balanced program for synagogue and center.

An Orthodox congregation (Beth El), organized in 1957 and housed in quarters that are already crowded, promises to meet the ritual requirements of its approximately one hundred families. It is as yet without the services of a full-time Rabbi, though it is guided by a young and highly capable Orthodox Rabbi who is presently serving another congregation.

Still another Conservative congregation, Mishkan Tefila, has erected a beautiful new temple, school building and community hall in Newton. Seven hundred and ten member-families are presently affiliated with this congregation, which observed its hundredth anniversary in 1958 and is the oldest Conservative congregation in Greater Boston.

Each of Newton's synagogues is, in short, a temple-center. A skillful interweaving of the social, cultural and religious elements has created the kind of synagogue which appears to be both the most desired and the most needed in suburbia.

In Fair Lawn (New Jersey) we find another of the many typical synagogue-centers which were originally intended to be primarily community centers rather than synagogues. The social and educational needs it was intended to meet are described in an editorial in a 1949 bulletin:[17]

We need a community center—not only will it be a place to meet in, to have parties in, to have our Sunday School in, to have a library in, to have lectures and concerts in—but it will be a place which will help us to become worthy Jews and real Americans.

Seventy-one per cent of the Jewish families who reside in Fair Lawn (as of 1957), or 1,075 out of a total of 1,500, are affiliated with the Fair Lawn Jewish Center (750 families), the Reform temple (150 families) and yet another Conservative congregation (175 families).

In an effort to foster a closer social relationship among Jews in the vicinity of Belmont, suburb of Boston, a few families decided to establish a "center of some kind." In 1931, the group organized as the Belmont-Watertown Jewish Community Center. Here, too, the center emphasis gradually gave way to the religious influence. By 1935, the religious school had assumed a major importance in the lives of these families. A Reform Rabbi was invited to minister to this congregation, and the name of the organization was changed to Beth El Temple Center.

"It is a center in the sense that all temples are centers of Jewish life."

In 1955, a new, commodious building was erected which has helped to knit the Jewish community together.

The Beth El Temple Center has a Sunday school of 300 pupils and a three-day-a-week Hebrew program of seventy pupils. In 1957, the temple had a membership of 370 families, which included many comparatively young professional people. There are many professors from Harvard, M.I.T. and Brandeis and numerous attorneys. Few indeed are the number of family heads over fifty-five years of age. By 1957 Belmont had some 400 Jewish families, while in 1940 there were but fifty families.

Sharon is another of the suburbs of Boston which has had a dual life. Located on Lake Massapoag, Sharon provided a highly pleasurable summer to a few Jewish families who, as early as 1950, had taken up summer residence there. The need for a place of worship was evidenced by the thirty families who worshipped at various homes on the Sabbath during the summer season. By 1933, the group had engaged the services of a Rabbi and set out to raise money for a temple of their own. Many years passed before Congregation Adath Sharon was able, on August 2, 1942, to complete its new synagogue. Most of the congregants still returned to their Boston homes in the fall, to return once again in the spring.

Sharon's major development occurred in the post-World War II years, when a housing development was undertaken in the community. This low-income project, known as Sharon Heights, brought 400 families to Sharon from Boston, Roxbury, Dorchester and Brookline. Other private building projects soon followed, and by 1949, with the help of eighty Jewish families, a new congregation, Temple Israel (Conservative) was built. By December, 1955, the congregation's program was expanded to include not only an improved Hebrew school but a youth center program as well. All of the community's Jewish organizations meet in the temple building. The major organizations are the temple's Brotherhood and Sisterhood, B'nai B'rith, Hadassah, O.R.T. and the Zionist Organization of America.

Temple Israel's membership is 550. Temple Adath Sharon has a membership of fifty families. A third congregation, Temple Sinai (Reform), with a membership of 125, has recently been organized. With an estimated 1,000 Jewish families in Sharon as of 1957, it appears that 72 per cent of the Jewish community is affiliated with a synagogue or temple.

Sharon's leading Jewish citizens believe that the Hebrew school and the youth activities program of Temple Israel are especially responsible for its rapid growth. Three hundred and ten pupils are enrolled in its three-afternoons-a-week Hebrew school program, forty-five in its pre-Hebrew school department, and twenty in its high school. Temple Sinai also has a Sunday school, whose classes meet both on Saturday and Sunday mornings.

The new Congregation of Euclid was also originally organized as a Jewish center.

"We were born on Yom Kippur night in 1947—on a front porch on Nicholas Avenue. A group of Jewish parents met there to formulate plans for the founding of the first synagogue in Euclid. So they organized Congregation Ner Tamid, the Euclid Jewish Center. There were fifty member families in 1949, and in 1953 the cornerstone was laid at our present site—E. 250th Street and Lake Shore Boulevard.

"The Congregation was named 'Ner Tamid' in honor of the 'Eternal Light' (Ner Tamid) radio program which had inspired these young people. It became a Conservative temple as a result of compromise of the opposing views of the early members."

The membership in 1957 totaled 300 families.

Along the foothills of the San Gabriel Mountains, from the flourishing city of Pasadena on toward the California desert, many well-established Jewish suburban communities may be found. The number of Jewish families who reside in this myriad of little towns, from five to forty-five minutes away from the center of Los Angeles, is increasing rapidly.

There are seven temples and synagogues in the San Gabriel Valley. Four are Conservative (El Monte, West Covina, Sierra Madre, Citrus Valley), two are Reform (Temple City and East Covina) and one is recorded as Orthodox (Montebello), although its Rabbi states that his congregation is "more nearly Conservative in its philosophy and practice than it is Orthodox."

Before 1931, the Jews who lived in Sierra Madre were looked upon with suspicion. Because they had no temple or synagogue, they were openly spoken of as "atheistic Jews." In 1931, the few Jewish residents, owners of chicken ranches, erected a temple which they called Beth Israel (The House of Israel). This congregation never engaged a Rabbi except on the High Holy Days. For a brief period it had a religious school, but not a particularly good one.

After World War II, when many young married couples moved into Sierra Madre, the question of religious education and worship became of major concern. Aware that the non-Jewish children of the town attended Sunday schools, the Jewish parents, with the aid of the Jewish Centers Association of Los Angeles, organized the San Gabriel Valley Jewish Center. A subsidy of $4,000 annually paid for the services of a part-time director. The major function of the center was to provide a unique Sunday school—as the center advertised in the Los Angeles Anglo-Jewish weekly, *B'nai B'rith Messenger*, "a Sunday School without religion." The philosophy of the Jewish residents was secular in the extreme: the group prided itself in the fact that "no religion was taught in its school."

"If you read a story to the children and the name of God was in it, the story was out."

In those days, the center had about fifty members. Although the temple still functioned as a house of worship, the center used the temple building for its Sunday school.

In the summer of 1948, the sponsors of the center decided that they "needed a Rabbi." In that year, the services of a Conservative Rabbi were secured, and by 1957 the congregation had a membership of 150 families. It draws its membership from such other Valley suburbs as Duarte, Azusa, Arcadia, and Monrovia. This Conservative congregation serves its people, but, in my opinion, has not yet developed a meaningful program for the community.

The origin of Temple Beth David of the San Gabriel Valley, located in Temple City, has already been recorded. This Reform temple, with a membership of 225 Jewish families, is certainly one of the most active in the entire Valley. Many of its members are professional men—among them doctors, chemists and engineers—who are either self-employed or find employment in the numerous new factories and enterprises in or near the Valley. The newest residents of Temple City and environs come from eastern cities and states. They find life less hurried, homes are less pretentious, and opportunities for businesses and professions are expanding in the Los Angeles area.

Though this congregation's general program is not much different from those of other congregations in the Valley, its emphasis upon the importance of worship is not often found elsewhere in the area. A brochure published by the temple invites membership on this basis:

Many of us have never shared sacrificially in the expanding program of a Temple. Through the generosity of others, we have been privileged to worship in Temples which have been built and maintained through the efforts of others. We now find ourselves placed together in a growing community *and our immediate task is to provide adequate worship and spiritual leadership.* This is a challenge to all of us! It is a call to service and sacrifice which offers each an opportunity and responsibility.

The members of Temple Beth David believe that there are many Jewish families who reside in the Valley who on principle do not belong to any temple or center. Their conjectures appear to be borne out by the accounts of the Whittier Jewish Center, the Citrus Valley Jewish Center and others in the area which began as "non-sectarian" institutions.

The consensus of estimates concerning temple-center membership in the Temple City area indicate that about 40 per cent of the Jewish families are presently affiliated. It is expected that the number will increase as Jewish children reach school age and are subsequently enrolled in Sunday and Hebrew schools.

The same sources believe that the growth of Temple Beth David's membership in recent years is due "ninety per cent to the fact that parents wanted their children to get some Jewish education in our school." This factor, positive and meaningful, must surely not be minimized in importance.

Whittier, another suburban community along the Valley, has a Jewish Center of its own. Organized in 1947, it was known as an institution "free from sectarianism." Many persons spoke of it as a "non-religious" center. As the months passed, dissatisfaction arose because "the center program has no Jewish content." The members have since rethought their position, and a religious basis for the center has been agreed upon. The Whittier Jewish Center recently affiliated with the Conservative movement. Although it has as yet no Rabbinical leadership, a layman has been appointed religious director for the 150 families who are now members.

The Citrus Valley Jewish Center in the San Gabriel Valley has about 150 member-families. Only five years ago, this community was nonexistent. The entire area had for years consisted of citrus orchards, when new housing projects brought hundreds of families into the area. Today there are 500 Jewish families in Citrus Valley and its environs. Here, too, the emphasis has been upon the need for Hebrew education of children and upon fellowship for young and old. This group, too, is affiliated with the Conservative movement.

A new temple-center, affiliated with the Conservative movement, has been erected in West Covina, the largest town in this district. It is expected to meet the needs of the town's 500 Jewish residents.

In East Covina, forty Jewish families recently organized a Reform congregation (Temple Shalom), breaking away from the West Covina Jewish community on the basis of a difference in religious philosophy.

In the suburb of Alhambra, too, the first Jewish organization was a Jewish center. A Conservative Jewish congregation has established a tenuous working arrangement with the center, and the two are now called the Alhambra Jewish Temple and Center. This institution has a membership of 200 Jewish families. (There are about 600 Jewish families in the area.) Because these suburbs are so near each other, many Jewish families, though they live in Alhambra, are known to be affiliated with temple-centers in other nearby communities. It is estimated that 50 per cent of the Jews in this area are affiliated with one or another Jewish institution.

Five hundred and fifty families are affiliated with the Jewish Educational Center of Montebello, another Valley suburb. This center, which draws its membership from the two adjacent communities of Montebello and Monterey Park, is officially regarded as Orthodox. There are about 1,500 Jewish families in these two suburbs; thus about 37 per cent of the Jews in Montebello and Monterey Park are known to be affiliated with the temple-center. Members of the center believe that another 10 per cent of the Jewish community belong to some other synagogue or temple, either in the San Gabriel Valley or in Los Angeles. In this community, too, the emphasis has been placed upon fellowship for young and old and upon the Hebrew education of the youth. This temple-center has had the services of a Rabbi since 1945.

Temple B'nai Israel of El Monte (another Valley suburb), with a membership of 100 families, is not a new congregation. It is distinguished from those already discussed in that it considers itself primarily a temple. Though it regarded itself for years as Reform, it became affiliated with the Conservative movement in 1957 and has already engaged the services of a Conservative Rabbi. Its simple, low-structured building, located on a main thoroughfare, is just around the corner from the Roman Catholic and Methodist Churches of El Monte. This congregation does not differ very much in its program from those already discussed. The desire here, too, is for fellowship and education of the youth.

Why do people affiliate with a synagogue? Reasons vary because people vary. From Euclid we are told:

"We want to give our children some kind of Jewish education, and we wish to be part of the Jewish community, and temple membership is synonymous with the latter."

There are those who say that "some Jewish families belong because of a sense of guilt which results from the expectation by their non-Jewish neighbors that they be affiliated with some religious body." From Belmont (Mass.) we are told:

"The temple represents us to the Gentile world. They know through it that there is such a thing as a Jewish community. I belong because in that way the temple helps me and my family to live as respected people."

Respondents in Newton say:

"We joined the synagogue because we felt we wanted our children to attend religious school. I feel that unless the children know enough about Judaism to be proud of it, being Jewish might offer problems and difficulties they would be unequipped to deal with even if they cope with their Jewishness only from an intellectual and cultural point of view."

Other interesting reasons come from various communities:

"I joined the temple to instill a greater unity in family life. I believe that it gives the children as well as the adults a greater sense of security and a feeling of belonging."

"My husband has always been a member of a synagogue, as was his father. It is a way of life for him. I had never experienced this and felt the lack of such closeness until we joined the temple. We find that our children are receiving an excellent education in Judaism."

"To 'join' is to become part of a whole. The 'whole' is the Jewry of my neighborhood and community. My child goes to Hebrew school in the temple to learn and, as a consequence, to be proud of his background, *not* to become religious or pious. I expect him to decide for himself what he wants to do about his Judaism, but I would like to influence him in the right direction through his own pride and complete acceptance of his people."

"We joined the temple to try to live a fuller life as a Jewish family unit. Our children attend Hebrew school in order that, through a rich Hebrew background, they can achieve the same purpose."

The education of the Jewish child in the tradition of his people is often expressed as the reason for synagogue affiliation:

"We want our children to know and appreciate their heritage."

"I feel that it is my duty to join a temple in order to show my children that Jews have a certain, special way of life."

"I want my children to learn more about Judaism as a way of life—to fill in the many gaps that I feel exist in my own knowledge. I think that it is important to subject my children to Jewish learning and thinking."

In St. Louis Park, a parent states:

"I belong to the synagogue because I have friends there. I have joined the synagogue where my children, my wife and I will be happiest, socially.

"It's true that we could get along without any synagogue, particularly us older people—but our non-Jewish neighbors cannot understand that. They want to know why we do not have a temple here in St. Louis Park. So we are building one which will be a source of pride to all Jews and the whole community."

A Silver Spring resident comments:

"I would be lonely out here unless I belonged to some Jewish organization. I want to identify myself with a synagogue. I can work for Jewish education, and I can help people through the synagogue."

From the San Gabriel Valley:

"I'm interested in business. This congregation needed help to work out its financial affairs. Someone thought I could help, and so here I am."

From Skokie:

"You can be a big fish out here. I like belonging to the synagogue because I can be 'somebody' here. I'm a respected member. I work hard whenever I am asked to do something."

From Temple City, one of the temple's founders explains his affiliation:

"My wife and I moved out to Alhambra. We had a child five years old at the time. Frankly, we had no desire to join any synagogue or temple. Then, one day, I met a friend who asked me, 'What are you going to do about the education of your child?' He was concerned about the same thing for his family. This got us to thinking about the matter, and we decided that we ought to start a temple. The purpose was simply to provide for the Jewish education of our children. Several non-Jewish organizations of the town offered to help us by providing a meeting place for the school. The Ministers Association and Kiwanis were particularly helpful. The Y.M.C.A. gave us a place to meet and on every hand we heard, 'You really need a temple here.'"

It is interesting to note also that 250 respondents to a questionnaire, or 41 per cent, state that their friends are members of the same synagogue with which they are affiliated. Friendships must therefore be recognized as an important factor in synagogue affiliation.

"Highly important also to many of those persons who join a synagogue is the matter of who is the Rabbi? What is his point of view? What kind of a *person* is he? Is he a real leader in both the Jewish and total community? What kind of Jewish education will be provided for my child in the temple school? Are the teachers professionally trained? Are the school facilities as good as public school buildings? Who are the temple's members? Are they friendly? Is there 'room' for us? Can we make friends through the temple and thus become integrated into the community more quickly? Is the temple located in an area to which my children and I have easy access?"

Fifty-two per cent of all respondents explain their synagogue membership in terms of what they consider their obligation as a member of the Jewish community and/or what their children require by way of Hebrew or Sunday school education. Sixty-eight persons, or 11 per cent, stated that their membership was based exclusively on the use of the synagogue's school facilities for their children's Hebrew education. Only eleven persons, or 1.8 per cent, gave as their reason that "I am religious."

A sense of identification with the Jewish people and a concern for the identification of their children with this people are thus clearly indicated as the two major reasons for synagogue membership.

Whatever the reasons for affiliation, it is noteworthy that the vast majority of members express satisfaction with the temple of their choice. Four hundred and ninety-eight respondents, or 83 per cent, believe that their congregations are "doing a good job." Only forty-two persons, or 7 per cent, expressed dissatisfaction with their synagogue. Ten per cent did not reply.

The "good job" to which these suburbanites refer may best be seen in the typical program of one of the large suburban synagogues included in this study.

Friday
EVENING   Sabbath Services

Saturday
MORNING   Bible Study Class
               Jr. Congregation Sabbath Service
               Adult Congregational Sabbath Service
AFTERNOON   Talmud Study Class of Adults
               Sabbath Afternoon & Evening Service
EVENING   Brotherhood Dance

Sunday
MORNING   Hebrew & Sunday School Classes
               Post Bas & Bar Mitzvah Services Breakfast & Class
AFTERNOON   Youth Club Meetings, including 3 United Synagogue Youth Groups and one Leaders Training Fellowship Group.
EVENING   Young People's Dance Party

Monday

AFTERNOON	Couples Club Supper and Forum
	Hebrew School Classes
EVENING	Athletic Program for Boys in Gym
	Social Dancing Classes of Children

Tuesday   Golden Agers—Meeting and Luncheon

AFTERNOON   Hebrew School Classes

EVENING   Committee Meetings $\left\{\begin{array}{l}\text{Youth}\\\text{Ritual}\\\text{Education}\end{array}\right.$

Home Study Classes
Boy Scout Troop Meeting

Wednesday

MORNING	Adult Hebrew Classes
AFTERNOON	Sisterhood Meeting
	Hebrew Classes
EVENING	Adult Study Classes

Thursday

AFTERNOON	Hebrew School Classes
EVENING	Congregational Committee Meetings

Friday   Sabbath Services

With minor variations, this program can be duplicated in most if not all suburban synagogues in America.

The Hebrew and Sunday schools have become the very heart of most suburban congregations. Temples and their religious leaders recognize their responsibility for the education of Jewish children. Usually a large portion of the temple budget is devoted to the support of the school. In our sampling, 41 per cent of the children of school age attend Hebrew school classes three afternoons a week or more, while 59 per cent receive their Jewish education in the Sunday school one morning a week.

In most suburban communities, the Hebrew and Sunday schools are under the direct supervision of the congregation's Rabbi or director of education. They are generally guided by the central city's Bureau of Jewish Education, if the congregation asks for assistance. Counsel and guidance are offered to all congregational schools in the greater Boston, New York, Cleveland, Chicago, Washington and Los Angeles areas.

In Minneapolis, the children from the suburb of St. Louis Park are transported by bus to one of America's best Hebrew schools, the Minneapolis Talmud Torah. This community-wide school has jealously guarded against the intrusion of any local synagogue or temple school in greater Minneapolis into the policy-making area of Hebrew education. In 1956, Talmud Torah optioned and later acquired a new and larger site for a branch in St. Louis Park. The new site covers ten acres and is planned to provide more adequate classroom space, playground facilities and room for group work agencies. Approximately 24 per cent of the Park's children, five to seventeen years of age, attend Talmud Torah classes, while 47 per cent go to Sunday school either in St. Louis Park or in a central city congregation. Thirty-two percent of the Talmud Torah's 1,200 pupils live in the Park.

The B'nai Abraham Congregation in St. Louis Park has established its own daily nursery school, which has met with an enthusiastic response. This congregation conducts its own Sunday school, which in 1957 had an enrollment of 250 children.

The schools on Long Island (Nassau and Suffolk Counties) are associated either with the Metropolitan Districts of the Bureau of Jewish Education, the Jewish Education Association, the United Synagogue of America, the Union of American Hebrew Congregations or the Union of Orthodox Jewish Congregations.

In the New York area, the Hebrew schools are more closely identified with the Orthodox, Conservative and Reform denominations than with the city-wide Bureau of Jewish Education.

In Boston the influence of the Bureau of Jewish Education, supported by the city's Associated Jewish Philanthropies, is marked. Most congregational Hebrew schools use its curriculum and otherwise voluntarily regulate their educational program to conform with the Bureau's standards. City-wide uniform tests are given annually in order that congregations may compare their schools with others in greater Boston.

In Newton, about 1,700 children of public school age attend

some Hebrew school. In addition, about 600 children attend Sunday school classes in one of Newton's five congregations. Many others are transported by bus to congregational schools in Brookline and Boston. Emphasis upon Hebrew education in the New England area is comparatively high; the more intensive programs are found in the Conservative and Orthodox congregations.

In Sharon, the Hebrew school of the Conservative temple is looked upon as the temple's primary activity.

"The school comes first with us. We know that we gain new members when families are ready to send their children to Hebrew schools. That is really all that most of them want from us. The parents want to return to their roots. They have no desire to run away from Judaism. They have no neurotic fears about being Americans and Jews. They know that they are Americans and now want to understand their Jewishness."

In Natick, a suburban community west of Boston, Temple Israel (Conservative) provides the Hebrew education for 131 Jewish children in the community. Forty are enrolled in the only other congregation in this suburb, Beth Am (Reform), which was founded in June, 1956. In all, 23 per cent of Natick's Jewish children five to thirteen years of age receive their training in Natick's congregation, while eleven other children acquire Jewish training from other sources.[18]

On the North Shore of Boston in the suburbs of Lynn, Swampscott and Marblehead, 61 per cent of Jewish children five to thirteen years of age are enrolled in Hebrew or Sunday schools.[19] Of these, 61.8 per cent attend a three-day-a-week Hebrew school, 20.8 per cent go to a four-or-five-day-a-week Hebrew school, and 13.7 per cent attend a Sunday school only, while 3.7 per cent of the children attend other types of schools. The number of children who receive a more intensive Hebrew education is remarkably high.

Although the number of children who receive some form of Jewish education has reached an all-time high of 80 per cent, the percentage of those who receive a Hebrew education is only 2.9 per cent higher than it was in 1947. Of those who receive some form of Jewish education, 51 per cent study only one day a week.[20]

In Euclid, Cleveland's United Hebrew Schools first assisted in the suburb by establishing a branch school there in 1947. By 1951, the Euclid Jewish Center assumed full control of this school, though the school still receives aid, guidance and assistance through Cleveland's Bureau of Jewish Education. The school has a total enrollment of 275 pupils, ranging in age from five to fourteen years. About 100 of these students are enrolled in the congregation's six Hebrew classes.

The suburbs on the West Coast present a different picture of Jewish education. Here, according to the record,[21] 69 per cent of the Jewish children who receive some form of Jewish education study only one day a week, and only 31 per cent are enrolled in three-days-a-week Hebrew schools. Though this falls far short of the national average, it must be remembered that these communities are among the newest in the nation and have not yet fully established themselves or their educational programs.

The degree of mobility, high as it is nationally, is even higher on the West Coast. Indeed, rootlessness is characteristic of the greater Los Angeles population. Jewish families have yet to fix their roots deep into the soil of their new suburban communities. It is not surprising, therefore, that interest in intensive Hebrew education is not yet marked in these communities. According to the records of the greater Los Angeles Bureau of Jewish Education, the San Fernando Valley has an estimated 105,000 Jews, but only 28 per cent of all boys and girls of school age receive any form of Jewish education. In December, 1956, 16,221 pupils were attending schools affiliated with the Bureau of Jewish Education of Los Angeles. Of these, 11,129, or 67 per cent, were enrolled in a Sunday (one-day-a-week) school. There has been an increase in the week-day Hebrew school population of 5.2 per cent.

The suburbs along the San Gabriel Valley have a high population of young people under twenty-one years of age. The towns of El Monte and Rosemead, for example, have a total population of 70,233, of whom 25,439 are under twenty-one. In Covina, Azusa and Baldwin Park, the total number of residents is 46,276, of whom 17,142 are under twenty-one. Montebello and Pico have a total citizenry of 39,960, of whom 14,353 are under twenty-one years. These figures hold true for practically all the suburbs along the San Gabriel Valley.

The Bureau of Jewish Education of Los Angeles incorporated the attendance records for the Jewish communities of the San Gabriel Valley in its report on the Jewish community of Los Angeles for 1953.[22] These records indicate that 66.1 per cent of the Jewish children in these suburbs were provided with a Sunday school education, whereas 26.8 per cent studied two or three afternoons a week. Informants agree that the number of those receiving a more intensive form of Hebrew education has since increased by about 10 per cent. It appears, then, that the Jewish communities of the San Gabriel Valley are providing their children with no more than minimal forms of Jewish education.

Limited facilities, an inadequate number of professionally trained teachers, transportation problems and inadequate finances are largely responsible for this "token" Jewish education. The communities themselves are seldom ready to give priority to a maximal program of Jewish education.

Although the number of pupils in the Hebrew or maximal program of study has hardly changed since 1946, it should be noted that the quality of instruction has vastly improved. Supervision of staff and curriculum by the Bureau of Jewish Education in the central city, as well as the expert guidance provided by the several national denomination school commissions, are responsible for this improvement. Whether Jewish education is actually flourishing is a moot question. We shall not know the answer to this question for another decade, when the results of present-day methods and curricula will be judged in terms of the attitude of Jews to Judaism, the Jewish people and concern for the welfare of their fellow man.

Adult Jewish education programs actively sponsored by temples afford another reason for congregational affiliation. The Jewish women of suburbia are the enthusiastic "students" in both day and evening classes.

The women, practically all of whom drive a car, get to and

from study classes without missing such important assignments as shopping, picking up Joey and Susan at school and getting them to dentists, doctors and dancing lessons. Rabbis in practically every suburban community speak enthusiastically of the women's encouraging response to the call for Jewish education.

"Our morning classes for women are really well attended. They study such subjects as conversational Hebrew, the prayer book, Jewish history, the Bible and fundamentals of Judaism. And they *really* work at it. It is fascinating to see how they undertake these classes and yet turn up at other study classes sponsored by Hadassah, which has some classes of its own."

Women complain that they cannot get their husbands to attend formal classes. Yet home-study courses, in which a select group of husbands and wives study or discuss some basic Jewish theme, are very well received. Rabbis and teachers in all suburban communities seem pleased with the results to date.

"The home-study groups are tremendously important because they provide me, their Rabbi, with an excellent opportunity to get to know these people in an informal setting. I teach them Bible and insist that they devote themselves to the study program assiduously. However, they really acquire much more through this medium for, in these home gatherings, people talk informally and give expression to their ideas about Judaism and the world. I have discovered that from these classes I acquire devoted friends and disciples."

Synagogues in suburbia often provide evening classes which meet in the synagogue building. These are usually lecture series or additional Hebrew classes. Though attendance records vary, the increasing number of persons who enroll in synagogue classes is definitely encouraging. Adult classes are exceedingly popular throughout suburbia.

In Newton, I have inaugurated special classes for the parents of our Bar and Bas Mitzvah boys and girls. I have found that, as the time approaches when their children will be formally confirmed in their faith through these religious ceremonies, the parents are even more receptive to formal classes for themselves. It is usual to have from seventy-five to one hundred fathers and mothers at each of these class sessions. Parents are receptive because they see that their Rabbi is interested in their children and in their training. They are often challenged by their own children and really want to keep up with their studies. Through this class, I am able to inculcate a philosophy about Judaism and an attitude toward Jewish life that is important both for the parents and their children. This is one of the healthiest Jewish experiences I have had in recent years.

Suburban congregations peopled by comparatively young families have not yet found it necessary to meet the needs of the Jewish aged within their communities, primarily because the number of "golden-agers" appears to be limited. Yet with the passing of years, this program may become increasingly necessary for all suburban communities. It is reasonable to suppose that the synagogue will gladly accept this responsibility, as it has already assumed other obligations with respect to its young people.

Often one hears the apprehension expressed that, though the synagogue is the formal symbol of a religion-centered way of life, it may very easily become a completely secularized institution if it limits its program to non-religious activities and interests rather than to deep-rooted spiritual needs. The Rabbis of many suburban temples are sorely troubled because many of their congregants appear to want an easy, relaxed kind of country club atmosphere, rather than a house of worship with a positive philosophy for Jewish life, with a strong belief in God and His purposiveness at its very center. Congregations and their lay leaders are indeed often misled by the growth in membership and the physical enlargement of the temple into believing that the millenium has arrived. This misconception is, of course, a source of grave concern.

"I get annoyed with those persons who answer my query: 'How are things coming?' by telling me how many persons have joined the temple in the past year and how much larger school enrollment has become or any number of things like that. What I am trying to find out is: 'How many of these congregants have had their lives spiritually enriched through their temple affiliation? How many persons have come to feel at home in this world because God is their Father?' It is this point which is all too often lost sight of."

Yet, as we shall note later,[23] synagogue affiliation is in its own right a highly important fact. It must not be looked upon lightly as evidence of the religiosity of contemporary Jewish families.

Criticism and caustic comment about suburbia's synagogues and their programs, though frequently heard, do not seem to me wholly justified. The synagogue is not now and never was *only* a house of worship. It is also a center of fellowship for young and old. It provides leisure-time and recreational activities, as well as Jewish educational facilities, for young and old. It is the primary means by which identification as a Jew is currently achieved. Suburban synagogues are, in fact, synagogue-centers. They offer each Jew the opportunity to come to know his own rich heritage and to live his life as an American Jew.

Chapter 5   The Round of Ritual

Ritual helps us to identify ourselves with the people to which we belong and to read the spiritual meaning for us of its historic experience. We can as little do without observances and practices that symbolize the religious meanings of our civilization as we can do without language to communicate our ideas and feelings to one another.[1]

The fundamental concept in Judaism is the belief in one universal and ethical God Who is directly interested in all His creations, including man. The Jewish people—whose ancestors, beginning with the patriarch Abraham, first offered this unique insight to humankind—has traditionally believed that its own distinctiveness is directly asociated with this basic concept. In order that the truth concerning the nature of God might be promulgated, it was essential for this people to lead "a distinct type of life calculated to realize the moral purpose of life and demonstrate its value."[2] Hence laws, practices and ritual regulating the life of the Jew were essential. A good Jew, according to the traditional interpretation, is one who fears the Lord and keeps His commandments —moral, ethical *and* ritualistic. According to this view, ritual is important not only because it helps to unite Jews in a bond of fellowship, but also because it reminds them of their ultimate purpose: to live the good life and to teach that the moral and ethical way of life is in fact God's way for man. From the Orthodox point of view, Jewish ritual practices must be maintained because God ordained them.

The rationale for ritual observance by those Jews who do not regard themselves as Orthodox is markedly different. While not accepting the premise that ritual was ordained by God, they affirm their belief in Judaism as the most moral and ethical way of life that has yet been devised. Further, they look upon Jewish ritual as an expression of the collective will of the Jewish people to survive and to preserve these supreme ethical and moral ideals which ultimately will gain acceptance in the heart and mind of man.

Many Jewish ritual practices are gradually losing their hold upon Jews throughout the world because men find it more difficult, in this age of science, to believe that these observances are divinely ordained. Ritual has lost its significance and meaning for them. They recognize that it may have served a worthy purpose in an earlier age, but they hold that men now aspire to form stronger bonds of unity and easier means of communication with their fellow humans, in contrast to their former tendency to keep aloof and separate from other people. This gradual reduction in religious ritual and observance has been noted among all contemporary religious groups.

Judaism, which has been termed "a ritualistic religion," has quite naturally been affected by these trends. The reduction of interest in ritual associated with the Sabbath, the Festivals and Holy Days, and particularly the Dietary Laws, is especially marked. Yet Jews in suburban communities, although less inclined to observe this type of ritual within their homes, seem to have found new, significant values in other ceremonial practices, such as the kindling of the Sabbath candles, the festive Sabbath meal, and the observance of the Passover festival, Chanukah (the Feast of Dedication, or the Feast of Lights) and Purim (the Feast of Lots). Though the *reasons* for ritual observance have changed radically, we may say that Jewish ritual observance is actually greater today among suburban families than it was a decade ago. Ritual associated with the child, the family and the people appears to be acceptable today.

The present interest in certain ritual practices is better understood if we realize that Jewish children are largely responsible for re-introducing (or sometimes introducing for the first time) Jewish ceremonial and ritual into the home. The child-centered home usually concerns itself with fulfilling the children's wishes. Because children have been indoctrinated in the religious schools in matters of ritual, and because "children must be satisfied," parents have returned to certain of their Hebraic traditions. It is generally agreed

that more Jewish families observe a Seder on the Passover than was
the case even a decade ago. The story of the exodus from Egypt and
explanations of the symbols of the Passover tale are taught through
the model Seder in the religious school, and children are urged to
repeat the lessons they have learned in their own homes.

"Parents often tell me that they have begun to observe the Passover rituals because they 'do not want to disappoint the children.'
What begins as a concession to the enthuisastic response of children
often becomes a rich experience for the parents as well."

Even though an increasing number of children are attending
Hebrew school classes and learning about these traditions, the observance of the Dietary Laws, generally regarded as the most basic
of all Jewish rituals, has markedly decreased in suburbia. According
to the traditional practice, all meat foods must be kept strictly
separate from milk foods, as the contact with each other—such as
meat with milk, butter or cheese—would render both unfit for consumption. This regulation involves the use of two sets of utensils,
both for cooking and eating, with one set reserved for meat dishes
and the other for milk or butter dishes, and the crockery and
cutlery of the two sets kept rigorously apart. Meat that is Kosher
("proper," or ritually prepared) must have been slaughtered in
accordance with a prescribed ritual, and the blood must be drained
from it in accordance with Biblical injunction (Genesis IX:4;
Leviticus III:17). The ritual with respect to Kosher food is complex, yet it was universally observed in the past.

But times change.

A sampling of 599 suburban Jewish families in over eighty
communities indicates that 76 per cent (456) of the respondents
questioned do not observe the traditional Dietary Laws within their
own homes. Even more—563 families, or 93 per cent—do not
observe the Dietary Laws *outside* their homes. Only 7 per cent of
those replying claim to observe a single standard of dietary observance.

A survey of the Rabbis in the suburbs of Levittown, Euclid,
Skokie, St. Louis Park, Montgomery County, Sharon, Newton and
the towns of the San Gabriel Valley reveals that no more than 10

per cent of the Jewish families maintain the traditional dietary ritual by purchasing Kosher meat for home consumption. It also confirms that only about 7 per cent of these families maintain a single standard of dietary ritual. Seventy-three Conservative and Orthodox Rabbis in sixty-one other communities believe that these figures are accurate for all of America's suburbs.[3]

"In Euclid, the number of Jews who purchase Kosher meat is certainly no higher than 10 per cent. Inasmuch as there is no Kosher meat market in Euclid, all meats must be purchased in Cleveland. Despite the lack of concern for the dietary regulations in the homes, the Euclid Community Temple and Center's dining facilities are *completely* Kosher."

"There are two Kosher meat markets in Skokie. However, there are many Jewish families who purchase their Kosher meat from butchers on the North Side of Chicago—merchants whom they patronized when they lived in the 'old' neighborhood. But it is estimated that no more than 10 per cent purchase meat from Kosher meat markets."

There is agreement by representative Orthodox, Conservative and Reform Rabbis in this community that fewer than 5 per cent of Skokie's Jews maintain a single standard of dietary observance within and outside the home.

"In Sharon, assuming that *all* families in the Orthodox synagogue purchase Kosher meat, and knowing that no more than eighty-five families of Temple Israel [Conservative] purchase Kosher meat, making 125 families in all out of a total 1,000 Jewish families in the town, we may say that, at the very top, no more than 12 per cent of the Sharon Jewish families buy ritually prepared Kosher meat. But we are quite certain that of the seventy-five families already referred to, all but six have a *double* standard of Kashrut [Kosher] food in the home and non-Kosher food is eaten outside the home. Thus, the number who really observe the Dietary Laws is almost nil."

"Jewish families living in the suburbs of the San Gabriel Valley simply do not maintain Kashrut with but one major exception. In the suburb of Montebello, there is a Kosher butcher who has been in the community for ten years. He is reputed to be doing a good business. Yet, at most, about 20 per cent of Montebello's Jewish families maintain Kosher homes. It must be noted, though, that no more than 5 per cent observe the Dietary Laws outside their homes."

Fourteen per cent of greater Los Angeles' Jews say that their homes are "strictly Kosher." Yet here, too, the number is reduced by more than half when a single standard of dietary observance is discussed.

"In St. Louis Park, it is believed that about 8 per cent of the Jewish families buy Kosher meat. The number who keep Kosher outside their home is infinitesimal."

"Most Jewish families who belong to the several Conservative congregations in Newton do not even pretend to observe the Dietary Laws. Although they all are the children of Orthodox parents, they have departed from dietary observance. The situation is such that in at least one of the several Conservative congregations, pastries and cakes baked in private homes may not be brought into the temple because the number of Kosher homes is so limited."

"Here, the number of Jewish families who purchase Kosher meats is less than 10 per cent of the total Jewish population. You can almost count the number of 'single standard' Jews on the fingers of two hands."

As for the three major suburbs in Montgomery County—Silver Spring, Chevy Chase and Bethesda—all the Rabbis agree that even the double standard of dietary observance is followed by no more than 7 per cent of the Jews.

Unless some new factors are introduced soon, we may expect that, though some vestige of Dietary Laws will remain, the number of ritually observant Jewish families will continue to diminish. Yet other forms of ritual observance appear to be increasing.

Reports from each of the suburbs studied reveal that more Jewish women are kindling the Sabbath candles in the homes on Sabbath Eve (Friday night) than at any time in the past decade. In fewer homes do men chant the Kiddush (blessing over the wine) at the Sabbath table, yet here, too, the number has increased greatly since 1946. A recent Los Angeles study [4] reports that 30 per cent of families in greater Los Angeles regularly light candles on Friday night. In the San Gabriel Valley suburbs, however, informants report that no more than 15 per cent of the families observe this ritual. In greater Washington (D.C.), only 29 per cent of all Jewish families kindle the Sabbath candles. Rabbis and other observers in Montgomery County believe that about 20 per cent of these suburbanites light the Friday night candles. In my opinion, these figures indicate a marked increase in this form of ritual observance by young Jewish suburban families.

How shall we account for the return to the Sabbath ritual? Rabbis and laymen offer their comments:

"Jews have no antipathy to ritual but they want the ritual to be simple, to be beautiful and to be meaningful. You can understand quite logically the positive Jewish values that result from the blessing of the Sabbath candles, the recital of Kiddush or the placement of the Mezzuzah on the door."

"What more beautiful way can there be than to kindle candles and offer a special prayer as one begins the Sabbath? These symbols have meaning for the people. Remember, whether Jews go to synagogue on the Sabbath or not, many of them do have a special Sabbath meal to which all the family comes. Mother prepares special delicacies. The candles make the occasion festive, 'partyish.' What's more, the children in these families have been learning these rituals in the Hebrew schools and Sunday schools. Parents recognize that they do have a responsibility to 'follow through' when it comes to the Sabbath—even if they do so only because of their children. So mother lights the candles and father says the Kiddush. It really doesn't matter if the Hebrew prayers may not be intelligible to all at the table. The simple fact is that—it's the Sabbath! And if the parents forget or ignore it, their children remind them or even perform these rites themselves. The melodies are so beautiful and the scene, as they or the parents chant, is inspiring. This way of observing the Sabbath, like the Passover Seder, which is becoming even more popular, involves the entire family and it is, therefore, well received."

The Sabbath Eve meal in which parents, children and often grandparents join is much more in evidence in the older eastern suburban communities, such as Newton, Marblehead, Swampscott and Belmont, than in towns like Euclid or the many suburbs along the San Gabriel Valley, excepting Montebello and Monterey Park.

Here again, proximity to a large and old center of population where ritual observance has been respected makes acceptance of these practices in the suburbs more likely. Skokie, even though a young Jewish community, derives its standards from Chicago's West Side, from which many of its residents have come. Here one expects and finds that the Sabbath Eve meal is much more of a ritual matter than it is in most suburbs.

Even when the Kiddush is not chanted, the occasion still provides a religious experience because the Sabbath candles have been kindled and the traditional blessings have been chanted. Sabbath Eve, because it brings the family together for a leisurely sharing of experience, is still an important factor in the survival of the Jewish people.

Eighty-one Rabbis in seventy-eight different suburbs throughout the country report that the synagogue or temple is only "moderately well attended" at the Sabbath Eve service and that "it is poorly attended on Sabbath morning, except when a Bar Mitzvah, confirmation or other special event takes place." And then "the people come to the Bar Mitzvah rather than to the service." Laymen within these congregations support these opinions.

One Rabbi summarizes the situation:

"Jews just don't pray these days. If they do pray, then they do so on special occasions only and do not seem to feel the need to do so most of the year. They certainly do not come to synagogue for daily 'Minyan' prayers unless it be for a 'Yahrzeit' [in observance of the anniversary of the death of a parent or other blood relative]. When you ask people why they don't attend Sabbath Eve services, they reply by saying that they do not manage to get together with their families very much these days, and if they do so on Friday night, they prefer not to rush. And besides, being with one's family is also a religious act. When it comes to Sabbath morning services, they simply say that they work on Saturday or 'are busy,' whatever that may mean to them. I believe that all it means is that actually other things are of greater importance and matter more. That is why they don't come. Prayer is fast becoming a lost art."

In order to bring more people into the synagogue at Sabbath services, many Rabbis invite the children or young people of their congregations to participate in the services. Thus, because parents and friends are likely to put in an appearance on such occasions, attendance is augmented.

"Some persons regard it as improper for me to use this method to get people into the synagogue, but I do not regard it as wrong in any way. Organized religion is obliged to compete with the numerous secular organizations, television, radio, theatres and other distracting influences. I, on the other hand, offer people the opportunity to see and hear their own children as they participate in a service. I try to make the service a rich and meaningful experience, and I preach or rather teach from the pulpit. Whether people come frequently or not, I try to have them come out of the service with a sense not only of personal ease, but a greater love and understanding of Judaism. This is all most difficult for me because I had hoped that people would come voluntarily. But it is a challenge to me, and I like it."

The twenty-one pupils of a confirmation class in one Newton congregation (Conservative) were questioned as to their parents' religious practices. Sixteen reported that their parents attended late Friday evening services in the temple on occasion; two stated that their parents worshipped at these services regularly; and three claimed that their parents never attended services. Fourteen pupils stated that their parents attended Sabbath morning services on occasion, while three declared that their parents never attended.

Ten of these twenty-one fathers do not work on the Sabbath. None of these parents works on Rosh Hashonah (Jewish New Year) or Yom Kippur (The Day of Atonement). Riding, shopping, writing and smoking are, according to Orthodox tradition, forbidden on the Sabbath, yet fifteen of the fathers smoke, nineteen write and all twenty-one ride and shop. Fifteen of the twenty-one mothers kindle the candles on the Sabbath Eve. Only one father chants the Kiddush regularly, seven others chant it occasionally "if they get around to it," and eleven never chant the Kiddush. All twenty-one of these confirmants reported that their parents never recite "grace" before or after meals.

With respect to the observance of the Dietary Laws, seventeen of the families mix meat and milk dishes, and thirteen did not use Kosher meat.

This sampling represents the degree of ritual observances on the part of parents whose children attend Sunday school in a Conservative congregation. Ritual observance by the parents who are avowedly Reform would be even less marked.

High Holy Day services, on Rosh Hashonah and Yom Kippur, are very well-attended in all temples and synagogues in suburbia.

"It's difficult to understand why they come. For so many of them come into services at a comparatively late hour and a good number do not remain to the conclusion of the service. Some know how to read the Hebrew prayers; others do not. Yet they come. Husbands and wives, parents and grandparents attend these High Holy Day services each year. Their children go on to special children's services in the synagogue. Every effort is made to make these occasions meaningful. Rabbis, ritual committees, congregational officers work zealously to inaugurate the religious year, on a high spiritual note."

Almost every new suburban synagogue structure has been built with the High Holy Day congregation in mind.

"We have 300 seats in our temple. That is certainly more than enough for the year. We may have a congregation of 100 to 125 persons at a Friday evening service. But we have built the temple in such a way that, by opening a series of doors, we combine the Community Hall with the temple. That gives us 500 additional seats. And even that may not be sufficient."

Why do people attend these Holy Day services in such numbers? Nostalgia; the feeling that parents, near or far, would approve; the conventions of society, which play a far greater role than is generally supposed; the urging by one's children who know about Holy Days and their significance through their religious school— all these tend to keep the number of Holy Day congregants high. There are those, too, who worship and pray in all sincerity and truth to a God in Whom they believe without equivocation or uncertainty. Still others believe that this spiritual "exercise" in the presence of their fellow Jews strengthens them in their resolve to live a better life. Whatever the reasons, temples are filled to capacity on the Jewish New Year and the Day of Atonement.

"I have noticed, however, that the very young couples with very small children are less likely to worship with us. They still 'drop in' at some service which their parents attend, or they stay away completely. When their children become old enough to go to Hebrew school, they join the synagogue and begin to attend High Holy Day services."

Here again, the congregational Hebrew school plays an important and dramatic role. Child-centered parents are guided by their children, who in turn take their cue from the school and the Rabbi.

The three pilgrimage festivals on the Hebrew calendar are Passover, the Feast of Weeks and the Feast of Tabernacles. Biblical in origin, each of these festivals has, through the centuries, enjoyed wide popularity and acceptance by Jews everywhere.

Passover, commemorative of the Exodus from Egyptian bondage, is still a major festival in the Hebrew calendar. Indeed, Rabbis throughout suburbia note that the Passover Seder services in the home are more popular and even better attended than they were a decade ago, with approximately seventy-five to eighty per cent of Jewish families conducting or attending a Seder.

"Passover is so important to us because the Hebrew school and Sunday school spend so much of their time teaching our children how to observe the ritual of this festival. All the blessings and traditional chants are taught. The many symbols, colorful and beautiful, are a source of pleasure to the children. Matzoh is 'different.' It looks and tastes different and is, therefore, acceptable for an eight-day period. The Seder is a home gathering where parents, children and guests join to tell the story of the Exodus of the Jews from Egypt, point up the importance of human freedom and the meaning of slavery. What lesson can have greater meaning to Jews in these days who remember Hitler, who know the evils of Fascism and Communism? So Passover, the Spring Festival, with its important message and its rich symbolism assumes greater meaning for Jews

today. I notice that people prepare their homes for Passover much
more carefully than they did a decade ago. Our children demand
it of us and today manufacturers of Passover foods have made them
so appetizing that they have become desirable."

Homes are carefully prepared for the advent of the Passover
Festival. All leaven is removed from most Orthodox or Conservative homes before special food, prepared for use on the Festival, is
brought into the home. The number of families of all denominations who refrain from eating bread and other products containing
leaven is believed to be increasing.

The Feast of Weeks (Shavuot), traditionally known as "The
Season of the Giving of the Law," would long ago have ceased to be
a major festival for Jews in suburbia were it not for the fact, that
in most congregational schools, confirmation or graduation services
take place on this day. The special occasion offers the Rabbi an
opportunity to deliver a sermon on the "giving of the Law at Mount
Sinai," which is traditionally the theme of this festival. The Yizkor
(Memorial Service) also takes place on Shavuot and brings still
another group of persons into the temple for reasons clearly dis-
sociated from the basic meaning of the festival itself.

The Feast of Tabernacles (Sukkot), with its emphasis upon the
need to trust in God, is less "popular" with adults because it follows
only five days after the Day of Atonement, and people have grown
"weary" of the Holy Day season. Synagogues and temples in suburbia erect beautiful Sukkot (booths), lovingly built by Sisterhood
and Brotherhood members assisted in their efforts by children from
the congregation's Hebrew or Sunday schools. The festival's importance in most communities is governed by the emphasis which
Sukkot receives in the school curriculum. Seldom do Jewish suburban parents observe the festival by attending synagogue or even
with special festival foods.

This festival is utilized in many suburban congregations for the
consecration service of new pupils in the Hebrew school. Again,
even though Jewish families seldom erect their own Sukkah or eat
their meals there, the festival can remain excitingly alive because

the pupils of the religious school enjoy both the beauty of this Harvest festival and the colorful fruits which decorate the interior of the tabernacle. However, though Sukkot remains on the Hebrew calendar, it no longer plays much of a role in the lives of suburban Jews.

The traditionally minor festivals of Purim, recorded in the biblical Book of Esther, and Chanukah, whose story is recorded in the Apocryphal Books of the Maccabees, have become major festivals in our day. The reasons for this are clear.

Purim, which relates the Story of Esther, Mordecai and Haman, reminds Jews of the uncertainty of their minority position in the world, of their dependence upon men of good-will in order that they may remain alive. It is charged with meaning for the Jew of today who remembers Hitler's crematoria and concentration camps. The Book of Esther reminds the Jew that intolerance is an old, old story. Because Jews understand this well, Purim is relevant and meaningful and serves as a pertinent reminder.

Purim is also an occasion for fun. Children enjoy it. They play an important role in all synagogue and temple services, which are built around the reading of the Megillah (Scroll containing the Book of Esther). The school conspires to make the festival even more meaningful through the child. Everywhere in suburbia, Purim is a major festival in terms of the emphasis placed upon it by children and their parents.

Chanukah, because of its coincidence with the Christmas season, has become exceedingly important and is often regarded as a major festival.

"How can we counteract the Christmas influence in our public school system? We must do it through our Hebrew and Sunday schools and in our homes as well. So we make Chanukah a season for colorful decorations. We kindle beautifully tapered little candles and distribute gifts and presents each of the eight nights of the festival. We arrange our beautiful school and home parties. We have our congregational book and gift shops present lovely gifts wrapped in especially designed holiday paper. In this way, Chanukah becomes lots of fun, aside from the story of the Maccabees and the Syrians and the implications of that story."

Everywhere, religious schools concentrate on the preparation of their pupils for the Feast of Lights. Anticipation of the pleasures and the aesthetic values of the festival help create a joyous mood among children and parents alike. Conversations with Rabbis, teachers and parents in suburbia make it evident that Chanukah occupies a unique place in the lives of American Jews. It is the symbol of the Jews' belief in man's inherent right to worship God in freedom, even as it attests to their hope for the future of mankind. Its major importance, however, lies in the fact that Jewish parents, disturbed by the introduction of a Christian religious spirit into the public schools, especially at Christmas time, and in degree fearful of its effect upon their children, are counteracting this influence through their religious schools by making Chanukah a thoroughly joyous festival, replete with gift-giving, food delicacies, candle-lighting and song. The Maccabees, symbols of the right of a minority to worship God in its own way, have helped American Jews win a major victory of survival in the twentieth century.

Written and oral statements by suburbia's Rabbis make it clear that, although the emphasis has obviously changed, the festivals, ceremonies and rituals of Judaism remain very much alive. Whether they are observed as "commandments" or as "folkways"—because the Lord commanded that they be observed, or because they help insure the physical and spiritual survival of the Jewish people—makes no significant difference.

On the other hand, young parents in suburban communities, even if they desire to observe certain Jewish ritual, find it difficult to do so because technical skills and modern procedures seem to have superseded religious ritual.

The birth of a child, for example, automatically creates a series of special problems for the parents. Hospitals usually urge the mother to return home after five days. This means that the circumcision rites (Briss) of the male child, which, according to Jewish Law, should take place on the eighth day following birth, must take place at the convenience of a physician on the fifth day, or else that some special arrangement must be made with the hospital. Then, too, many hospitals object to the use of the traditional

"Mohel" (the skilled performer of the religious rite of the circumcision) and insist that a medical doctor, who is not necessarily a religious or devout Jew, shall perform the "operation." Thus the "ritual" takes second place to the "operation."

The secularization of the circumcision rite is especially disconcerting to a new parent who wishes to retain his ties with the traditions of his fathers and finds himself frustrated.

"I know that my son is supposed to be given his Hebrew name at the Briss. How can I do this, if the doctor who operates doesn't know the first thing about Judaism and cares even less? Just exactly what am I supposed to do?"

These experiences are often reported by Orthodox and Conservative Rabbis in suburban towns. The same problems arise in the central city as well. In the big city hospitals, these problems might long ago have been solved if Jewish doctors on their staffs had viewed these situations sympathetically.

If the newborn child happens to be a girl, the child is usually given her Hebrew name at a synagogue service at which the Rabbi officiates. Suburban Rabbis urge parents of newborn children to bring these ceremonies into the synagogue. Thus the child and the parents are warmly and officially received into the household of Israel.

"I can understand the Rabbi's appeal to me to come into the synagogue with my joys even as I appeal to him for his aid when I am confronted by some sorrow. He is correct when he helps me to realize that I am really turning to him not so much because he may be a special messenger from the Almighty, but because he and his congregation, to all intents and purposes, represent all Jews everywhere."

Another heartening experience to suburban Rabbis is the fact that the English names now being given Jewish children are often Biblical in origin. Names like David, Michael, Samuel and Jonathan are much more frequently given than they were a generation ago, and girls' names such as Judith, Rebecca and Rachel have once again become popular with Jewish parents. The trend is away from such names as Montague, Hillary, Scott and Gregg, for these were often used in an attempt to hide or obscure Jewish identity. If names may be used as a gauge, it can be recorded that Jews in suburbia are no longer fearful about identifying themselves as Jews. They are definitely secure as American Jews.

The Bar Mitzvah is a religious rite in which a youth who has attained his thirteenth birthday is permitted to ascend to the pulpit of the synagogue. There, with the Sacred Scroll of the Torah (Five Books of Moses) before him, he recites the traditional blessings before and after the weekly reading of the lesson from the Torah and chants the prophetic portion of the service. This rite is required by Jewish tradition of every male, on the Sabbath nearest his thirteenth birthday; by following these practices, the youth becomes the equal (in this one respect) of any other Jewish male. The ceremony is known as Bar Mitzvah; that is, "He who has, in the presence of the congregation, formally accepted the responsibility of observing the Commandments that are contained in the Torah."

The occasion is traditionally one of rejoicing. It is a "simcha" (joy) which is recognized as highly significant. This *rite de passage* is an important milestone in the religious life of the youth.

A Kiddush (Thanksgiving to God—Praise of the Almighty) over a goblet of wine and a simple repast are usually provided by the parents after the service, either in the synagogue or in the home. It is, after all, the ceremony itself as an integral part of the Sabbath service that is traditionally regarded as the primary concern of the parents and their friends.

In more recent years, some parents have tended to use the occasion of a son's Bar Mitzvah for increasingly elaborate "partying." In most cases, in my experience, the social hour which follows the ceremony is conducted with dignity and decorum. In others, unfortunately, this does not hold true. The Bar Mitzvah serves as the pretext for "the party," and the youth, who a few minutes before was the object of raptured attention, is all but forgotten. The "ceremonies" following Bar Mitzvah will be discussed in another connection in Chapter 8.

The newer ceremony of Bas Mitzvah, which approximates the same religious rite for the Jewish girl thirteen years of age, has most often added another significant spiritual experience to Jewish life. Its general adoption and use in recent years indicates that there is both awareness and recognition of the "right" to equality in religious practice for the Jewish female.

Nearly all Jewish marriages are officiated at by a Rabbi. More than half of the marriages which take place in suburbia are performed either in the temple or in the Rabbi's study. Whenever the congregation is housed in an adequate temple building, the member-families prefer to arrange for the religious ceremony to take place there.

Brides in suburbia who have been pupils in the temple Hebrew or Sunday school invariably arrange for their marriage ceremony to take place in the temple. It is not only the fashionable thing to do; it is also a further means of identification with the Jewish religious institution—the temple.

"I want *my* Rabbi to officiate at my wedding. He confirmed me and I know it means something to him as it does to me to bless me under the 'Chupa' [wedding canopy]."

When a Rabbi is not asked to officiate at a marriage, it is usually because an elopement is involved or because one of the parties is not Jewish. The incidence of mixed marriage, presently around 7 per cent, appears to be increasing. (The Washington, D.C., area reports a high of 11.3 per cent.) Seldom is a Christian clergyman asked to officiate at a mixed marriage because the Jewish bride or groom does not usually "give up" his religion. On the other hand, conversions *to* Judaism are reported in each of the suburban communities studied. The convert is usually a non-Jewish girl who is marrying a Jewish youth.

Most Rabbis insist upon intensive study of Judaism by the individual who seeks conversion. The length of time involved in study is seldom less than two months; frequently it lasts a year. Conservative Rabbis in most suburban congregations insist upon following the Orthodox ritual for conversion. This means not only study of Prayer Book, Hebrew and Jewish history, customs, ceremonies and theological concepts, but also the ceremony of immersion

(Tevila). Orthodox Rabbis rarely officiate at conversion ceremonies; in many cases, however, they invite their Conservative colleagues to do so. Reform Rabbis who officiate at these rites usually insist upon a prescribed course of study and do not require the Tevila.

The situation with respect to divorce among Jewish suburban families is not clear. Rabbis report that many young couples turn to them much more frequently than is generally known to help resolve family disputes.

"I find that most of the husband-wife problems are those in which young couples find that there is too much interference in their lives by well-meaning parents, and resentment is created. Well-intentioned parents could help their children so much if they permitted young couples to run their own lives."

Perhaps because of the very youth of so many suburban families and the number of children who bless these marriages, husbands and wives are less prone to think in terms of divorce. Divorce is still a highly unpopular institution in Jewish suburbia.

The observance of the anniversary of the death of a parent or other blood relative by the recital of the Kaddish (Mourners' Prayer) is still general throughout the country.

In Orthodox and Conservative synagogues, ritual prescribes that both an early morning and evening (sundown) service take place in the temple every day. The congregants at such services consist almost entirely of those who are observing the anniversary of death (Yahrzeit). According to Jewish law, they are expected to attend the daily service for a period of eleven months and one day following the death.

In larger suburbs such as Newton, a daily Minyan (a worship convocation of at least ten males required for a religious quorum) takes place in two Conservative temples, one Orthodox synagogue and one Reform temple. There is no Minyan in the third Conservative congregation. Euclid, in its only house of worship, usually has a daily Minyan. In Skokie, two of the four congregations have daily services. The three communities of Montgomery County differ among themselves in this respect. The several Conservative congregations maintain a daily service, while Silver Spring's Reform

temple has no Minyan and Bethesda's Beth El is not always able
to secure a Minyan. At the Montgomery County Jewish Community in Chevy Chase, there is usually a daily service. St. Louis
Park's B'nai Abraham is unable, to date, to maintain a daily service.

With the one exception of Montebello, no congregation in the
San Gabriel Valley has a daily prayer service. This is due, of course,
to the inability to secure ten males, thirteen years of age or over,
who will join in such a service. Hence even the practice of reciting
the Kaddish is gradually losing ground.

One Rabbi [5] in a suburban community, unhappy about his congregants' neglect of the Kaddish and the opportunity afforded them
to observe the anniversary of death in a traditional manner, edi-
torialized on this theme in his congregational bulletin. He wrote:

DO YOU REMEMBER?

What is the ultimate affront to any man? The denial of his
deepest legitimate need. Such is his need to be remembered after
he has left this world. Say what we will, the thought that we will
be forgotten shortly after we are gone, that our living, and hence
our departure, will ultimately make no significant difference to
anyone, is a thought no one can truly accept. To be unremembered
is to die a second death. To forget someone whom we once loved
and whose life we shared, is the ultimate impiety—the deliberate
denial of what they wanted most—to be remembered.

I am moved to this reflection when on Friday evenings I read
the names of those whose Yahrzeits are supposed to be observed
during the week coming. In many instances, neither on Friday
evening, nor during the week, does a son or a daughter rise in the
congregation to recite the Kaddish. A name is called and there is
no one who remembered (though they were duly reminded in
advance in written form).

There is nothing we can do for the dead; nothing except remember them.

If we fail them there, nothing else matters. Elaborate expensive
caskets and monuments—frowned on by the Tradition—are no substitutes for acts of loving kindness of truth that is gracious memory.
To do a man's desire, says the Talmud, is to honor him. It was our
parents' desire, even as it is our own, to be remembered once we are
gone. In Judaism, we neither sanctify nor worship the dead. We
do something infinitely more meaningful. We remember them by

our recitation of the prayer—the Kaddish—that accepts and glorifies and anticipates the coming of the Kingdom of God, that Kingdom in which both we and our departed are citizens.

On the Day of Atonement and three other occasions throughout the year—the concluding day of each of the Pilgrimage Festivals: Passover, Feast of Weeks and Feast of Tabernacles—the Yizkor prayers are recited in the synagogue. Mourners usually attend in considerable numbers for this special prayer service.

Reports indicate that, if this festival day occurs on a weekday, there is every likelihood that far more women will attend this service than men. Here, too, men leave a sacred duty to be performed by their wives.

Jewish homes in the suburbs, particularly in the eastern communities, are recognizable today much more often from the Mezzuzah attached to the doorpost than has been true in well over two decades.

The Mezzuzah (the small piece of parchment on which are inscribed the verses "Hear, O Israel, the Lord, our God, the Lord is One" and the longer passage beginning, "Thou shalt love the Lord Thy God with all thy heart, with all thy soul and with all thy might" is enclosed in a little metal or wooden container and affixed to the door. Well over 50 per cent of all Jewish suburban homes are said to have a Mezzuzah.

There are sound reasons for this increase. Within the past decade, very beautiful Mezzuzahs—decorative, distinctive and Jewish—have been designed and made in the State of Israel. Jews are taught through their Hebrew schools, PTA's and wherever else they gather that one proper way to announce their symbolical identification with the Jewish people and the Jewish way of life is through the Mezzuzah.

"This is our way of saying, 'The home you are about to enter is a Jewish home.'"

Although Jewish ritual is less frequently practiced today by suburban families than in past generations, it still plays an important role in Jewish life. Jews do not seem to feel that Dietary Laws are as important or meaningful as did their grandfathers. They work on the Sabbath and otherwise show little regard for the details of Jewish law that seemed so important a generation or two ago. Still, they observe and practice that ritual which is associated most directly with their family life and with the home. They choose the ritual they will observe, less often on the basis of Jewish Law than on a far more practical basis—what appeals to them and their families, what has significance and relevance for them, and what they believe identifies them as Jews.

Fortunately for the Jewish people, many of the practices of contemporary Jews help to maintain their distinctiveness and are rich in positive values. Thus suburban Jews and Judaism seem to gain in spiritual and moral strength, despite the changes in emphasis in matters of ritual.

Chapter 6   The Search for Religion

The outer edges, at least, of Judaism have indeed been changed under the impact of American culture. Jewish society has taken on many new forms and appurtenances. . . . But there do seem to be certain cultural values which continue to be expressed, through these new forms as they have been expressed, through older forms, by the many long generations of Jews.[1]

The evidence gathered for this study shows clearly that Jews in suburbia are preponderately non-Orthodox in religious ideas and practices. Although affiliated with synagogues and temples in ever-increasing numbers, they do not place the same emphasis as earlier generations upon the importance and relevance of ritual. The Sabbath, traditionally accepted as a day of rest and re-creation of the spirit, or even as a day of prayer, is not observed in or out of the synagogue, though this is enjoined by Orthodox Judaism. The Dietary Laws, too, are fading in significance.[2]

The number of Jews who pray in accordance with any practice—Orthodox, Conservative or Reform—is generally regarded as minimal, both in suburbia and elsewhere. Religious leaders in suburban communities studied agree unanimously that few persons observe the traditional practice of reciting their morning prayers in their homes. If, as mourners, they attend the daily morning or evening service in the synagogue, they must often become reacquainted with the ritual of the service. Without such mourners, who are expected to attend daily services throughout the first eleven months of the mourning period, as well as on each anniversary of the death of a blood relative, most suburban synagogues would find it difficult to maintain the traditional daily prayer service.

According to a 1955 nation-wide survey by the American Institute of Public Opinion, Jews trail in attendance at worship services.

This Gallup poll significantly reveals that when the adult population was asked, "Did you attend a church or synagogue in the last seven days?" Catholics claimed to be the most faithful in attendance at church services, with 74 per cent; Protestants were next with 42 per cent, and Jews followed with 27 per cent.

Synagogue attendance among the 599 respondents to our basic questionnaire is rather anemic. Though only fourteen persons never attend a synagogue service, only two men worship in synagogue daily. The largest group (307 persons, or 51 per cent) "seldom" worship in the synagogue. One hundred seventy-nine persons, or 30 per cent, attend services once a month; while 73, or 12 per cent, attend weekly. Seven persons worship twice a month, and thirteen attend only on the High Holy Days.

In a recent study [3] the Jews of one community were asked: "Why do you go to the synagogue?" The most frequent answers were: "It gives me a good, peaceful feeling" 26 per cent; "It's every Jew's duty" 18 per cent; "I like to follow the services" 17 per cent; "I enjoy the sermons and find the Rabbi instructive" 16 per cent; "I went to learn about Judaism" 13 per cent; and "I go to meet other people" 12 per cent. Another 6 per cent offered miscellaneous reasons; 11 per cent replied "don't know" or gave no answer.

It is significant that not one answer suggested prayer and worship as the important motivations for synagogue attendance.

Asked why they joined (not attended) a temple, Jews in another community replied:

"Because I am a Jew and I want my children to be Jewish. I believe that a belief in God is essential. We must feel deep down that there is a God and that he watches over all of us—rich or poor, good or bad."

"I have a firm belief in the Jewish way of life and while I am no longer Orthodox, I cannot conceive of another way of life for me or for my children."

"I have joined a temple because I feel the need for belonging in a spiritual sense to some organization that represents Jewish tradition."

"I have since my early youth had a strong desire and need for prayer and temple attendance. I also have a need for belonging to a temple."

"I feel the need of a synagogue for spiritual and moral uplift. I like to attend services and feel better for it."

"I feel at peace and at home when I am in the temple. It seems to be part of me to want to be close to a house of worship."

"My husband and I feel a definite need for religion in our lives."

"Religion has played a great role in my everyday living. How else and where else can one turn to but the temple and its religious leader to lead me in the way of my tradition? I find that I cannot meet many of life's situations alone. The temple gives me strength and courage."

"Joining a temple brings me closer to people of my own faith and creates a common bond between me and them. Coming from a community which had a very small Jewish group, I can appreciate how important it is for Jews to have this kind of bond. No matter to what degree we feel that our leanings are Orthodox, Conservative or Reform, and even though we often say that we are belonging because of our desire to give our children a Hebrew training, we know that we are benefiting ourselves because we are enriching our own lives through religious knowledge and our closeness to others of our faith."

"We feel that religion plays an important role in every stage of our lives."

"I come from a very religious home. We always belonged to a synagogue and this was instilled in me. I always took it for granted that when I married and had children we would become members of a temple and feel that we belong to a religious institution."

"We joined a synagogue in order to be part of Jewishness. We have roots in the Jewish faith but not too detailed a knowledge of our rituals. This we hope to learn. We have a strong faith in God."

"I was born a Jew. I was raised in a Jewish environment. I wish to be a Jew not only by birth but by choice, by association and by knowledge."

It is worth noting that 92 per cent of all respondents to this study answered, "I believe in God." Rabbis in this community in-

dicate that their congregants "take God for granted." There appears
to be a belief in God the Creator, Whose immanence in the affairs
of men is nevertheless open to question.

"Somehow I believe that there was One by Whose will the
world and all that is in it was created. I like to believe that He
created the world—whether in six days or six epochs or stages—at
any rate, that there was a purposive beginning to it all—but I am
inclined to believe, too, that the Biblical account concerning God
and creation is really correct. God created the world in six days
and rested on the seventh day—and He has been resting ever since."

Doubts concerning God's immanence, the role He plays in the
lives of men *now* and His justice and fairness in His dealings with
humans (if He is concerned with each of us) trouble the minds of
young Jews in suburbia. They doubt also that prayer can change
the course of human events in any degree. These young men and
women, recipients of college educations, are deeply moved and
disturbed by the Nazi holocaust and the annihilation of six million
Jews and keenly aware of the role which science and natural law
play in contemporary civilization. Like so many other thoughtful
people, they are uncertain and even confused in their ideas about
God and the meaning of human existence. The following statement is typical:

"However much I would like to believe in a personal God Who
is looking out for me and my family, I'm afraid I cannot do so. I
remember that my grandparents thought that God was directly interested in them. They had only to ask for God's help through their
prayers, and they were certain that they would get it. They really
had faith in Him. It isn't that I don't believe in God. Rather, I
would say that I don't believe in that kind of a God Who is willing to upset the rest of the world in order to please me. I believe
that there was a Creator of the world, but now I feel that we understand natural law and know that it is law that is the most important
element in this world. I believe that there is something 'special'
about the Jewish people. No other people has given the world a
Bible like the Hebrew Bible. I'm proud to belong to this people and
to have my children learn its history and its values. Frankly, I
find my strength these days in this people and its values. That's
why I prefer to remain loyal to it above all else."

The Jew has never been required to reaffirm his unquestioned acceptance of a creed. Except for a vague "God-consciousness," theology has played no more than a minor role in the life of the average Jew. In effect, Jews possess a "crisis" religion. They appeal to a *personal* God in critical moments; they turn to prayer or ritual in desperation when life seems particularly hard or its burdens oppressive. When "things are normal," however, they feel no urgency or need for God or prayer.

This approach to religion is hardly unique, according to liberal Christian clergymen. They report the same "crisis religion" response among their own congregants.

According to the traditional view, a Jew is to be judged by his deeds rather than by any words he may offer concerning his creed. Inasmuch as the ritual of Judaism is described in terms of "Mitzvos" (commandments, duties or responsibilities incumbent upon the Jew because his Torah, his Divine Teaching, has prescribed them), a Jew's faithfulness is judged by his observance of the ceremonies, rites and observances of Judaism, as well as by his ethical and moral practices. Hence we may understand why Jews often say, "I'm really not religious," when they really mean, "I do not observe as much of the ritual of Judaism as Orthodoxy expects of me."

Suburban Jews, most of whom have not affiliated with Orthodox synagogues in their respective communities, must then be regarded as digressing from "normative" Orthodox Judaism. For Orthodoxy defines the norm primarily in terms of ritual observances, particularly with respect to the Sabbath, Festivals and Holy Days and the Dietary Laws.

Yet, as we have noted elsewhere,[4] certain ritual *is* being observed today, even though emphases have changed[5] and the amount of ritual observance of the Sabbath—and particularly the Dietary Laws—has been markedly reduced. And certain basic values remain fixed.

The desire by Jews for identification with the Jewish people is generally recognized to be greater today than in the past half-century of American Jewish life. Suburban Jews, many of whom represent the third and fourth generations of American Jewish families, seek active affiliation with the Jewish community, particularly through synagogues and temples. Young Jewish families voluntarily become members of an organized religious body. Such identification, it must be stressed, could be avoided if Jews so desired it. About 40 per cent of America's Jews, in fact, *do* refrain from such a committment.

Rabbis in suburbia agree that, in the past decade, Jews' affiliation with synagogues and temples has increased at a much faster rate than their population. This important fact is often explained in terms of man's insecurities and anxieties in this troubled world, his need to conform to the standards of society and his need to "belong" in order to acquire status. These factors, however, are not a sufficient explanation. In my experience, only one motive—ethnic interest in the Jews as a people—really explains suburban Jews' affiliation with the one institution which is openly labelled "religious."

This is not to imply that all Jews who join synagogues do so from religious motives. I do suggest, however, that more Jews today are turning to the synagogue in search of religious values than has been true since the 1930's.

"We are not dealing with people who are antagonistic to religions in my community. I find that they really *want* religion. They are trying to understand Judaism and what it expects of them. They may not be religious Jews in the sense that Orthodoxy uses the term because they often fail to maintain many of the traditional ritual practices, but I feel that there is a *genuine search for religion* that should not be ignored or minimized."

Although uncertain and equivocal about the meaning of this wave of religious identification, spiritual leaders of suburban congregations—Orthodox, Conservative and Reform—generally agree that it is somehow not simply a matter of "belongingness." Some of these Rabbis speak of it as a "religious revival," though most seem uncertain on this point. Their comments provide interesting analyses of the situation.

Those who see hopeful portents for the future in the current experience comment as follows:

"This is a suburban community. Most Jewish families had no previous synagogue affiliation or had negative attitudes to religion. Membership in temples is often motivated by social or child-centered reasons. But, for a minority, there *is* a genuine interest in religion."

"An intensification of Jewish affiliation is apparent. The increase in participation in all activities plus increase in temple attendance certainly constitutes a 'revival' to some extent."

"People who were not interested in Judaism are attending services and sending their children to Hebrew school."

"Compared to the people's religious interest before they moved from [the central city], there has been a remarkable change. But it still leaves much to be desired."

"There is greater participation of young families in temple life than ever before."

"I have found that 90 per cent of my people never attended a synagogue for twenty years prior to their moving here. The activity is amazing."

"This is a new Jewish community. People who have joined this congregation for social or educational reasons have also come to participate in the religious aspects of congregational life."

"Something has happened if we realize that children whose parents were estranged from Jewish living are enrolled in our religious schools. This tells us something about their parents and their concern for religion."

"There is a revival. It is marked by an increase in the number of affiliated and an emphasis upon Jewish education. A spiritual revival, definite in form but restricted in numbers, has taken place."

"There is a definite revival of interest."

"There is a growing hunger for and interest in the fundamental issues of life and man's destiny on earth."

"There is a greater interest in the synagogue in discussions on religious topics and also a desire to pray (without knowing how, as yet)."

"There is a revival of Jewish consciousness. This may be due to something inherently Jewish plus the pressure which results from living in a church-going Christian environment."

"There is a revival in the sense that parents are concerned that their children should receive a religious education. Sometimes the interests of the parents themselves are aroused thereby."

"As the community becomes more mature, religious interest increases. More people are participating in the religious aspects of our temple with sincerity and genuineness."

"There is certainly renewed interest in Judaism. I'm not sure that it ought to be called religious revival."

"There seems to be increased opportunity to provide for religious instruction, influence and statement of aims. I judge that there are more religious programs, services and courses offered and the chance for a religious person to express himself than formerly. People are willing to support religious functions in the synagogue for the benefit of others, especially for the children."

"I feel that there is a religious revival in the sense that people seek identification with a religious institution and want their children to receive a religious education—but they are not yet ready to express this as a personal commitment."

"The people are searching after something. What is happening is something more than the urge to identify with the synagogue. There is a yearning for values that must be called religious."

On the other side, though in no instance does any Rabbi deny that "something of moment is taking place," many agree with a recent comment:[6] "Indeed we may say it is 'congregationalism' rather than faith which is experiencing a revival." They describe the marked increase in synagogue membership as "social and even educational" but certainly not religious.

"Our temple membership is high. Religious school attendance is regular. But Judaism is absent in the personal lives and homes of our people. A 'religious revival' is *not* membership and clatter."

"More people belong to synagogues, but I see no evidence of intensified piety or heightened religious loyalties."

"The temple is growing because I believe social pressures make parents want to send their children to a religious school. But most people are overly absorbed in 'establishing' themselves economically. That is their greatest desire."

"A return to the synagogue is not to be equated with a return to religion."

"A revival of religion is *not* shown by an increase in the number who worship or in an increase in Kosher homes. A true revival of Jewish religion would be shown in the desire and loyal determination of young people to be Jewish, to cherish Jewish sentiments and teachings and to remain Jews."

"It is true that affiliation with a temple is important, but there is little religious content in what is presently occurring."

"Young people affiliate with synagogues in large numbers for a variety of reasons in our community. However, the prime motivation for some does not seem to be a religious one."

"There may be a renewed interest in congregational affiliation, but whether it can actually be identified with 'revival of religion' is, to my mind, questionable."

"There has obviously been an increase in Jewish identification and an awareness of being Jewish, but this has not necessarily involved any religious commitment."

"Religion as a personal experience is missing. 'Joiners' do not even really participate in the life of their congregation. They just belong."

"Nothing more has occurred than a revival of interest in Jewish affairs because of people's relocation in the suburb."

"People are not more religious. There is rather more interest in the temple activities."

"Those who affiliate do so for social reasons more than religious. Less than 50 per cent of my community are affiliated with a synagogue."

"Synagogue membership bears no relationship to religious revival. I see no intensification of personal observance. There is an uplift though in parents' desire to give their children a better Hebrew background than the parents have. To this extent only is there any revival."

"Group identification is all that has occurred. Affiliation with a synagogue is often a manifestation of a peculiar type of assimilation. Because non-Jews build churches, so Jews, in order to follow the general trend, build synagogues. The exact nature of the present formal pro-synagogue orientation can perhaps best be explained and defined by a psychiatrist."

"There has been a revival of religious *interest* and affiliation only. But there is no real personal commitment."

"Those who are interested in the synagogue place it on the same level as their lawn or perhaps slightly lower. It is part of the community set-up and indicates no interest in the religious."

"Most of the people who are affiliated with the synagogue are members only because they want their children to attend Hebrew or Sunday school, and not because of a personal religious interest."

"There have been no changes in practices of Jewish families to warrant the statement that any form of revival of religion has taken place."

"There has been a revival of social forces, making for conformity and belonging. There has been little change in people's attitudes toward faith."

"I do not consider affiliation with a synagogue as indicative in itself of a revival of religion."

"There is greater interest in joining than interest in religion. People will come to hear reviews and lectures *on* religion but that is *not* a revival of religion."

"There is a greater amount of affiliation but mainly for the schooling of children. After having enrolled their children, they begin to haggle over standards and length of years of a child's education and seek to reduce the school period of study."

"No great spiritual deepening has taken place except for a few. Mostly what has occurred is a new sense of responsibility, community and an appreciation for *some* religious values."

"There is considerable interest in the temple and its activities. Whether this interest has had any impact upon the religious inwardness of people remains to be seen."

"There is a revival in terms of synagogue affiliation and greater interest in things Jewish, but the revival of religion is really superficial."

"I have been able to discern only an increased interest in congregation affiliation and activity. I am not certain about the full religious character of this affiliation."

"I would not admit to a religious revival in the sense of a greater influence of religion in the lives of our members. However, there is a greater identification with the synagogue. There is a greater awareness of need for belonging for the sake of the children."

"The religious revival in my town appears to be a 'desire to know more about Judaism.' As for Faith, Belief or Prayer, we haven't much of that."

"There is no depth of religious thinking nor is there very much of a philosophy concerning Jewish life. The members of the Adult Jewish Study Group seem to respond more positively to religion and religious values than do others. These people are certainly not irreligious or anti-religious. They are simply not moved much by religious thought and values."

The quest for religion does not express itself in the same way or with the same intensity in all communities. In suburbs adjacent to those central cities that are themselves comparatively young and whose cultural roots are not deep, the search for religious values appears less marked than in areas noted for their deeply planted cultural roots. The New England Jewish communities appear to be more devoted to this search than the suburbs in the far West. The suburbs and cities of the West Coast, particularly the Los Angeles area, though less noted today for their quest for religion, are also beginning to feel this upsurge manifested by a strong minority. Five Rabbis in West Coast suburban communities speak of it typically as follows:

"We ought not to discount the significance of this interest. These people are not primarily concerned with the synagogue as a play center or even as the center for activities. They look upon the synagogue as the religious center and upon the Rabbi as their religious teacher. Even though their numbers may not be great, they make up in quality for what they lack in quantity. They are the 'remnant of Israel' of whom the Prophet has spoken."

Most suburban Rabbis doubt that a "revival of religion" has occurred. They appear to agree with Glazer [7] that while there is much "Jewishness" (which he defines as "all the activities which Jews come together to carry on *without* the auspices of religion"), there is little of "Judaism" as "the historic religion of the Jewish people." The reasons for their skepticism are clear:

(1) Jews are generally less observant today than in earlier generations.

(2) When observant, they are less inclined to observe those rituals and ceremonials which have consistently been emphasized in Judaism.

(3) The moral and ethical standards of the Jewish people do not seem to be different from (i.e. superior to) the general standards of the people around about them.

(4) They have neither more or less faith in God, His goodness and justice, or His immanence than all of society. God's existence seems to them utterly irrelevant in this age of science.

Dr. Mordecai M. Kaplan has commented: [8] "Changes have taken place in men's conception of the nature and function of religion. Those changes have made it impossible for most Jews to accept many of the traditional beliefs and assumptions concerning God, man and the world. The current crisis in religion has certainly not left the Jews untouched."

Kaplan's interpretation [9] of the "spiritual" may help us to understand how even such a word as this may acquire a new relevance and meaning in a new age.

Spirituality is a quality not only of the individual, but of the group personality. As long as they [the Jews] seek the welfare of all mankind through the Jewish people, they are spiritual.

Jews do not know what to make of the God-idea. Unable to understand His relation to man or His role other than that of Creator, they have chosen to bypass the problem. Instead, they pursue the more immediate goals in life and, *while not denying God,* concentrate rather upon the immediate problems of life here and now. In this sense, then, they are regarded by some as "secular" Jews. This "secularism," however, is not to be mistaken for anti-religion or non-religion; it is rather concerned with "living the good life" in this world.

Though there may be wide gaps and uncertainties in their system of belief concerning the nature of God, and though they no longer regard ritual and ceremonial practice as divinely ordained, all the evidence I have been able to gather indicates that they believe in themselves as Jews—as part of a people that has made a unique contribution to the world in envisaging the universe as an entity, as one. They believe, too, that the insights and values promulgated to all the world through the children of Israel represent the highest, most ennobling way of life that man has yet conceived. They believe that man is one, whatever his color, class, creed or national origin, and that life is basically good. Even though so much about man and the universe remains outside their understanding, they seek to live in such a way that the highest ethical and moral ideals are realized in their own lives.

This enriching way of life, with its emphasis upon man's conduct in relation to his fellow man, is for them incorporated in a written document and an oral tradition which together are called "Torah." It is Wisdom, so ennobling and so concerned with the growth of man's spirit that it represents the will of an eternal and infinite spirit, whom they call God.

The Jewish people is for them the vehicle, the agent through whom this Torah has been promulgated. They desire to be an integral part of the life of this people by practicing its highest ideals of "Zedakah" (righteousness, charity and justice), "Ahavah" (love), "Gemilat Chesed" (the performance of acts of loving-kindness) and "Rachmanut" (compassion)—to name but a few. To participate with their fellow Jews in the synagogue, which has as its primary purpose the teaching and the promulgation of these values, is for them a *religious* act.

The significance of this voluntary act of belonging to the Jewish people through membership in the synagogue is surely not to be discounted. To be sure, this is not "normative Judaism" as Orthodoxy defines it, because ritual and ceremonial are, for them, less "commandments" than "sancta" and tradition—the honored mores of a distinctive people. God is more a power, a will, a cause, a force, a personality than a person. Yet this is still Judaism.

The will to be a Jew—to belong to the Jewish people; to provide a knowledge of Torah to one's children and to acquire some of that knowledge for oneself; to live by certain, if not all, of Judaism's traditional practices, and to accept its basic values in theory and, as far as humanly possible, in practice—is a significant and voluntary act that constitutes a *commitment to a distinctive people,* the Jewish people. He who belongs to a religious community and actually identifies with it indicates thereby a desire for a particular goal, a purpose and value in life.

Fromm[10] offers an interesting theory for "belongingness" which helps us understand why Jews in suburbia wish to "belong." He reasons that affiliation with a synagogue provides the Jew with something more than the opportunity to belong: it helps him "to relate himself to [a] system which would give meaning and direction to his life."

Men cannot live without some sort of cooperation with others. In any conceivable kind of culture, man needs to cooperate with others if he wants to survive, whether for the purpose of defending himself against enemies or dangers of nature, or in order that he may be able to work and produce. . . .
Unless he belonged somewhere, unless his life had some meaning and direction, he would feel like a particle of dust and be overcome by his individual insignificance. He would not be able to relate himself to any system which would give meaning and direction to his life, he would be filled with doubt, and this doubt would paralyze his ability to act—that is, to live.

Most Jews belong to the synagogue today precisely because it is a religious fellowship. Theirs is no clear-cut belief in a God; many Jews are groping and seeking, often desperately, to understand the God in Whom they profess to believe. Yet even if they have not yet discovered the certainty of God or experienced His reality, they believe, with a firm conviction, in man and in a people.

The Lander brothers [11] suggest that 90 per cent of American

Jews have identified themselves with the synagogue for social and secular reasons rather than for genuine religious promptings. Even if this were true—and the Landers' assertion does not constitute verifiable evidence—we should not forget the other 10 per cent whose motives and purposes are beyond question.

Further, it is not improper to suggest that many Jews throughout the past century may have observed the Orthodox ritual for reasons which may best be described as the conventions of the society of which they were a part, rather than because of any personal convictions.

An ancient Hebrew cabalist book, the Zohar, has it that "God, Israel and Torah are one." [12] This cryptic comment assumes special significance today if we think of its implications for Jews who "belong" to our synagogues and temples.

Judaism has traditionally affirmed the intricate relationship among these three—God, Israel and Torah. It reminds us of their indivisibility. Each requires the other if it is to fulfill itself. It is the people Israel that makes possible the relationship between God and Torah. Torah itself could have little significance without a people that attempt to live by its teachings. The name of God could hardly be blessed without a people that feels a distinctive relationship to that God. Finally, the people Israel is the agent through which Torah may lead all men to God. In all these ways, "God, Israel and Torah are one."

The Hebrew sages say: "The ladder of Heaven has three rungs —Israel, Torah and God." [13] That is to say, if the Jews were to disappear, Torah would disappear, and God Himself would lose the most effective witness to His presence.

In this age, the emphasis upon the people is greatest. The Jewish religion is Jewish only because it functions in and through the Jewish people. If the religion is to survive, Jews must remain aware of their identification with the Jewish people. Ritual and religious symbolism are the main techniques for insuring this "consciousness of kind," or what is commonly called "Jewish consciousness."

The will to be identified with the Jewish people, and concern for its survival and enhancement, are expressions of the Jewish religion at one level. There are, however, higher levels. Ascending the sages' "ladder," the Jew becomes increasingly concerned with Torah itself. And the top rung is occupied by those whose faith in God is clear and certain—men and women who are free from doubts and uncertainties concerning His nature and His relationship to man. These religionists indicate by the manner in which they live that they are motivated by the highest values of morality and ethics incorporated in the tradition. They employ ritual as a reminder of their commitment to God and their devotion to their people.

Different ages use different methods and media to express their values and ideals. Today's Jews appear to express the values they cherish through the people. The Jewish family, despite the pressures of the times, remains intact. The love of man is nowhere better and more realistically indicated than in philanthropy, in which the Jew excels. The conviction that human freedom and human brotherhood must remain man's highest goals is evident not only in many of the Hebrew Festivals, which are still carefully observed, but also in the marked interest manifested by Jews in secular organizations and movements dealing with these concerns.[14] The love of human learning and education for their own sake remain deeply entrenched in the Jewish way of life. There is faith, too, in the people Israel and its law-givers, prophets, priests and sages. Given an era of peace, this people may once again bespeak "the word of the Lord" to this troubled age.

All these beliefs—and more—are symbolized by the synagogue. To seek affiliation with it is ultimately to recognize the primacy of these Hebraic values. The Talmud has noted:[15] "Even if one enters into an activity for an ulterior motive, it is still possible to arrive at the correct principle." Affiliation with the synagogue, even though for an "extraneous reason," may lead to a more meaningful understanding of God.

The synagogue helps to concretize the meaning of Torah by emphasizing the importance of learning and knowledge in general and of the study of Torah in particular. To educate all Jews, young and old, in the way they should walk is a recognized function and duty of the synagogue. Moreover, the synagogue, more than any other institution, has helped to keep alive through the centuries the relationship between an ancient land, Israel, and her descendants in each new generation.

There are patterns of conduct and relationships between men by which the common origin and unity of man can be demonstrated. By adopting these high standards as our own, we can share in the very act of creation. These truths, too, are the message of the synagogue.

Heschel,[16] in the spirit of the mystic, has interpreted the purpose of the synagogue in terms both eloquent and relevant. He writes:

What does a person expect to attain when entering a synagogue? In the pursuit of learning one goes to a library; for esthetic enrichment one goes to the art museum; for pure music to the concert hall. What then is the purpose of going to the synagogue?

Many are the facilities which help us to acquire the important worldly virtues, skills and techniques. But where should one learn about the insights of the spirit? Many are opportunities for public speech; where are the occasions for inner silence? It is easy to find people who will teach us how to be eloquent; but who will teach us how to be still? It is surely important to develop a sense of humor; but is it not also important to have a sense of reverence?

Where should one learn the eternal wisdom of compassion? the fear of being cruel? the danger of being callous? Where should one learn that the greatest truth is found in contrition? Important and precious as the development of our intellectual faculties is, the cultivation of a sensitive conscience is indispensable. We are all in danger of sinking into the darkness of vanity; we are all involved in worshipping our own egos. Where should we become sensitive to the pitfalls of cleverness, or to the realization that expediency is not the acme of wisdom?

We are constantly in need of self-purification. We are in need of experiencing moments in which the spiritual is as relevant and as concrete, for example, as the esthetic. Everyone has a sense of beauty; everyone is capable of distinguishing between the beautiful and the ugly. But we also must learn to be sensitive to the spirit. It is in the synagogue where we must try to acquire such inwardness, such sensitivity.

To attain a degree of spiritual security one cannot rely upon one's own resources. One needs an atmosphere, where the concern for the spirit is shared by a community. We are in need of students and scholars, masters and specialists. But we need also the company of witnesses, of human beings who are engaged in worship, who for a moment sense the truth that life is meaningless without attachment to God.

Jews, though not necessarily given to such elevated sentiments, intuitively sense these purposes and goals in far greater numbers than many suppose.

The suburban Jew is generally not oriented toward ritual, certainly not toward the same rituals—the Sabbath and the Dietary Laws—that characterized his grandfather's generation. He does not regard ritual as God's specific commandment; indeed, he is not clear about the nature of God, and he is utterly confused about the authority he should attribute to "Commandments." He "believes" in the value and importance of the Sabbath, but his observance centers about the Sabbath Eve family meal, the Kiddush and the kindling of the Sabbath candles, rather than the synagogue services. He has little or no feeling about the importance of Dietary Laws as a religious rite.

The ceremonials and rituals that the suburban Jew does observe are those which help him strengthen the family and ethnic units and counteract the assimilating influences of other religions. He possesses a strong desire to remain an integral part of the Jewish people. He has affiliated with the synagogue because he appreciates the ethical and moral values which he associates with this people and its ways of life. He believes that there is something distinctive and unique in his tradition, even though he may not be able to identify it precisely.

Although he believes that there must be a God Who created this world, he cannot understand His continuing association with the Jews or, for that matter, with humankind. He has seen so much misery and wretchedness, suffering and death in this world! The fate that recently overtook six million Jews in Europe has shaken what little faith was left in him. Today he sees a world of anxious and troubled men and women, of angry and suspicious nations, and he stands aghast. Industrial power, the machine, the state, science— each has at some time or other within his lifetime served temporarily as a god to be worshipped. Each in turn has failed him. Today he begins anew to search for a God Who will give him a sense of security and at-homeness in the world. He turns to his people, the Jewish people, and hesitantly seeks to understand his ancient Torah. His quest is real, and the challenge to organized religion and its spiritual leaders is great.

The upsurge we are witnessing today may not be a completely unqualified revival of religion. It is, rather, a quest—a search for the meaning of human existence. Jews are re-examining their faith and their obligations and responsibilities to their group and its institutions. The number of Jews who are searching for values which can give meaning to their lives as Jews appears greater today than it has been in the past four decades of American Jewish life. Suburban Jews, through their synagogues and temples, are leading this search.

Chapter 7   Tension and Unrest

*Our society is composed of a multiplicity of elements, each
of which seeks to shape the institutions of American culture according to its own scale of values. Out of this never-
ending competition comes America's pluralistic culture,
ever-dynamic, ever-changing, ever reflecting the stresses
and pulls of the multifarious and contradictory elements
and yet somehow coming out as a substantially harmonious
orchestration of these components.*[1]

Although overt anti-Semitism is not a serious problem in
suburbia today, one may intermittently detect latent indications of
an unfavorable attitude toward Jews. It may show in a surly reply
to an innocent question or in a real estate broker's attempt to divert
a Jewish client from looking at a house for sale in a particular neighborhood. On occasion it takes the form of a teacher's comment to
a pupil about "your kind." Dislike of the unlike is universal even
if it is officially frowned upon. Yet nothing resembling the virulent,
bitter anti-Semitism of pre-World War II days appears to exist in
suburbia today.

Three hundred and eighty-eight respondents, or 63 per cent
of those suburbanites who replied to my questions on this subject,
believe that there is *no* anti-Jewish feeling in the suburb in which
they reside. Eighteen others indicate that if there is any anti-
Semitic feeling, they "are not aware of it." Yet 190 persons, or 33
per cent, believe that there is or may be "some" anti-Jewish feeling,
even though they could not often particularize.

That this "feeling" is something more than a figment of the
imagination is pointed up by a recent survey, made by the Anti-
Defamation League,[2] of the policies of real estate agents in the
suburbs around Detroit. This survey revealed that more than

half of these brokers practiced discrimination in varying degree against members of the Jewish faith:

——33 1/3 per cent of the agents surveyed clearly indicated that they did not wish to sell or rent to Jews and discriminated against them in one way or another, blatantly or subtly.

——6 2/3 per cent used delaying tactics to discourage prospective Jewish home purchasers.

——16 2/3 per cent tried to avoid selling to Jews by attempting to direct them to other neighborhoods.

——43 1/3 per cent did not discriminate.

Despite these startling facts, it is generally agreed that antipathies with respect to the presence of Jews in the suburbs are not so marked as in past years.

One reputable real estate broker (non-Jewish) remarks:

"Twelve years ago [1945], prejudice against Jews was really a problem here. As a real estate man, I ran into it all the time. Today [1957], however, it is really a rarity." *He adds:* "But there was prejudice here not only against Jews but against any group of non-Protestants. It was then more difficult to get owners to sell to Jews."

Although discrimination against Jews in the matter of housing in suburbia is less marked than it was a decade ago, anti-Jewish discrimination is still a source of grave concern to Jews, as it must be to all Americans who are concerned with the goal of equality of opportunity for all. Recently [3] the Anti-Defamation League pointed out that such discrimination exists in a great number of communities throughout America. The Incorporated Village of Bronxville, a suburban community in Westchester County (New York), has acquired the reputation of admitting as homeowners or renters only those who profess to be Christians. In this mile-square community with a population of some 6,500 persons, there are no known Jewish families. Surrounding suburban towns—Tuckahoe, Yonkers, Mount Vernon, Eastchester, Pelham, Crestwood and New Rochelle among others—have no such religious barriers.

Suburban communities in and around Chicago are almost completely closed to Jews. Among those on the North Shore where Jewish families are persona non grata are Kenilworth, Lake Forest,

Barrington and Palatine. The ADL reports, too, that the North
Shore suburbs of Glenview, Winnetka, Northbrook, Northfield,
Wilmette and Deerfield are in part closed to Jewish residents. There
is reason to believe that, primarily in the older sections of most of
these towns, Jewish families are not welcome. New sections, pro-
moted and built by Jews, do have Jewish residents. Housing discrimination and restrictions against Jews also exist, according to the
ADL, in the suburban community of Lathrop Village and other sections of Oakland County (Michigan), in the Kansas City suburb of
Leawood and in suburban developments in the far West, particularly in the Seattle (Washington) metropolitan area.

"Gentlemen's agreements" and other devices tending to discriminate against Jews are found in the South, the District of
Columbia and even in such areas as Montgomery County, where
Jews reside in large numbers. In the environs of Boston, the suburbs
of Winchester, Weston, Wellesley and Needham are said to have
road-blocks barring Jewish home-seekers.

There is sufficient information and evidence to indicate that
these restrictive covenants and other devices used to prevent Jewish
settlement in suburban communities are part of a discriminatory
pattern that exists throughout the country. True, the situation is far
better than it was a decade or two ago; yet the fact of discrimination
must be carefully noted and regarded as a challenge by those who
are opposed in principle to blanket discrimination against any people
or group of peoples.

It is worthy of note that Fair Housing Practices Committees
have recently been organized in Newton, Natick and Wellesley
(Mass.). The high-minded, non-Jewish sponsors of these committees, concerned about discriminatory practices against Negroes, Jews
and other minorities, believe that by making the general public
aware of such un-American practices, they can gradually overcome
such tendencies.

It should be noted that Rabbis and ministers in suburbia are,
almost without exception, members of the same Ministers' Association. An interchange of pulpits usually occurs during Brotherhood
Week, as well as on other occasions during the year. Both Protes-

tant ministers and the Rabbis attest to proper and often cordial relations among themselves. City officials often turn to Rabbinic leaders as the recognized spiritual leaders of the Jewish communities,
and the Rabbi and the temple are formally respected. Yet despite
these surface pleasantries, there are signs of tension, discomfort,
unrest and disturbance.

Invariably, Jewish residents of suburbia, when pressed for a
more careful examination of Jewish-Christian relations, point out
that Jews seldom come to know non-Jews any better in suburbia
than they did in the big city.

"Our husbands do business with them. We see them in the
town's shopping area. It's always a very pleasant, 'Hello, how are
you?' kind of superficial conversation. We may even meet at a
meeting some afternoon or even perhaps at a PTA school affair,
but it is seldom more than that. It is a kind of '9 to 5' arrangement.
The ghetto gates, real or imagined, close at 5:00 P.M. 'Five o'clock
shadow' sets in at sundown. Jews and Christians do not meet socially even in suburbia. If we do, you bet that it is to help promote
some cause or organization where they think we Jews may be helpful. But after five o'clock there is no social contact, no parties,
no home visits, no golf clubs—no nothing!"

This is not an isolated opinion expressed by an unhappy and
unaccepted Jewish person. On the contrary, it is the most representative comment made by Jews and is generally confirmed by Jews
in suburban communities all through America.[4]

To what extent is this condition the result of Jewish self-
segregation? Scrutinizing each of the communities in this study
with this question in mind, I discovered first of all that, although
Jews earnestly desire the friendship and company of their non-
Jewish neighbors, their closest friendships are reserved for other
Jews who have the same community, class, synagogual and organizational interests. This primary friendship relationship is natural—
and characteristic of every kind of suburb. This was true in every
kind of suburb—the oldest (Newton), the mass-produced (Levittown; Skokie), the suburban-industrial town (Euclid) and the
dormitory town (St. Louis Park).

The social segregation of Jews and non-Jews at dusk is, however, not to be explained as voluntary self-segregation on either side. It would be more correct to suggest that the same interests and attitudes are not yet mutually shared by suburban Jews and non-Jews.

"When Jews take a fancy to a particular suburb, build a temple, organize a Hebrew school or establish a youth center, it is natural that other Jewish families will move into the general area. They like to live near the synagogue and school, and that, I think, is to their credit. More Jews move into the general neighborhood. Jewish stores come into the area, and a little colony often develops."

Jewish families are highly concentrated in suburbs like Silver Spring—especially that area known as Langley Park—and Wheaton (Maryland). Certain neighborhoods in the Essex County suburbs of Newark (N.J.) are spoken of by city officials as "Little Israel" even though no suburban community is in fact a ghetto, golden or otherwise. Jews live together in considerable numbers, but under no circumstance do they seek to live in all-Jewish towns.

In certain areas, school districts are almost totally Jewish. In two precincts in Newton, the elementary school population is almost completely Jewish. In 1957, the Jewish enrollment in one elementary school was 468 out of 486; in another, 311 out of 319. On the San Francisco peninsula, Jewish families are found in considerable numbers in Piedmont, near Oakland, especially in the Hillsborough area, where the most expensive homes are found. On the other hand, there is no indication that Jews are clustering together to any degree in the suburbs of Seattle.

The Chicago suburb of Northfield, is a divided community in which the older part of the town is largely closed to Jews, while in the new development a majority of the residents are Jewish. In the Chicago area, Jewish real estate developers are reported to have built large housing projects in sections formerly restricted to Jews and to have offered these new homes for sale to Jews and non-Jews alike. The choice of place of residence is thus made by the new homeowner rather than by the real estate broker.

Even though such phrases as "The Golden Ghetto," "Little Jerusalem" and "where the Jews live" call attention to neighborhoods in which Jewish families live, it must not be assumed that even these districts are exclusively Jewish, or even that Jews constitute a majority of the residents. Minority groups, particularly those easily identifiable through their houses of worship and religious schools, often tend to characterize a neighborhood in this manner.

Jews usually live in areas that have more Jews than others, not just because they like to be near "their own kind," but because non-Jewish families tend to move out from streets on which a few Jewish families have bought homes. The availability of good housing very quickly brings other Jewish families to the same streets. Jewish neighborhoods, then, are created to a great extent by the sudden withdrawal of Christian families, creating a vacuum which in turn is filled by newer Jewish families.

Yet in all the suburbs studied there are only a few in which almost-all-Jewish neighborhoods exist (Newton, Swampscott, St. Louis Park, Skokie). Jews, in fact, live in all sections of many suburbs, including those already mentioned (Belmont, Sharon, Natick, Levittown, Silver Spring, Bethesda, Chevy Chase, San Gabriel Valley, St. Louis Park).

New residents are anxious to establish friendships and positive relationships in their new community. They not only join synagogues and send their children to Hebrew and Sunday schools, but also join non-sectarian organizations with alacrity. This is especially true of women.

"Consider the case of the League of Women Voters in Newton. This was, not so many years ago, one of the most popular general organizations in the community. The officers and directors of the League were Christian women. Then Jewish women were invited to join, and their number kept on increasing. Now you would expect this would be one organization where civic-minded Jewish and Christian women would work side by side—but that is not the case. One-half of the members are Jewish, and five of the six officers are Jewish. Twenty Jewesses out of twenty-three persons served on the organization's committee. Ten out of fourteen village chairmen are Jewish. What has happened to the non-Jewish women? They have simply pulled out of the League. They have left it flat. It is no longer the organization to which to belong. Now I'm reasonably certain that these women are not anti-Semites. They just don't care to be part of an organization having so many Jews. This is much more delicate, to be sure, but it is a fact that cannot be contraverted."

Jews find it difficult to understand why they are not yet accepted socially. With rare exceptions, most of these new Jewish suburbanites are native-born. They know no country other than America. The men of suburbia have, almost to a man, served in the armed forces of America in World War II. Many are graduates of colleges and universities. They maintain lovely homes and look out for the welfare of their children with infinite care and patience. They participate in general communal activities and generally comport themselves in a manner that requires no apology. They become members of a synagogue or temple and provide their children with religious education.

Despite this social freeze, Jews believe that they "belong." Their sense of "at-homeness" was strikingly and humorously illustrated in the Easter egg-rolling contests staged on the White House grounds on April 7, 1958.

Another Easter Monday went its egg-shattering way on the White House south grounds today. . . . New this year was a pan of matzoh balls, one dyed green, brought by Paul Lazar, 15 years old, of Langley Park, Maryland [a suburb]. "It's the Passover as well as Easter," he explained.[5]

Participation by Jews in the activities of the total community is not easily measurable. Yet community officials, including Red Feather executives, agree that Jewish residents contribute liberally to these and other philanthropies, including the Red Cross, the Salvation Army and numerous medical funds. Jews are also among the solicitors and workers. Jewish parents on the San Francisco peninsula, who had rarely taken much interest in community organizations when they lived in San Francisco, suddenly threw themselves into school and recreational programs when they moved to the suburbs. In Levittown, they participate in Red Feather drives, Salvation Army fund-raising and the like, and work hard on campaigns for cancer and muscular dystrophy. In the Overlake groups around Seattle, Jews are active in the service clubs, local PTA's and the Scouting movement.

In Sharon, they participate in practically every civic enterprise. They assist in the Heart Fund, Red Cross, Health Fund and other drives of all kinds. They are active in the Parent-Teachers Association, the Sharon Civic Orchestra and Choral Society and the Sharon Players.

Open opposition to the establishment of Jewish synagogues and youth centers has been voiced from time to time, and suburbia's public officials occasionally refuse to grant permits for building programs. Jews are becoming increasingly annoyed with such cold receptions. They speak of the "un-Americanism" of those very persons who, ironically, believe that they in fact are America's very best sons.

"How are we to interpret the attitude of some of these people? Not all, mind you. Sure, we are Jews and they are Christians. But this is America where there is no one state religion. All men are supposed to be equal before the law, and the differences of men with respect to religion are not only acknowledged but respected. Some of them still act as if they believe that Jews have horns. I don't know what it is, but there is something wrong about the way in which certain of these old settlers act. They are polite, all right, but so condescending, it is frightfully embarrassing. No, I won't call their attitude anti-Semitic. I must say, however, that they give one the impression that this town and all America belongs to *them*, and *they* are always passing judgment upon us Jews."

In 1948, Cleveland's Euclid Avenue Temple was faced with the need for moving to the suburbs, where most of its congregants lived. It took an option on thirty-one acres of land in the village of Beachwood, on the eastern border of Cleveland. Almost immediately, opposition to this move occurred within the City Council of Beachwood. Only after a series of law suits, in which the Council was charged with bias, did this temple win the right to erect a building in this suburb.

In another case, Temple Israel of St. Louis (Missouri), denied a permit to erect a temple and religious school in the suburb of

Creve Coeur, filed suit against the official whose two zoning amendments had resulted in denial of the permit. Community sentiment made it clear that anti-Jewish feeling had brought about the zoning amendments. The St. Louis County Circuit Court recently ruled that the community of Creve Coeur must permit Temple Israel to build its synagogue.

In the suburb of Shorehaven, adjacent to Norwalk, Connecticut, residents sought to bar the Norwalk Jewish Center from establishing recreational facilities at a recently acquired building, a large mansion. They explained that the Center would create traffic hazards and depreciate the value of the property.

Congregation Tifereth B'nai Jacob in Minneapolis, whose members have moved from the heart of the Jewish neighborhood on the city's North Side, wishes to erect its new synagogue structure near the suburb of Golden Valley. A Golden Valley ordinance would keep the synagogue out of this area. Because the congregation would build in a residentially-zoned area, some Minneapolitans regard this denial as basically unfriendly. The issue has not yet been tested in the courts.

In a law suit involving the Community Synagogue of Sands Point, Long Island, the congregation argued that local authorities had refused to it permission to develop—on an estate known as "The Chimneys"—the building and meeting rooms to which it felt legally and morally entitled. Even though the local authorities insisted that their action was free from prejudice, the belief was engendered that prejudice was certainly a factor. On July 11, 1956, the Court of Appeals of New York State overruled the lower courts and permitted the congregation to build.

These are but a few of the cases which have received considerable public attention. It should be remembered that rejection of such applications by city councils may, in fact, have nothing to do with anti-Semitism. Such acts may quite naturally result from fear of overcrowding, the need to safeguard property values, and other such important considerations.

Sometimes, efforts by older residents to keep would-be newcomers from taking up residence in suburbs arouse suspicion. In

Westport, Connecticut,[6] one selectman "suggested that new residents moving into Westport be charged 'a flat sum' immediately for use of the town's 'excellent facilities' in the manner of an initiation fee. . . . 'Some people move in for eight to ten years, get their children educated and then move out,' he said." A chairman of the town's Tax Study Committee of the Board of Finance replied that "he was afraid that if such a fee were imposed, there wouldn't be too many people anxious to move into town."

Although the reception to Jews and their houses of worship has not always been cordial, movement of Jewish families into suburbia continues without abatement. Many of the new suburban communities were built on vast areas of land often thought to be undesirable by the older townspeople. It had not occurred to them that there might be gold in the potato fields that ultimately became Levittown or the vegetable patches that became Skokie or the citrus country that bore suburbs in the San Gabriel Valley.

The sale of land proved exceedingly profitable after World War II. Such a financial harvest could hardly be resisted. Then, too, many of the developers purchased unused areas in well-established suburban communities, paid handsomely for it and later sold the newly erected homes to whoever would buy. In cases where "gentlemen's agreements" never to sell to a Jew had existed, they were frequently violated; real estate brokers were more determined to make a sale than to perpetuate biases. Given such determination, coupled with an often unreasonably high sale price, the sale was usually completed before anxious neighbors could take counteraction.

Established suburban communities were, in fact, themselves responsible for their own remarkable growth. Their comfortable living, commodious homes, good schools and leisurely appearance excited the interest of middle-class Jews, who sought these very comforts for their own families. Zoning laws, especially the fixing of the size of lots upon which homes might be built, were not changed until old-timers complained that the newcomers constituted a threat to the future growth, development and status of the suburb.

We seem to have learned little of any permanent value from

World War II, in which boys whose creeds, color and class were different fought together as a unit. However, in the wake of the war, some legislation against discrimination *was* enacted on city and state levels, and people *did* talk about the wrongness of religious and racial discrimination. There were also practical monetary considerations. It was possible to reap rich dollar rewards by selling to Jews—and then "escaping" to another, even further-removed suburb.

In my own city of Newton, neighborhoods change in a fairly consistent pattern. If a Jewish family purchases a home at the *end* of any given block—the corner house, let us say—the non-Jewish neighbors remain on the street for a minimum of two years. However, if the Jewish home is in or near the center of the block, the neighbors on both sides almost immediately list their homes for sale and remain only as long as necessary to complete the transaction.

Although Jews have moved into Newton in considerable numbers, there has been only one "incident" in which the question of anti-Jewish feeling was formally raised.

In February, 1953, a Jewish youth on his way home from a youth program at Temple Emanuel was viciously beaten by three teen-agers. Just before the beating, one of the attackers asked the boy: "Are you a Jew?" When the boy acknowledged his faith, the bitter attack took place. Several other Jewish youths had narrowly escaped the attack by running from the scene. The Newton police quickly apprehended the attackers, who were subsequently punished. The community was thoroughly aroused, however, and Jewish members of the community were shocked. It seemed incomprehensible that such an attack could have occurred in the "Garden City." It was particularly disturbing because this case appeared to be something more than sheer juvenile delinquency: anti-Jewish prejudice was definitely involved.

A representative group of Newton citizens convened to analyze the nature of the incident and to consider what, if any, action should be taken. A careful study of this and other incidents which then came to light made it clear that:

(1) Juvenile delinquency existed in Newton as it did else-where, and

(2) Hostility to Jews had to be reckoned with in the community as a fact.

It would serve no purpose to ignore this hostility or to minimize its importance by suggesting that these were isolated cases which need not be considered seriously. The consensus of those school, church and social leaders who counseled together was that Newton was in transition. The ever-increasing numbers of Jewish families moving into the suburb appeared as a threat to some of the older residents. Juvenile hoodlums might seize on the Jewish issue to rationalize gang attacks.

This volunteer committee undertook the important task of educating the public to its responsibilities. The double threats of incipient juvenile delinquency and anti-Semitism were carefully studied. Weaknesses in the community structure, particularly the paucity of programs and facilities for young people, were brought to light. The danger to the total community from attacks based, overtly or covertly, upon prejudice were exposed.

The volunteer committee then advocated and proposed legislation to establish a city-sponsored Human Relations Committee. Although a strong effort was made by certain city officials to prevent the establishment of an official committee, the legislation was finally passed and the committee was appointed in November, 1953. The years have passed, however, and there is still little indication that this committee believes that any prejudice really exists in Newton. It is true that Newton appears to be quite free from *overt* anti-Jewish feeling. However, if opinion of experts in the field of human relations are to be relied upon, this suburb, among many others, is minimizing or even ignoring latent and undercover prejudices and antipathies.

Bizarre notions about the attitudes and practices of Jewish families have often been expressed by Newton's older residents. In April, 1954, a special PTA committee considered such charges and formally replied to them. Some of the questions which this committee was asked were:[7]

Do children have huge sums of pocket money for which they do not have to account?

Is there an increase in the number of people who go off on winter vacations, leaving their children with inadequate and irresponsible supervision?

The committee replied:

It is not a common practice for Newton parents to give large sums of money to their children.

Although some cases were found where parents go off on winter trips, leaving their children with irresponsible supervision, this is not the common practice. Most parents are unwilling to leave children in the care of others.

In no case was the word "Jewish" used. It was clear in context, however, that these charges were directed against the newer, Jewish residents.

A study prepared in 1955 by a committee of the Parent-Teachers Association Council of Newton noted "tension between the old and new residents of the city." This report found that "new residents thought that conflict between new and older residents in the community was a major problem. On the other hand, older residents often regard the children of newcomers as lowering standards of behavior." Evidence of rowdiness at public exhibitions and "lack of consideration for the rights of others" were also attributed to the children of Newton's more recent residents. Certainly the records of the Newton Police Department give no evidence of a major increase in juvenile delinquency, and what delinquency there is has until recently been ascribed to the older, more crowded areas of Newton, in which few Jewish families reside.

More recently, evidence has come to hand of a small group of delinquents living in Newton's Oak Hill section, in which some of the suburb's newest and most luxurious homes have been built. These Jewish youths, all of high school age, have already come to the attention of high school authorities, and a few have been checked on by the police because of suspicion that they may be actively involved in petty thievery. It has been difficult to explain their actions, inasmuch as these youths come from "good" homes and families. Psychologists who have been studying this situation believe that these delinquents, who have arrived in Newton recently from other areas of metropolitan Boston, are seeking status for themselves. "They want to be somebody. Back in —— they knew everybody. Here they are quite alone, or were until they began to get into trouble." This group is, however, exceedingly small. Although there is concern about them, there is no indication that they constitute a major threat to the well-being of the community.

Sometimes the police are obliged to call some Jewish youths to task for disturbing the peace, "i.e., loud talks on the street, the use of horns on motor vehicles, etc."

"We sometimes are annoyed by these people who are so busy running around that they fail to bring up their children properly, but that criticism applies to only a few families."

There have been "incidents" also with respect to anti-Jewish feeling in relation to the public schools. An official of the public schools once received an anonymous letter. Referring to an elementary school which has a preponderantly Jewish enrollment, it asked: "How long are you going to permit Jews to take over?"

On another occasion, when the children of an elementary school were jointly celebrating Christmas and Chanukah, they kindled the little candles which commemorate the miracle (recorded in the Books of Maccabees) of the little cruze of oil which burnt for eight days. An indignant non-Jewish parent phoned a Newton Fire Department marshal to report that the law was being violated when these candles were kindled in the school building. According to the informant, the parent's primary objection was to the introduction of any symbol of this Jewish Festival.

"It never occurred to him that there might be some question, as Jewish tax-payers view it, of celebrating Christmas in our schools. Most of our people take this for granted because they say 'this is a Christian country.'"

Some suburbanites resent what they speak of as "inroads of Jewish teaching" in the public schools; at times, they threaten school officials in the hope that additional Christian teachings will be introduced to counteract these Jewish values.

Not even young children are left unpoisoned by prejudice. In one of the elementary schools in a predominately Jewish section of Newton, an "anti-kike" club of youngsters in the sixth grade was discovered.

Due to the overcrowded condition of Newton High School, a new high school is now under construction. It so happens that the greatest growth of school population has occurred in an area which is largely populated by Jews. The high school will be built in this district. Designed to house fifteen hundred students, the new school will be of unusual design and will provide facilities which no school in Newton has ever had. One hears of people asking: "Isn't it strange that the Jews should be getting the new high school, while the rest of us get only what's left? We all pay taxes, but the Jews get the best of us all."

If wishful thinking continues to prevail, these and other incidents within the suburb can be passed off as insignificant. But if they are viewed in the aggregate and analyzed, they must be viewed as sources of irritation and increasing tension that must somehow be alleviated.

Despite these undercurrents of tension and "feelings," the formal relations between the Jewish and non-Jewish communities in Newton is good. If, on occasion, a remark by a teacher in a classroom or a policeman on his beat provokes Jewish protest, Jewish families generally recognize this as an isolated, often ill-considered statement, rather than an indication that a virulent anti-Semitism is sweeping the suburb.

Invitations to speak at various Protestant and Unitarian churches in Newton are frequently extended to the several Rabbis. Interfaith luncheons and "get-togethers" have been sponsored by the women of the synagogues and churches in Newton for some years with marked success. In 1957, the women of the Sacred Heart Church (Catholic) and their priest, accepted the invitation of Temple Emanuel's Sisterhood and thus became the first Catholic organization in Newton to visit with their Jewish neighbors under synagogual auspices. On the occasion of the 150th Conference of the Congregational Churches of New England, two major affairs

—a luncheon and dinner—were housed in Temple Emanuel's spacious Community Hall.

When, in 1956, a great fire destroyed the Eliot Church (Congregational), this 175-year-old congregation accepted the invitation of Temple Emanuel to use its sanctuary for its Maundy Thursday and Easter Sunday services. This act helped to cement the interfaith relationships within the community. These Christian services housed in a Jewish house of worship were characterized by one local commentator as "worth a barrel of sermons."

On occasion Jews become indignant when a community-wide action is taken by suburban officials without regard to the interests of this religious minority. The following newspaper report [8] from Milton, another suburb of Boston, explains the nature of one such problem:

SPECIAL TOWN MEETING CALLED FOR MAY 27TH

PETITION SEEKS CHANGE
IN TOWN MEETING DATES

The Board of Selectmen last night (Thursday) signed a warrant for a special Town Meeting to be held Monday, May 27th, at the Town Hall.

The meeting was called at the petition of 200 members of Congregation B'nai Jacob who requested the town to change the date of the two sessions of the annual Town Meeting from the traditional Saturday to a Tuesday. The first session of Town Meeting is the election of town officials on the first Saturday in March, while the second is held the following Saturday to appropriate funds to transact town business during the year.

The petition states that the Saturday date interferes with participation in our government by members of the Congregation, since both sessions fall on the Jewish Sabbath.

There has been much controversy over the petition, but the town by-laws require that on petition of 200 or more citizens—or two percent of the electorate, the selectmen must call a special Town Meeting within a forty-five day period.

Meanwhile, it was rumored around town that some of the instigators of the petition had reconsidered their request and wish to withdraw the petition.

Debate centered around the question as to whether or not this could be done, and opinion seemed to indicate that it could be consummated if a request signed by all of the original petitioners was made to the Selectmen before the Warrant for the meeting was signed. No such request was made to the Board of Selectmen up until 10 P.M. Thursday night, and the Board signed the Warrant for the special Town Meeting, which it is believed will be a short one.

The Warrant Committee will study the proposal and make its recommendations to the townspeople in advance of the special session. . . .

Obviously, the members of Congregation B'nai Jacob acted within their rights: a meeting held on the Jewish Sabbath might have disfranchised all Jewish residents. Yet their action, taken independently of other Jews in the suburb, came as a surprise to members of another Jewish congregation in the community. As a net result, this independent action seems to have been costly to the town of Milton. It is said to have aroused the ire of the community's "old-timers" against these more recent suburbanites who happened also to be Jews. "The Jews are trying to tell *us* how to run our community!"

"Because Jews in suburbia are comparative newcomers, they are on occasion regarded as 'foreigners' who have no right to thwart the will of the older settlers. The Jews, on the other hand, believe that as tax-paying citizens in suburbia they must safeguard their rights as citizens.

"We do not ask for special privileges; we do claim that the right of any minority must be protected. Even though this often inconveniences older citizens who have never before had to concern themselves with any minority, it is our duty to call attention to the fact that community living, in order to be happy and successful, must concern itself with the welfare of *all* citizens, whether they are old-line Americans or recent arrivals."

The non-Jewish residents in suburbia are also subject to tensions. The status quo is often disturbed by the rapid growth in the town's population: new and more expensive school buildings are required, as are expanded sewage, water and other public utilities, roads, police and fire protection and numerous other services. Each new requirement produces a higher tax rate for *all* the town's citizens. Some dissatisfaction with the new residents is almost to be expected. This, however, is a matter of economics, not of anti-Jewish prejudice.

The suspicion often exists that these new residents wish to assume some role in the political and organizational management of the town. Since old-timers are generally quite certain that matters are going along very well, they often object to new residents—who presumably would introduce changes—serving on boards of education or other official bodies. There is always the fear that the suburb's political complexion may change. And old-timers frequently resent the increase in traffic, the intrusion of new shopping areas, the overcrowding of schools and public utilities and the generally faster tempo resulting from suburbia's increased population.

"It's getting so you can't come to the center any more without running into a lot of shoppers. I used to like to come up just to talk with my shopkeeper friends, but I can't do that now. They are just too busy. All this may be good for business, but this town isn't what it used to be."

New residents are even more a cause of aggravation if they happen to be members of a different faith. They prove doubly annoying if the communities from which they have come are regarded as socially inferior. It is assumed that cultural levels and standards will necessarily be low.

Sources of annoyance with Jews vary from community to community. In Newton, for example, teachers and pupils in the high school indicate their concern with the tendency of some Jewish boys and girls to have lunch together in the school cafeteria.

"Some of these Jewish girls always dress as if they were going to a party. It annoys the rest of us to see the attention these Jewish children pay to fine clothes even while at school."

"Why do some of the boys bring their father's car to school and ride around after school as if they were important?"

"If the Jewish kids stay out of school on their Holy Days, why don't they remain at their synagogues and pray? What's the idea of hanging around school in the afternoon and just getting the rest of us angry?"

"When a Jewish child gets up to make a report on current events, he usually reports on trips he has made to Nassau, Bermuda, Miami or some other vacation spot which he and his family have visited. He thinks nothing of it, but we teachers notice that this often creates tensions in the other children."

There is little association between the Jewish and non-Jewish boys and girls except in their classes and school clubs. They share little social life during or after school hours.

These sub-surface tensions have their counterpart in most American suburbs. In Levittown, for example, informants have noted that few opportunities are afforded the children of the community to work and play together, except in school. Although there is no evidence of organized anti-Semitism, there is a "feeling" that some prejudice against Jews exists in this community, whose population is approximately 50 per cent Catholic and 30 per cent Protestant. Rabbinical leaders deny this, yet admit that they have heard reports about the veiled antipathy.

In Euclid, too, there is general agreement that "there is no anti-Semitism." Yet a discerning Jewish leader has commented:

"The young people here, ages thirty to forty, feel that there is some feeling of tension, even though there is no organized anti-Semitism, here in town. They don't really pin it down or point out just where it is. Sometimes they say, 'You will find it in housing restrictions.' Others say 'there are restrictions in the matter of jobs which Jews may hold in the factories.' I suppose there is some, but frankly, I cannot cite chapter and verse. Besides, the younger the Jewish couples who talk about it, the less they feel that there is any kind of anti-Semitism."

Relations between Jew and Christian in Euclid appear to be good. However, here too there is little social contact between these groups.

Jews and Christians maintain an excellent relationship in Silver Spring and, in fact, in all of Montgomery County. Rabbis are well received by the Christian ministers and the Ministerial Association.

Jews participate actively in the civic life of their respective suburbs. They are a highly respected group, one non-Jewish leader reports, because their intellectual standards are reputedly high and because their skills, scientific and other, have won them important posts with the Federal government. It may be, too, that inter-religious frictions and tensions are few because the major developers of the area, notably Silver Spring, are Jews.

A recently formed Niles Township Human Relations Council, which encompasses every major official organization in the Skokie area, seeks "to improve the general welfare of all the inhabitants of the various suburbs that comprise Niles Township." Before and during World War II, Niles Township was considered by many to be the active scene of operation of the German-American Bund and was regarded by many to be the most anti-Semitic area in metropolitan Chicago. Skokie has had its share of tensions for well over a decade.

In 1946, a Jewish community club devoted to the care of mentally retarded children was organized in Skokie. "This group was formed out of a sense of isolation felt by the small Jewish group as well as by the lack of total acceptance of these individuals into the general social life of the community." [9]

In the early years (1946-50) there were indications of anti-Jewish prejudices, taking the form of "gentlemen's agreements" among homeowners not to sell homes to Jews. The inability of Jewish candidates for the school board to get elected has also been cited as evidence of prejudice,[10] yet it is more than likely that Jews themselves did not support these candidates. Today Jews participate in many of the general community organizations and activities; there are, for example, three Jews on the Advisory Board of the YMCA. Some of the youths in Skokie go to the YMCA for their fun. But characteristically, there is little if any social intermingling between Jewish and non-Jewish residents among the more recently arrived settlers.

In some cases, old Jewish residents and their children had established close relationships with non-Jews. The increased Jewish population has, in some cases, resulted in the decrease of intensity of Jew, non-Jew friendships. One has the feelings that there is a strain involved in the maintaining of the relationship.

Typical of the tensions which are increasing in the suburbs is the following, reported from Fort Lee, New Jersey:

"A conflict had developed within the Jewish community with respect to the question of whether or not Jewish children should join the Tri-Hi-Y organization of the high school when they were invited. Some time before, the local Catholic parish had ordered all Catholic children to withdraw from the Y organizations at the high school. This act resulted in certain evidences of tension. The Tri-Hi-Y is a status-giving organization and is generally highly regarded by students and faculty alike. Upon becoming a member, a pledge must be taken to 'develop Christian attitudes in home, school and community.' This pledge is recited at each meeting. Other factors tend to give the impression that the Y is basically a Christian religious character-building organization. The Jews were split in their attitudes with respect to the Tri-Hi-Y.

"Following a series of meetings with friendly, understanding officials of all groups involved, it was agreed that there was need for the creation of a non-sectarian service group in the high school. That this problem was resolved in a manner satisfactory to all concerned is fortunate indeed."

On the peninsula, out of San Francisco, there are three country clubs; several have a few Jewish club members. It is alleged that one club, in San Mateo, will not accept Jewish members. Jews on the peninsula do not expect that all country clubs will be open to them. In this case, however, there is both hurt and chagrin, because the local Community Chest, the Red Cross and other charities use the club's facilities.

"It is as if community officials were saying to us, 'We want your money, all right, but it doesn't matter whether you Jews are accorded treatment as equals otherwise.' "

Resentment, in this instance, has resulted in the building up of certain Jewish youth organizations in the area.

"If our young people cannot be accepted in a first-rate country club just because they are Jewish, we will build our own Jewish youth groups and make them absolutely the best."

It should be reported that "there is considerable amount of inter-dating" between Jewish and Christian youth on the peninsula. In the entire Bay area (San Francisco) there is no indication of any form of anti-Jewish housing discrimination.

Jewish families express their concern about the scheduling of football games and other sporting events on Jewish Festivals and Holy Days. Even more Jews are disturbed because Jewish Holy Days are so frequently ignored when examinations are scheduled in the junior and senior high schools.

"It almost seems deliberate. The teachers either set examinations on a Jewish Holy Day or else they set it on the day following such a Holy Day, thereby making it impossible for our children to go to their synagogue and worship in peace. And when you raise any questions about it, you get such replies as 'Well, the Jewish festival is not on our calendar,' or, 'Teachers are autonomous. We cannot control each and everything they do,' or, 'How were we to know this was a Jewish holiday?' (even though the principal is known to have received a Jewish calendar giving all the festival dates for a year ahead)."

The major source of tension in suburbia becomes evident around the Christmas-Chanukah season. Jewish children then feel most exposed and unprepared, and their parents are generally indignant about the manner in which Christmas has been incorporated in the public school programs, from kindergarten through high school. Preparation for the school Christmas program, emphasis upon gift-giving, discussion of the New Testament's record of the birth of Jesus, the carols with their Christological character—all these are regarded as intrusions into the public school system by perhaps well-meaning citizens who, ignoring the public non-denominational support of the school system and the Constitutional guarantees of separation of church and state, insist that "this is a Christian country" or argue that "the rights of the majority must not be ignored by the minority."

Jewish parents, often disturbed by this issue, react to this situation on different levels. Children are told that they need not (often should not) join in singing Christmas carols or participate in other activities directly associated with preparation for Christmas. Children, especially in schools where there is known to be a Jewish minority, sometimes ask for the right to introduce the theme of Chanukah, which usually occurs at the same season. To counteract the influence of the Christmas season upon their children, Jewish parents have converted this minor Jewish festival into one of major proportions within their homes as well as in their religious schools. Through their national and local Jewish agencies, as well as through their congregational leaders, they carry on a consistent campaign to root out purely religious sectarian festivals from tax-supported public schools.

These tensions are far greater in the suburbs than in the urban schools because the direct, personal, face-to-face relation between principal, teacher and parent is so much greater. What transpires in the suburb is not only more personal but more frustrating.

Because Jews feel at home in suburbia, they do not hesitate to "view with alarm" those tendencies which would have caused no more than a shrug of the shoulder in the big city.

"We feel that teachers have no right to make our children recite Christian prayers at the beginning of the school session. Church and state ought to be kept separate. But if the school system insists on beginning with prayer, at least make it impossible for some teachers to decide on what is right and what is wrong. I don't think that inclusion of the Lord's Prayer is right because that is a Christian prayer. It is not one which Jews and Christians have in common."

In Sharon (Mass.), Jewish parents of high school pupils justifiably objected strenuously to the principal when an Arab speaker at a high school assembly delivered an intemperate attack on Israel.

In Ross, a suburb of San Francisco, community relations were disturbed by the Jewish protest of a performance of a Nativity play before a Parent-Teachers Association. A Jewish mother of six children, who is also a practicing attorney, attended a meeting of the Ross School District Board and soundly criticized it for allowing the teaching of the Christmas story in the grammar school.

"The religion it reflected was not the religion of my children. It confused them, and they brought their confusion into our home.

It was an experience outside our faith. The presentation violated a basic constitutional right separating church and state. Our laws proscribe the teachings of any religious doctrine in institutions receiving state support."

She recommended the singing of Christmas songs and a Santa Claus play instead of the Nativity. School officials in the suburb have not yet arrived at a satisfactory solution.

Jewish parents in suburbia are often deeply offended by the school requirement that their children should sing Christmas carols or participate in Nativity plays.

They believe, too, that the reading of the Bible in the public schools constitutes another violation and that the Christian majority is mistaken in its impression that such efforts will assure moral character and better citizenship. The recitation of the Lord's Prayer and "released time" programs (in which children are excused from their regular school classes to receive denominational religious instruction) are also viewed by Jews as forces that make for divisiveness within the community.

"Something must be done about all this. It has already gotten out of hand. We Jews have no right to sit back and let such things take their natural course. All that means is that, in the eyes of public school officials, there will be no question about either moral or legal rights to place religion in the schools."

The desire to find some solution to the "church-state impasse" has often led to compromise or "accommodation." In East Orange, New Jersey, for example, the problem created by a Nativity scene set up on the lawn in front of the Town Hall was resolved by erecting a huge Chanukah Menorah across from it.

Certain suburbs have compromised by authorizing the observance of both Christmas and Chanukah (Lynbrook, Long Island; Plainview and Plainedge, New York). This compromise was objected to by Rabbinical and other Jewish leaders of Plainview.

Tensions were reported to have increased in 1957 in Oak Park, with its 40 per cent Jewish population, and Huntington Woods, with its 20 per cent Jewish population—both suburbs of Detroit— when Chanukah was celebrated partly at the behest of individual

Jewish parents, even though Detroit's Jewish Community Council and other Jewish organizations had opposed the idea.

A similar situation, in which the local Rabbi became the central figure, was evidenced at Yorktown Heights (1957). Catholic and Protestant clergy objected to the Rabbi's assertion that there ought to be no religious emphasis in the public schools.

In Evanston, Chicago's most populous suburb, the problem has been officially noted by the School Superintendent, Dr. O. M. Chote, who has pointed out:

"There was an increasing number of inquiries from parents of the Jewish faith concerning the observance of the Christmas season in the public school. Your Superintendent, therefore, has given this matter considerable thought to see what appropriate action might be taken to make sure that our schools are within the law on this matter. . . . Your Superintendent takes the position that we have not only the right but the obligation to recognize in some appropriate way any holiday or event that is of wide-spread interest to people in the local community, whether it be related to our general heritage or a religious festival. There is a fine line in religious matters where information and education stop and indoctrination takes over. It is our hope that we will not violate the legitimate religious sentiments of our patrons or indoctrinate children in a manner unbecoming to a public school."

In Valley Stream, Long Island, in 1957, a Christmas play to be presented by children in the sixth grade of a public school was banned after heated debate and charges that Jewish pressure groups had interfered with the schools. Christian parents, aroused by the action of the district superintendent, were bitter. One well-known citizen suggested that "pressure groups were destroying brotherhood and good human relations in the community, making it advisable and necessary for Christians to organize to defend Christianity in Valley Stream."

A qualified Jewish observer has remarked:

"At the present time there is more tension, prejudice, anti-Semitism and hatred in Valley Stream, in the opinion of most residents and observers, than there has been in a decade. Within the school itself, all of the friendly relationship among Jewish and

Christian teachers has evaporated. Only strictly official conversations are carried on, and tension and hard feelings are evident in all staff meetings as well as in other contacts between teachers and the school."

Jews believe, as do their Christian neighbors, that religion can play a vital role in solving many of the vexing problems that have arisen in contemporary society. The rise of totalitarianism with its philosophy of anti-religion, the increasing social and economic tensions, the changing status of the family and the marked increase in juvenile delinquency—all these have heightened the belief that the moral values of religion can, if properly taught, counteract the evil influences of this day. Jews deny, however, that the tax-supported public schools are the proper place for such teaching.

As Jews see it, the major source of the tension building up between them and their non-Jewish neighbors is the issue of religion in the public schools. In the suburbs, where direct contacts with school and city officials occur much more frequently than in the central city, parents voice their concern and ofttimes their indignation when individual teachers and/or whole school systems, however subtly, urge Christological references and values upon their pupils.

Before Jewish families became a sizable minority in many suburbs, the Protestant Christian majority was seldom obliged to consider the specifically religious values in the schools' observances at Christmas and Easter. Jewish children were expected to accept the standard of the majority.

Today, many suburbs are definitely religiously divided. Today's Jewish parents believe that religious freedom requires the elimination from the public school of any form of moral teaching or practice that is not acceptable to everyone. They object to Christmas carols, Nativity scenes, Christmas plays and pageants, readings from Bible (both New and Old Testaments), released time programs and other forms of sectarian religious expression because, they believe, these are divisive influences in the tax-supported public schools. They voice their concern not only because they desire to safeguard their own way of life, its sancta and values, but also because they are concerned with the rights of other non-Christians whose children also attend the public schools.

Jews believe that the home, the church and the synagogue are the proper settings in which sectarian religion should be taught. Respectfully but firmly they remind proponents of religion in the schools to examine their own church-school educational programs: to ascertain if the teaching staff is equal to its task, if the textbooks and curricula are stimulating and relevant, and if classrooms and equipment are equal to those of the public schools. Above all, they ask if the guidance and direction in church schools is genuinely expert, not just well-intentioned.

Jews remind their Protestant neighbors that they, the Jewish families, in suburbia as elsewhere, are spending huge sums in order to provide for the religious education and training of the Jewish child *after school hours* on weekdays, and on the Sabbath and Sundays as well, through professionally trained and directed teaching staffs. The training of Jewish children in the ways of their fathers is of paramount interest and concern to most Jewish parents today, as it has been through the centuries.

The principle of separation of church and state, as America has understood it, is important not only because it is recorded in the Constitution of the United States, but also because divisiveness among the American people must be reduced whenever possible. The right of all Americans to worship God in accordance with the dictates of their own prescribed pattern has been accorded them by the law of the land. Shall we increase tensions by dividing our children into separate camps within a public, tax-supported school system, while professing our desire for the brotherhood of man? Do we not know that there is still so much prejudice and intolerance of different religious and racial groups that we dare not add fuel to the fire, even if we claim to be doing so in the name of God? Those who support a program of religion in the public schools are playing into the hands of persons and churches who favor parochialism. Is that what we Americans really want?

There is no indication that Jews will recede from their present position. They are convinced that the rights of conscience and the Constitutional freedom of each individual must be safeguarded. As Americans and as Jews, desirous of perpetuating both heritages, they are determined to press for an unequivocal answer to this problem. The fuse has already been lighted. Only major statesmanship and continued mutual respect can reduce the effect of the explosion which may result.

Chapter 8   The Homogenized Society

The greatest threat to American liberty today comes not from outer coercion but from inner weakness. . . . The greater danger is . . . less from the people who do not want others to be free than from the people who do not want to be free themselves, who feel themselves rendered guilty by deviation and threatened by dissent, whose whole aspiration is to merge their identity with the group.

What liberalism must resist is the tendency to turn America into one great and genuinely benevolent company town—the bland leading the bland. It must oppose the drift into the homogenized society. It must fight spiritual unemployment, as it once fought economic unemployment.[1]

Historians, social scientists and, in fact, all students of contemporary American life agree that since World War II there has been a marked increase in the tendency toward standardization and conformity.

A devastating picture of the uniformity in both thought and practice which characterizes contemporary American society has been drawn by Lerner [2] and other analysts of the American scene. We are paying a high price indeed for our technological skills, our ability to mass-produce both the goods we desire and the machines by which they are manufactured. Uniformity in our dress, our homes and even the thoughts we think is becoming an integral part of the American pattern of life. There is sufficient reason for grave concern.

It is almost impossible for this generation of Americans to escape the trend to conformity. Uniformity and standardization are the natural consequences of mass-production. Advertising, too, is geared to this type of appeal. A recent study [3] estimated that members of an average suburban family are exposed in a typical day to

510 display ads in newspapers; 113 car, bus, train and subway cards; 281 billboards of various sizes; 53 radio ads; 64 television commercials; 447 magazine ads; 50 ads in a couple of comic books read by children—a total of 1,518 advertisements aimed at the average suburban family. In each case, the family is being urged to (a) "live modern," (b) follow the crowd, (c) be a good fellow, (d) be popular, and (e) accept another man's standards. The pressures that result from such advertising are overwhelming.

Suburbia is a fertile field for observation and study of conformism because the overt forms of unformity are so clear. The mass-produced houses of the newer suburbs, erected from a few simple and similar architectural designs, have been the subject of much humor and commentary for the past decade. The army of commuters who move as a mass from their homes to the railroad station to the big city and then back each day gives one pause for critical concern. Most significant of all, our thinking, too, has become standardized; our ideas and opinions reflect the oracular comments of the syndicated columnists and radio and television pundits.

We use the phrase "the homogenized society" as a term of opprobrium. Ideas and values seem to be suspect if they differ from those held by other members of our society, but many fear that the standardization of ideas and the consequent loss of individuality will ultimately destroy us. When ideas and values are mass-produced; when it is assumed that values and opinions which deviate from the average have no right to be heard; when to be average is considered not only safest, but best—then the spiritual well-being of the nation is in danger. And this standardization and conformity are markedly evident in the suburbs.[4]

Various reasons have been suggested for the high degree of conformism. Paul Tillich, noted theologian and a professor at the Harvard Divinity School, sums them up in three factors: (1) the fact that ours is a technical civilization; (2) the intentional imposition of patterns on the masses by interested groups; and (3) the common striving for security, especially by the younger generation.[5]

Conformity often follows when freedom has become a frightening experience to man. The average individual is quite literally afraid to make decisions. The very opportunity to make a choice among several courses of action forces him to reject several of them. He thus begins to feel that he is isolating himself. This, in turn, becomes a major source of anxiety. It is therefore easier—and it certainly provides greater security—for a man to have others make decisions for him. For this reason, says Fromm,[6] so many of us seek an "escape from freedom."

How desirable it appears to be like everyone else, especially when our security seems to be directly involved! We are reminded frequently how important it is to join with others against those forces that threaten ultimately to destroy us—against atom and hydrogen bombs, satellites and missiles, and against war generally. These factors alone are sufficient to make strong men feel uncertain and weak men quake with an unholy fear. And there is some validity: annihilation of the human race *is* today's major threat.

We also fear our own talents. We believe that we can escape our responsibilities as individuals by joining the crowd and letting it (or some of its leaders) do our thinking for us. At least, we hope, we shall then not be noticed; we can hide ourselves within the group. Thus many persons deliberately seek to lose an important part of their identity as individuals, to submerge it in the mass of men among whom they live. They choose to ignore human problems, to act as if these problems did not really exist. Our generation has concluded that it is unwise to "stick your neck out" or to be vocal in criticism. Consciously and quite deliberately, we conform.

There are also group pressures which tend to restrict our actions. The McCarthyism of a few years ago represented the attempt of one group, wittingly or unwittingly, to silence all those who disagreed with them. Any who spoke out faced the danger that they might be tarred with his brush. Such group pressures, often exerted in the name of democracy, tend to confuse otherwise good citizens into believing that as long as the majority approves some idea or action, the minority has no right to question it further. It had better join with the majority and do as it proposes.

To become a member of this "homogenized society," we are

often informed, is to "adjust" to it. Since "adjustment" means nothing more than to have the approval of our fellow man, we ought surely to recognize its importance to our personal welfare.

Maslow [7] points out that "adjustment means a passive shaping of one's self to one's culture, to the external environment." He continues, "But supposing it is a sick culture? Adjustment is a passive rather than active process; its ideal is attained in the cow or in the slave or anyone else who can be happy without individuality, even, e.g. the well-adjusted lunatic or prisoner." Inasmuch as it has nothing to do with goodness or rightness, conformity that is requested in its name is decried as but a snare and a delusion.

To receive the approval of others in whatever we do and say appears to be of greater concern today than ever before. To be sure, this is not a *new* value. It is rather the *degree* of our clamoring for approval which seems to have increased. We fail to be as discriminating in that for which we seek approval.

Suburbanites are as anxious as all other Americans to be "accepted" by their neighbors, friends and community. To be accepted is to acquire status as an individual, and what can be more desirable?

If the ranch-type home is generally approved and accepted by suburbia, most families will make an effort to acquire one. If our friends use a certain interior decorator, we will most likely turn to him. If a new car or membership in a particular golf club are required for acceptance, then every effort will be expended to secure one or both. Midwinter vacations, clothes, the school which our children attend—these are all dictated in large measure by the standards and values of the community.

"If I want to get some practice accepted within my church, I try to get one of the better known families to accept my standard. If I succeed, I am certain to have the idea generally accepted in quick order. People like to follow the leader. Only the trouble is that they do not question the leader on his values. They assume that the leader, especially the social leader, is right, and do as he does whenever possible."

"Success" is measured in terms of the possession of material things. Businessmen who are known to have acquired great wealth, therefore, are all too often assumed to have special qualities of character which should be emulated not only in business but in all other areas as well.

We are often led to believe, too, that differences among Americans tend to destroy national unity. Individualism, so often honored in theory, is often frowned upon in practice. The homogenization process by which personal distinctions are obviated and even eliminated, in order that we become "of the same kind" with little to distinguish each of us from the other, goes on apace.

"You find that people in this suburb don't even think for themselves any more. They read only what they are told are "best sellers." They vote the straight Republican Party ticket even though they have been Democrats in the big city. They keep doing and saying the things expected of them by their neighbors. Their children have to be dressed like all the other children. They must go to a summer camp, just because the other children go. Parents don't dare express honest thoughts on anything for fear of being looked upon as queer. It isn't too much to say that, of all the people I know, suburbanites are no longer free men and women. They are part of a well-oiled machine which bears a warning for all to read, 'Adjust yourself.' "

Robert Hutchins [8] has commented:

By definition, a moron is a person who cannot think, and one of the benefits conferred upon us by the industrial revolution is that it has made it possible for morons to be successful. Thinking leads to criticism and criticism brings on controversy.

Hutchins might just as well have been talking about the people of suburbia. They fear criticism and they seek to avoid controversy. They generally refrain from participation in any situation which makes one appear different. Acceptance by the larger group requires that one conform to its standards.

"He's a brainy fellow—got good ideas. He is honest and sincere in all that he does. But he hasn't got a friend in this club—and all

because he tells us what he thinks. Why can't he be a good fellow
—smile pleasantly and cut out this business of taking exception to
what our leaders want?"

The same problem of conformity confronts the youth in
suburbia as well.

"One kid sets a standard and soon all the others follow. Many
times, I tried to get my daughter to be independent of the group,
but I just didn't succeed. She wants to be popular, and to be
popular you *must* do what the others do. I'm pleased with one
thing, though. These are really nice youngsters. If they weren't,
we would really be in trouble."

In certain important respects, the standardization of materials,
gadgets and products of the machine is a blessing. Though it has
deprived us of much of our individualism, it has instead provided
us with material comforts and satisfactions. We may denounce the
mold into which we have seemingly been poured, yet standardization of goods constitutes a major source of our benefactions. The
machine has helped to make available to millions of humans what
would otherwise be accessible to but hundreds. Costs have been
sharply reduced, and distribution has been increased. The comforts
of life, produced inexpensively, have become available to most
Americans through the very process of standardization we so frequently decry.

What of Jews in suburbia? Is this uniformity characteristic
of them? Are there perhaps differentiations and distinctions among
Jews who live in far separated areas of the country, or in suburbs
as different from each other as Newton and Levittown?

Suburban standards of dress, food, automobiles, clubs and games
differ, in the main, according to the suburbs' economic status. More
Cadillacs are found in Newton than in Skokie. Homes in Marblehead and Swampscott have more likely been planned by an expert
interior decorator than have those in Silver Spring. Parties and
socials are far more lavish in the New England suburbs than they
are in Euclid.

Since Jewish suburban communities vary in terms of the economic income of all their residents, Jews often choose the suburb into which they move on the basis of its social and economic status.

"When I was in business, I would check the credit rating of my would-be customers in Dun and Bradstreet. This was the rating book. Anybody who was anybody had his credit rating listed in that book. I am always reminded of that book when I think of the suburbs. If someone tells me, 'I live in Sharon,' I get a pretty good picture of his economic condition. If, on the other hand, I'm told, 'We live in Wellesley,' I get a completely different picture. Now, in most cases, the standards of Wellesley—how the people entertain, the cars they drive, the quality of the clothes they wear— differ in marked degree from those of another suburb."

Into those suburbs containing upper-middle-class Jews have come many families whose personal insecurities and lack of cultural background have made it necessary for them to emphasize their material and economic success. Frequently the objects of pronounced disapproval by other Jewish residents, they go merrily on their way, flaunting their lack of knowledge and their ignorance of their rich spiritual heritage by calling undue attention to themselves and their possessions. Failing to recognize that culture is something more than a surface cover-all, they practice a hedonistic approach to life which leads their fellow Jews to describe them as "pagans" and even vulgarians.

"They have a peculiar kind of logic. They reason that if enough is plenty, then 'too much' is even better. These are the people, luckily a minority, but a powerful minority, who, lacking roots in their Hebraic tradition, seek to emulate the undiscriminating standards of the rootless in the larger community."

"When I visit X suburb, I know that I cannot expect to find the kind of expensive socials that I find in Y suburb, just one hour distant from each other. The people who live in X are in most cases the children of the people who live in Y. But they are trying to establish themselves as much as possible without papa's financial help. Now, mind you, the kitchens of both homes are modern and up to date. They both have all the gadgets. But the kitchens of X suburb homes are smaller, more compact. The living room in Y suburb has wall-to-wall carpeting. But you won't find that sort of thing in X suburb."

A suburban Rabbi coments:

"Most of my people have really nice homes, comfortable and well appointed in all respects. I find them to be really good and devoted parents, too. But, I am disturbed about a certain small group within the community who are 'dollar mad.' All that matters to them is money. They think they can buy anything and anybody with money. They live in outlandishly extravagant homes. The women are often spendthrifts, and the husbands are either genuises or fools—the way they are working to make money. With all that they have, you do not often find these people very charitable. They live for themselves alone. They and their clique cause me to be ashamed for them."

A layman, bitter because of a recent unhappy experience, expresses his indignation:

"Just about everything is 'all right' with those people. They have little culture, Hebrew or secular. They respect the dollar and what it can buy more than anything else. They negate the spiritual and accent the material. They judge everything by the standard of the market place. Their idea of Heaven is the country club. Their idea of Hell is having to spend any time by themselves. They judge all men by what they have. They are the vulgar ones who defile everything with which they come in contact. Luckily, they do not predominate in my community."

The "country club mentality" with which America's church members have been charged is also found to a degree in certain suburbs in which Jews reside. In most of the pre-World War II suburbs, many Jewish families regard their synagogue as a social club. Just as membership in a country club is said to give one status, so membership in certain suburban synagogues is urged on the basis of social appeal: "The right crowd belongs."

"You really ought to join the synagogue. The best people go there. They don't take just anybody. You're lucky if they accept you."

Lerner [9] classifies the five major goals in American life as success, prestige, money, power, and security. Many acculturated Jews in suburbia accept these standards as avidly as most other Americans.

"Even though we know many Jews whose cultural values are truly high, it is disturbing to find that money and the things that money can buy have tempted so many of these suburban Jews to build their lives around it as the greatest of life's goals. I'm not disturbed when I see other money-mad people, but when Jews forget that they are the People of the Bible, whose prophets gave the world such majestic values, it is enough to make one cry. I feel sorry for them."

Often unable to distinguish between the real and the apparent, the substance of worth and the tawdry yet glittering imitation, their ersatz values attest to their basic superficialities. Lacking the understanding and support of their Hebraic traditions and group life, some suburban Jews fall prey to the current cultural "success system" and, in their own insecurity, scramble madly after prestige and power. They believe that the undiscriminating expenditure of money alone will assure the attainment of their life goals.

Whatever the economic level of each suburban community, there are class differences *within* each community as well. Friendships are developed and maintained on the basis not only of economic status, but of intellectual or professional status as well. There are as many class divisions within the Sharon and Skokie Jewish communities, for example, as there are between them, though each of these suburbs may be classified in a different economic bracket. In Euclid, the social stratification of semi-skilled worker and professional is generally fixed, as is the division between the several very wealthy families and the semi-skilled. Professional men and their families are accepted as friends by the upper-middle class or lower-upper class because skill and learning are still generally appreciated.

Though most Jewish parents in suburbia remain levelheaded despite their improved economic status, some adopt standards and values that, if continued, can only lead to the extinction of the tradition-directed Jew. In upper-middle class Jewish communities, class-conscious parents sometimes help to implant false values in their children.

"One day, my son, who had just concluded a phone conversation with one of his pals, called upstairs to tell me that he had accepted an invitation to go to the museum with his friend. That sounded good, so I readily consented to let him go. Within a few minutes, I heard the honk of the auto horn and my boy dashed out of the house. I thought nothing more about it until my boy returned about three hours later. He had been to the museum with his friend, all right, but that was only a part of the story. My son's friend had called, not in the family car driven by his mother, but in a city taxicab. His mother and father were out of town. And he —a nine-year-old youngster—had been given enough money to do with as he pleased. Here he was with a pocket full of spending money, making decisions one had no right to expect of one so young. What is disturbing is—what is that boy going to be like ten or fifteen years from now, seeing that money means so little and he has had just about everything already? Besides, what are his standards going to do to my son and *his* standards? Is my boy, too, going to get the notion that money is about the most important thing in the world?"

Jewish mothers in these class-conscious families are often accused of setting false standards for their daughters:

"When I see mothers going to such extremes with their daughters, buying such expensive dresses, making their children feel a sense of competition with other children in whatever they do or wherever they go, I get sick about it all. Why must they say—and I have heard them—'You should be the best-looking girl at the party' or 'the best dressed'? Why is that so important? Are these the values that these mothers really want to have their children stress? These women set such standards and all the other youngsters get envious and nag at their mothers until they enter into the same kind of competition by trying to outdress the others. They have impossible values!"

A Girl Scout leader in one suburban area recently indicated her concern because Jewish children in that community were expressing their dissatisfaction with scouting.

"These girls are so accustomed to more costly and grown-up forms of entertainment that they make it almost impossible for us to carry out a simple and character-building but unsophisticated Girl Scout program. They have been given values by their mothers and/or others in their group that make them disinterested in scouting. They disturb group activity rather than help it."

False values often creep into occasions that could otherwise evoke a wholly precious religious sentiment, elevated and spiritual. The Bar Mitzvah, which solemnizes a youth's becoming "a son of the commandment," offers an enriching spiritual experience. The boy, by this religious rite, is accorded his rightful place as a responsible member of the "holy nation." He is, however, likely to receive the impression that the party which follows the religious rite is the most important phase of the ceremony.

In a recent case before the New York Supreme Court, the parents of a boy who had a trust fund of $600 (resulting from a personal injury case) asked the court's permission to use the money toward payment of a planned Bar Mitzvah dinner which would cost $700. The Court ruled:

The Bar Mitzvah is the solemnization of a boy's becoming a "son of the commandment." The spiritual values the occasion symbolizes may not be relegated to second place in favor of a gesture of conspicuous consumption. It would be more fitting if the funds belonging to this boy were utilized to initiate or to continue his education in faith and in morals.

While it is manifest that it was never intended that the principal feature of the Bar Mitzvah festivities be an epicurean adventure, the solemnity of the occasion need not render it less joyous. For the psalmist has enjoined us to "serve the Lord in gladness." In this spirit, the Court grants the application to extent of permitting a withdrawal of $200.00.

A midwestern Rabbi [10] recently warned against three possible abuses in connection with a Bar Mitzvah. First, the Bar Mitzvah ceremony may mark the end of the child's Jewish education. Second, "in school we try to inculcate the power to discriminate between what is important and what is trivial, between the good and the merely glittering. Then comes the Bar Mitzvah party which so often neutralizes all that the school has attempted to teach, and influences the child to believe that ostentation is better than modesty, and that money spent on elaborate entertainment is better spent than money spent on books or charity or the Synagogue."

The third threat, according to this Rabbi, "is to the service in the Synagogue. When relatives and friends, who do not generally attend the Synagogue (except for such occasions), converse loudly during prayers, visit and kiss each other conspicuously, sit with arms folded, not even glancing at a prayerbook, carrying large bundles of gifts and otherwise desecrating the atmosphere of worship, they certainly do not add to the dignity and significance of the service."

What this wise Rabbi has written about his own community could apply with equal cogency to certain Jewish families throughout suburbia.

Bar Mitzvah parties are most frequently simple affairs in those suburbs where the mother is in direct charge of arrangements and where her friends help her prepare the repast which usually follows the service. In those suburban congregations where "everybody knows everybody," informants say, such functions are generally simple but lovely gatherings in keeping with the religious nature of the occasion.

In my experience, undue attention is given to the social aspects of the Bar Mitzvah in those congregations which tend to emulate a segment of the Jewish upper-middle class. Jews too have their *nouveaux riches*.

Levittown, so near Manhattan and its numerous catering establishments, is said to have more such "affairs" than Euclid or the suburbs of Montgomery County. Skokie, though very close to Chicago, is less prone to conduct lavish Bar Mitzvah parties than are the more fashionable Glencoe and Highland Park, Illinois. In St. Louis Park and along the San Gabriel Valley, the few Bar Mitzvahs already conducted appear to be generally free of extravagant display. In some cases, Bar Mitzvah receptions are conducted in a nearby country club immediately after the synagogue service. Rabbis, in such cases, complain that the religious emphasis of the Bar Mitzvah is often lost in the purely secular, though elegant, club settings.

In greater Minneapolis, which includes St. Louis Park, Rabbis have decreed that all marriage ceremonies must be performed either in the synagogue or the home, not in hotels and other public establishments. Most other Jewish communities have no hard and fast rule about where the marriage service may take place. Suburban

Rabbis indicate, however, that an increasing number of such services are taking place in the temple sanctuary.

"I find that if the bride or groom knows the Rabbi well, and if the Sanctuary is well appointed, young folks like to be married in the temple and have their own Rabbi officiate. I notice that the number of marriages in the temple or in my study has increased in recent years. I guess that one of the reasons certainly is the fact that I have been the Rabbi for almost eight years. This means that the families know me better and this makes a real difference to all concerned."

More than half of the Jewish marriages in Newton are solemnized in its synagogues and temples. This is true, partly because the Rabbis are well established with their congregations, but more especially because each of the congregations has erected a modern community hall—as beautiful, in fact, as most of the hotel ballrooms in greater Boston.

After careful observation of suburban Jewish communities throughout America, I believe that flashiness and disrespect for ritual are *not* characteristic of the vast majority of suburban Jews. Most Jews remain tradition-directed and conscious of the uniqueness of their own spiritual heritage. In the face of powerful efforts that seek to force them into a standardized and uniform mold of thought and action, Jews have demonstrated their independence by their continued loyalty to their age-old values.

Whatever may be said about the lessening of interest in certain of the traditional ritual practices, the modern Jew is still very much concerned with the physical and spiritual welfare of his fellow man. Philanthropy means to the Jew exactly what it says—love of mankind. This value, biblical in origin, is almost as meaningful to him today as it was to his fathers. In 1956, for example, Jews throughout the United States contributed the huge sum of $135,-000,000, through their locally organized Jewish Federations and welfare funds, for the welfare of other humans at home and overseas. In 1957, American Jews purchased $50,000,000 worth of bonds to support the State of Israel. In 1958, their contribution to this cause alone was authoritatively estimated at $47,000,000.

In 1958, five and one-half million Jews contributed approximately $200,000,000 to Jewish causes, movements, and hospitals, Jewish family service organizations, and Hebrew educational programs. The nation's Community Chests and United Funds in 1957 had raised a total sum of $400,000,000; the Red Cross, $85,000,000. The contrast between Jewish philanthropies and these secular causes (to which Jews have also contributed liberally) points up the high value which the American Jew still places upon philanthropy. His concern for humankind is clear.

Two thousand years ago a Hebrew sage described his Jewish contemporaries: "They are merciful, they are chaste and they are charitable." These values may be said to characterize most Jews today. The very newness of suburbia and the comparative youth of its Jewish residents make a detailed account of their contributions to specific charities well-nigh impossible. Yet, of the $775,000,000 expended by Jews for the construction of religious edifices in 1957, well over half of that sum was contributed by suburbanites for their own synagogue centers. Community leaders believe that Jewish suburbia will, in ever-increasing degree, support and maintain not only houses of worship but other worthy causes that are directed toward freedom, equality and human brotherhood.

We have already noted [11] the high value that the Jew places upon the family and family life. His regard for the child and his continuing devotion to the ideal of marital fidelity are beyond question. Despite the weaknesses that are presently manifest in his family relationships, students agree that the standards of the Jewish family remain high.

The movement of so many Jewish families into suburbia is another indication of the desire to maintain an elevated standard for family living. The material cost of such a move is often higher than can be afforded, yet sacrifices are made in the family interest. That the suburban Jew places so high a value upon his family— that his devotion to his wife, his children, and their physical, educational and spiritual welfare is so marked—is cause for satisfaction.

These values, having their source in the written and oral tradition of the Jew, are surely the values that dominate his life.

Whatever words or phrases may be used to describe them, they remain what they have always been—religious values. In the character of Jews in suburbia, then, these positive values stand beside the negative, materialistic values generally accepted by contemporary American society.

Suburbia, with its seeming emphasis upon conformity and standardization, has affected the lives of some Jews adversely. But for the vast majority of Jews living in suburbs all through America, it may be said that the basic values upon which their lives and families are founded are indeed sound.

Chapter 9   The Larger Community

Democracy is not of itself a guarantee of human brother-
hood, of racial and religious tolerance. A realization of
these facts should be both an admonition and a challenge
to us—an admonition not to be too naïve in our optimism
or relaxed in our vigilance—and a challenge to defend at
all times the basic traditions of American life which may
at any time and, in fact, are frequently imperilled, and to
resist to the utmost of our material and spiritual resources
the forces of darkness and disruption both here and
abroad.[1]

Though Jewish males in suburbia appear to be little interested
in local politics, their wives are increasingly active and concerned
with all the political aspects of their suburban community life.
Membership in such organizations as the League of Women Voters
and the Parent-Teachers Association often provides the setting for
this new interest, for new and better schools can be built only if
the voters stand ready to approve a bond issue. The pressures frequently exerted by real estate firms and property owners to change
the character of a suburb by erecting apartment buildings and stores
in areas zoned for private residences and the need for improved community services and utilities impress themselves more directly upon
the suburban housewife than upon her husband, for it is the housewife who really *lives* in suburbia.

"After all, it's the woman who really knows the town she lives
in. She is in it all day and every single day. She sees the town in
all its glory, but she sees it, too, in all its weakness. And she is
more likely to want to do something about these things on the
local level."

Although the number of registered women voters is, according
to all reports, increasing in suburban communities, there is as yet

little indication that Jewish women are becoming affiliated with a particular party—Republican or Democrat. Their attention is focused upon certain local issues rather than upon the political party as such. Unless a political scandal occurs, the local officials are likely to remain in office; apathy of the voters is more likely to decide a suburban election than any other factor. To date, Jews have not played much of an active political role in any suburb, even though their numbers in certain suburbs has attracted the attention of politicians.

In the entire metropolitan Washington area, including Montgomery County, 30 per cent of all Jewish women belong to one non-sectarian organization, and 21 per cent are affiliated with two or more non-Jewish organizations.[2] We may conjecture that the number of Jewish women in the suburbs alone who belong to such organizations is not markedly less. Although the number of men in the metropolitan area who are members of non-sectarian organizations is slightly greater (31 per cent), these organizations include business and trade associations, chambers of commerce and service clubs like Rotary, Lions and Kiwanis. Seldom is a political organization mentioned.

In St. Louis Park, Jewish men and women belong to an average of 1.17 non-sectarian organizations each. The percentage is the same for each sex.[3]

We have already noted[4] that Jewish women in suburbia participate actively in other phases of the organizational life of the community. They are often the leaders in the League of Women Voters, Community Fund or Red Cross. They join with friends and neighbors in promoting one or another of the recently created organizations, particularly health societies concerned with aid to the blind or with such diseases as cerebral palsy, nephritis and cancer. Luncheons, campaigns, fund-raising—all these require careful planning, devoted effort and generous periods of time if they are to be performed adequately. Leaders of these national societies agree that their best and most devoted workers live in suburbia.

Jewish women appear to be playing an important role in the growth and success of these organizations, which represent specific human needs and are, therefore, appealing to these suburbanites. The fact that these causes serve not Jews alone, but humanity at large, provides special attraction. The need to acquire status through such activity, especially if such effort may lead to the improvement of human life, is evident everywhere. The much vaunted "leisure" of suburbia is, so far as the Jewish woman is concerned, largely a myth. She is an "organization lady."

In contrast to their wives, the Jewish men of suburbia are less often involved in or even concerned with organizational life. They claim that they have little time for such activity. Evenings are spent mainly at the PTA, which they attend with their wives, and at home with friends and television. House repairs and lawn-tending fill their free afternoons. They campaign on behalf of Community Fund and the central city's United Jewish Appeal in limited numbers, though they generally contribute to these causes rather liberally.

The men of suburbia, including its Jewish residents, become directly concerned with the politics of their community only when some special issue or problem arises.

"You will see the men get worked up when some proposed action is likely to affect real estate values on their street, or more particularly the value of their own property. Then they really get excited about such matters and appear at City Council meetings or elsewhere, more often to protest than to propose new legislation."

Since suburbia is economically middle class, the interests of its residents often change from what they were in the central city. People tend to become more conservative in their political views, for they now have more of economic value to safeguard and protect. They are less likely to support or sponsor bond issues for local improvements when they know that their own tax rate will be increased.

When economic conditions are favorable and "times are good," one may expect little change in the political climate. This is particularly true in older suburbs, where houses have been privately built rather than mass-produced. Political party changes are more likely to occur in those communities where homes are less expensive and where generally it costs less to live, than in the older, more staid, suburban communities.

Reports from men and women, religious and lay leaders, young and old, seem to agree that Jews in suburbia, though they express concern about political issues within their own social groups, are not stimulated to the point of action or organization.

"Why should I join these organizations and get my name on some list that will make me appear to be a Communist? I would rather keep away from these groups, think my own thoughts and mind my own business."

There are many others who, sympathetic to liberalism, join an organization but refrain from active participation in its affairs.

"There is nothing an individual can really do other than pro vide dollar support for a cause. So that is what I am doing."

The commuter feels that he has little time to devote to social action.

"When I get home from my place of business, I am really tired. My wife has had a hard day with the children, and she would like to go out somewhere. So we don't bother about these organizations. Let others who can give them the time worry about them."

Yet it is interesting to note that 47 per cent of the respondents to our questionnaire (344 persons) belong to some organization or otherwise participate in the work of some communal and worthy cause within their community. Only 112, or 18 per cent, claim no affiliation with any organization, either Jewish (excepting the synagogue) or non-Jewish. Twenty-three per cent are members of a temple, Sisterhood, Brotherhood or Parent-Teacher Association. Twenty-three per cent express their interest in the State of Israel by joining some Zionist organization, including Hadassah (the Women's Zionist Organization).

Thirty-five per cent of all respondents are affiliated with some organization in which fellowship and social life are emphasized. Only 17 per cent belong to a golf club; of these, 60 per cent are members of exclusively Jewish golf clubs, while 40 per cent belong to non-sectarian clubs.

A recent study [5] has revealed that Jews are generally more concerned with and interested in foreign and international affairs than any other group of people in America, and that they constitute 18 per cent of the readers of such magazines as *The Atlantic Monthly* and *Harper's*. Twenty per cent of the readers of the liberal magazine *The Reporter* are Jews. The study indicates that Jews are "more likely to participate in an organization where international affairs are the subject of discussion than any other kind of society. They more frequently read those newspapers containing coverage of foreign affairs even when news about the State of Israel is omitted. They tend to be more basically liberal than their counterparts."

Jews' general concern with the welfare of their fellow men and their interest in liberal movements is further attested by these facts. Yet such interest, real though it may be, does not always express itself in direct social action in their own communities. Suburban Jews tend to act only in crises.

Apathy toward social reform and the "general welfare" has been noted by numerous citizens and social scientists. Bernard Barber,[6] in a thought-provoking study, declares that what we speak of as "apathy" is, in fact, an important phase of the American pattern of government. American society, he declares, has never operated on the assumption that each man will take an active part. On the contrary, though it is characteristic of the American people to join organizations to support a specific purpose or "cause," they have always turned active leadership over to a comparatively small number of persons who "run the organization." This, he points out, is no different today from what existed in the "golden age" of the town meeting in New England. The active minority who carry on the business are recognized as the leaders, who are assumed to act in the interest of the majority.

Apathy is not, then, a new condition which has arisen in our day. It is rather a tradition: we cannot be active everywhere, so we permit an active minority to make decisions for us in many areas. Yet the serious charge remains that "apathy is our fifth column." [7]

In August, 1957, Boston newspapers were not published for

three weeks, due to a strike. When the papers resumed publication, one-half page of the *Boston Herald* was devoted to "bringing you up to date on the comics."

Columnist Bill Cunningham, in the first issue after the strike, commented:[8]

The real education came, however, from answering the phone calls in the Herald-Traveler City Room. . . . Not once, to me, nor within my hearing, did anybody call to ask how the Civil Rights Bill was making out, whether Khrushchev had left East Germany, or whether it looked as if the London disarmament conference would fail. Instead—well, one lady called to know if we knew anywhere she could get a list of the movies offered by the various drive-in theatres.

A popular song of a few years ago, "Que Sera, Sera" (What will be, will be), aptly describes the contemporary attitude. Senator Herbert H. Lehman's comment[9] in this connection is particularly worthy of note:

Many, if not most, Americans act as if they lived in isolation booths. . . . The national atmosphere is heavy with lethargy and escapism. The chief emphasis of today is on *not* worrying about what might happen *tomorrow*.

Suburbia obviously prefers not to be disturbed. Its residents would rather *avoid* differences of opinion and controversy if, by so doing, they can be regarded as "regular." That high moral or ethical issues may be involved, or that we may become engulfed by the tidal waves of totalitarianism as a result of our own complacency, does not disturb suburbia.

Suburbia's Rabbis, in keeping with the biblical prophetic tradition, speak from their pulpits on the social issues of the day. It is to the credit of both lay leaders and members that Rabbis are seldom discouraged from speaking on pertinent themes. Their sermons deal with war and peace; the implications of the hydrogen bomb; missiles and satellites; foreign affairs; colonialism; the Near and Far East; integration and segregation; race hatreds; civic righteousness; civil liberty; and other relevant themes. Indifference to these themes appears to be surprisingly large.

The *Christian Century*[10] complains of the apathy and lethargy of church members throughout America:

The church lives and lets live. It gives no one any trouble. It drags no sordid messes from the outside to outrage us. It is very careful not to mess the conventional broadloom of our conforming lives. . . . We no longer poke our prophetic nose into injustice.

It may well be, however, that our silence in the face of our present difficulties may be due in part to our having nothing to say. Few, if any, of us have any major insights that may help to free the world from inner and outer conflict. No leader, statesman or prophet has yet appeared upon the national or world scene to clarify our thinking and point out the direction mankind should take.

The problems are tremendously new and all are novices, all are fumbling. In this agitated anthill which is our home, not greatness, not God-like insight, distinguishes one man or woman above the rest; but only the little spark of courage to say and do the rather difficult and different thing, to think new thoughts, to follow small insights, not working for big ones.[11]

Silence, according to this view, is not necessarily apathy, any more than the High Priest Aaron's silence at the death of his two sons was indifference or lack of concern. At times, in the face of overwhelming problems and all-engulfing situations, our very humanity demands that we remain alertly silent as we struggle to find the solution to our problem.

The characteristic tendency in these days is to avoid any overt act that may single us out and direct attention to us. Personal conformity with what is assumed to be the general political or cultural pattern is generally regarded as desirable and right.

Until the end of World War II, it was assumed that wage-earners and "little businessmen" voted the Democratic Party ticket as an indication of their "liberalism." Since 1946, however, the improved financial status of so many American families, the increased security of wage-earners through the entrenchment of their powerful unions, and the move of so many of these families to suburbia have made for the tendency toward "conservatism." The move to suburbia is supporting evidence of the wish to retain that security—economic, cultural and social—already achieved and to resist further change. The new status and outlook which result from the purchase of one's "own" home (no matter how heavily mortgaged) should not be underestimated.

Jewish suburban communities are affected not only by these factors, but by another of considerable importance. Jews are members of a cultural and religious minority; their "different" practices, rites and ceremonies make them a *recognizable* minority. Some Jews, therefore, decry any deed or word that may further set the Jewish community apart. They believe that the best protective coloration for the Jew who wishes to live free from identification *qua* Jew is to refrain from taking any action or making any statement which suggests that he is not conforming to the mores of the larger community.

"Jews oughtn't to be seen or heard. Every time a Jew gets appointed to some office, he creates some problem of anti-Semitism. It isn't a question of whether I like it or not, or even whether it is right or wrong for a Jew to act or speak as he wishes. What is more important is whether such action or office-holding is 'good for the Jews'—that is, whether it will help them to survive in peace. That's why I think that Jews should not take sides on public issues."

There are those, too, who move to suburbia in order to play a kind of game with life itself. It is a game of "let's pretend." Let's pretend that life is all good, that there are no bothersome problems of war or peace, of bombs, missiles and satellites, of segregation or non-segregation, of intolerance or good-will, of a United Nations or a disunited world. "Let's escape from it all by shutting our minds and refusing to face the facts of life."

Judaism has always opposed this attitude. Prophet and sage, from Bible times to the present, have urged the Jew to confront life steadily, realistically; to regard problems and difficulties as his opportunity to demonstrate that he is indeed God's co-partner in the creation of the world. "The Almighty did not complete all the acts of creation within six days," say the sages. "The continuing act of creation requires that we mortals shall utilize our God-given talents, our knowledge and our strength toward the end that the world shall be improved and perfected."

It is the privilege and the duty of the Jewish community—particularly in the suburbs, in which so many young Jewish families reside—to help create a better world. So much remains to be achieved in improving human relations that to shirk our responsibilities is to offend ourselves, our children, our fellow men, and God, in Whom we profess to believe. The task of the synagogue in suburbia is, in part, to awaken men to their responsibilities—to help build a positive life for the Jew and, through him, for society.

It was good to discover that suburban synagogues and temples have, officially at least, recognized this responsibility. They have appointed social action committees in considerable numbers.

In 1955, at the 43rd General Assembly of the Union of American Hebrew Congregations, consisting of 550 Reform congregations, the delegates urged the establishment of congregational social action and community affairs committees in their respective temples. A national budget was set up and national personnel appointed for this purpose.

The United Synagogue of America, the national organization of Conservative congregations, also has a national Social Action Committee, as does the Union of Orthodox Jewish Congregations.

The National Women's League of the United Synagogue of America, through its national office and active Social Action Committee, provides materials on such subjects as civil rights, Federal aid to education, immigration, the Middle East, and Arab-Israel relations. It supplies these materials to its Sisterhoods and their Social Action Committees all through the nation.

The National Federations of Temple Sisterhoods and Brotherhoods, affiliated with the Union of American Hebrew Congregations, performs a similar and highly regarded task.

The Rabbinical organizations of all three movements in Judaism have for many years provided the religious motivation and the Rabbinic leadership which have inspired and directed Jewish congregations in both urban and suburban areas.

Mr. Albert Vorspan, Executive Secretary of the Commission on Social Action of the Union of American Hebrew Congregations, wrote me his impression of the role of the suburban synagogue:

I must say that my experience does not confirm the judgment that "no progressive moves in the field of social justice come from suburban communities and their religious leaders." On the contrary, it has been our experience that some of our best social action programs stem from new suburban congregations. Because the suburban congregation is usually made up of young people whose Jewish lives revolve around the synagogue, and because there is usually a void not yet filled by the old established Jewish civic groups, there is frequently a tendency for the synagogue to play an active role in community affairs. As a matter of fact, I would say that the chief resistance we have met in social action, aside from the South, which is another matter, has been from the large, old established congregations in the metropolitan centers. I could cite many, many experiences, but I think the most helpful thing I could do would be to send you some reports of what some social action groups in suburbia have been doing.

His reports indicate that these committees set up programs of "self-education." Each member of the committee is assigned a subject and is responsible for informing the whole group about developments in that area. These subjects include interfaith and interracial activities, problems of civil liberties, evaluation of mayors' committees on community relations, problems associated with changing neighborhoods, Federal security programs, anti-discrimination legislation (including housing), juvenile delinquency, religion in the public schools, action to "clean up" local political scandals, support of the United Nations, separation of church and state, and revision of the McCarran-Walter Act provisions for immigration.

Nearly three hundred of these Reform congregations have active, well-directed programs for social action, approved and supported by their Rabbi, board of trustees and congregation.

The enthusiasm of this and other national Jewish organizations for social action is understandable. Jewish suburbia may ultimately, through its synagogues and other national organizations, take the lead in the fight against social inequities and in behalf of civil rights.

Synagogual committees on social action, like the individuals who comprise them, seldom act except in a crisis. A case in point is the social action taken by the Jews in the five-year-old suburban community of Levittown (Pa.), with a population of 60,000. Despite the threat of anti-Semitism, Jews lined up solidly in support of the right of a Negro family to live in the community. "The Dogwood Hollow Social Club," which played a prominent role in seeking to keep the family out, was openly opposed by more than 1,000 residents, who signed a "Declaration of Conscience" deploring acts of violence and intimidation.

The Jewish Community Council, in a written statement, made its position clear:

We welcome to Levittown Mr. and Mrs. William Myers, expecting no more, no less than is expected of any member of our community.

Believing that reason and loving kindness, blended with firm faith in the future are true guides in developing wholesome relationships among men;

Holding that pre-judgment is neither wise nor adult; knowing that an upright man is a blessing to his community and that the color of a vessel gives us no clue to its content; affirming that each generation of the American citizen has been handed an inheritance and is responsible for its protection and transmittal; "that all men are created equal, that among these are Life, Liberty and the Pursuit of Happiness," understanding that to "love thy neighbor as thyself" means to protect his right to enjoy his inheritance.

Though vandals expressed their anger with one Jewish family who befriended Myers, by painting red letters "KKK" on the walls of his home, they did not deter this and other Jewish families from giving active support to integration forces within the community.

Jews in many suburbs have demonstrated their readiness to take sides on such issues as separation of church and state, religion in the public schools and minority rights. In Silver Spring, for example:

"It is exciting to find that many of the government employees take stands on issues almost directly contrary to that taken by their employer, the Federal government. These, of course, are highly skilled people. They seem to be completely unafraid. They discuss, argue and study the major issues of the day with great care."

The Jewish community of Mount Vernon (New York) is reputed to be "social-action conscious." Its interest in such matters has recently been awakened by a special problem:

"In Mount Vernon, we find that in recent years the Protestants have been moving out of town and Roman Catholics have been coming in in large numbers. We became concerned because there is great need for a new, up-to-date high school. It is really desperately needed. But we cannot get the voters' approval for it because the Catholics are known to oppose being taxed for a new school when they have their own Catholic schools. I can feel for them having to pay for two school systems. But they are simply against expending any money for the new school, so all the others of us who want a really first-rate public high school are at their mercy. We Jews are doing everything we can to arouse interest in the town's needs. Whether we will succeed remains to be seen."

The Montgomery County Jewish Community (Chevy Chase) has no social action committee. Yet individual members of this congregation and Jewish residents in the suburb are actively interested in social issues. Though government employees under a Republican administration, many of these people have been strong and open supporters of the Democratic candidates for president.

On occasion, complaints are registered by members of the community against those who do not support liberal causes.

"There are a fair number of people who are afraid of their own shadow. They try to make themselves as inconspicuous as possible. They are not among the most highly respected, even though they seem to be pretty well off."

The Jews of the San Gabriel Valley tend to be conservative in their political reactions. Rarely does one hear of any action which demonstrates strong convictions on issues involving social justice. In one instance, however, a Rabbinical leader, supported by his congregants, took a stand which might have caused some eyebrow lifting among the more conservative members of the community.

Yet he was warmly applauded. Because Negro infiltration into the San Gabriel Valley is a source of concern to some, it was significant that this Rabbi extended a public welcome to these newcomers.

All the available evidence suggests that Jews do not vote as Jews in suburbia.

In Newton, when a well-known Jew ran for Congress on the Democratic ticket against a non-Jewish incumbent, the Jewish candidate was defeated. Political experts in the area are convinced that Jews did not support the Jewish candidate.

"We believe that many Jews here voted the Republican ticket and supported the Republican incumbent. Had the present congressman taken some action in Congress which might have aroused their ire, the result might have been different. But there is no reason to believe that, excepting for an act which might be regarded as anti-Semitic, Jews would have supported the Jewish candidate just because he is Jewish."

The continued growth of the suburbs' Jewish population is generally expected to increase the number of votes for the Democratic Party. The facts, however, indicate that Jews vote as individuals, not as Jews.

In Nassau County (New York), for example, Jews have voted along conservative lines. Although the Democratic vote has increased considerably (6 per cent in four years) in the area, it is hardly as great as it was in the Bronx or Brooklyn, from which so many of these voters originally came. In Levittown, the Republican Party has had the voting support of many of its Jewish residents.

The independence of government employees, many of them under Civil Service, has been noted by local community leaders in Montgomery County. Though their employer is a Republican administration, support of the Democratic Party is indicated.

Observers in Skokie declare that Jewish residents support the Democratic Party as they did when they lived in Chicago.

"We have noted that people here vote for the man rather than for the party much more than they used to do in Chicago. Still, there is a strong pull toward old party ties."

In St. Louis Park voters go along more frequently with the incumbents in local politics and tend to support the Democratic party along national lines.

Euclid voters are far from agreement in their political choices. Many young Jews employed in the numerous industrial plants in and around Euclid vote as independents. They are inclined to vote for the man rather than for a party.

Most of the suburbs in the area of San Gabriel Valley vote Republican and have remained in the Republican column in the past decade. Jews have voted with the majority and it is expected that this tendency will continue for some time.

Jews who reside in upper-middle-class communities are, according to all accounts, usually aligned with the Republican Party. Even then, they are known to cross party lines if, in their opinion, a candidate is strong on such issues as civil rights or Israel. Seldom, however, is their interest in the welfare of Israel alone enough to change their vote.

Democratic political leaders believe that, though it may take more time than they wish, the present Republican strength in the suburbs will be dissipated. Suburbanites who voted as Democrats in big cities and switched to the Republican Party when they changed residence are, according to the Democratic National Committee, coming back to the Democratic Party. Democratic leaders report the trends as follows:

— —Newton, a traditionally Republican stronghold where 39 per cent voted the Democratic ticket in 1952, increased that vote to 43 per cent in 1956;

——Nassau County (Long Island), with its many suburbs, voted 23 per cent Democratic in 1952 and 29 per cent in 1956;

——Westchester County (New York), a Republican stronghold for years, increased its Democratic vote from 26 per cent in 1952 to 28 per cent in 1956;

——Suffolk County (New York) was 18 per cent Democratic in 1952 and 22 per cent in 1956;

——Brookline (Massachusetts) gave the Democrats 40 per cent of the vote in 1952 and 46 per cent in 1956;

——Arlington and Fairfax Counties (Virginia), voted Democratic by 39 per cent in 1952 and 43 per cent four years later;

——Montgomery County gave the Democrats 37 per cent of its vote in 1952 and 43 per cent in 1956.

Thus, reason Democratic leaders, in the political tug-of-war now being waged, the "country club set" will lose to the "supermarket set." [12]

It is generally argued that, assuming "normal" conditions in the next few years, the swing to the Democratic Party will be greater in those suburbs into which most new residents will move.

Opinion among the respondents is divided as to whether they live in a progressive, conservative or reactionary community. Only ten persons regard the community in which they live as "reactionary." Three hundred eleven, or 51 per cent, say that they live in a "progressive" suburb, while 40 per cent think that their home suburb is "conservative." Nine per cent either have not replied or believe that their community may consist of an intermingling of all three.

Most suburban Jews have a friendly, though at times uneasy, feeling about the State of Israel. They read about its problems, its successes and its failures with avid interest. They are aware that their Hebraic tradition and even their Torah is directly associated with this ancient land. They are proud of the *chalutzim* (the pioneers) whose devoted efforts have converted swamp land or arid desert into gardens, rich farmland or cities. They are moved by the heroic men and women of Israel whose physical courage and bravery have created the new state. They are impressed and even inspired on occasion when they realize that the gates of immigration have remained open to receive Jews from other lands who are obliged to flee from their homes and begin life anew. They are excited by the Hebrew University, Medical School, Weizmann Institute and numerous other scientific and intellectual enterprises so ably carried on by scholars and teachers. The courage and fortitude of a Ben-Gurion fascinates them, and the flexing of Israel's muscles during the Suez campaign moved them deeply.

Yet the men of suburbia do not enroll as members of any

Zionist organization in great numbers, though they do support the National United Jewish Appeal Campaign. Their wives, however, are more frequently members of Hadassah or Mizrachi, the women's Zionist organizations. A survey of the record of affiliation reveals that women outnumber men in Zionist organizations by three to one in such suburbs as Newton, Sharon and Swampscott; and by two to one in Euclid, Skokie, Levittown, Chevy Chase, Bethesda, Silver Spring, St. Louis Park and the suburbs of the San Gabriel Valley. Hadassah was one of the first national organizations to solicit memberships in suburbia. Combining philanthropic, Zionist, cultural and social interests through its various chapters, Hadassah has succeeded where the Zionist organization of America has seemingly failed. However, membership alone is not the sole means of identifying a Zionist.

"America is my home. I'm an American citizen. I was born here. I fought in World War II. I don't have to apologize to anyone for my feelings about America, because this country is my home and I love it. But I love the State of Israel, too. I love it as an Irishman loves Ireland and feels for it when something happens to it. I love it because I know that my Torah came through the Children of Israel from there. I love it, too, because the people have had courage to win a homeland for themselves. I think I'm more proud to be a Jew now than I have ever been in my whole life."

There is an interest in and a readiness to support the State of Israel, even though Jewish suburban men do not belong to any organization specifically dealing with Israel. This is further attested by the response of young Jewish suburbia to the regular campaigns for the purchase of State of Israel bonds.

"These young people do two important things. First, their wives actually join the teams to sell bonds to their neighbors. In ever-increasing numbers, they are undertaking this major responsibility and really beginning to get good results. Second, they buy bonds themselves. True, they do not buy them in quantity nor do they purchase large denominations—but they buy bonds and that is an indication of their interest in Israel and their sense of involvement with it."

Everywhere in suburbia one hears talk about the desire to visit Israel "sometime." Most of these suburbanites are not yet in a financial position to be able to undertake pilgrimages to Israel, but improvement in their economic status and growth to adolescence of their young children may change the picture in the future.

Although the number of official Zionists is small, the feeling for Israel is widespread. Israel, whose achievements have astonished the world, has become the symbol of the Jew reborn. Jews in suburbia know enough about Israel to be deeply moved. Yet what the attitude may be should Israel suffer any reverse in the years ahead, it is difficult to say. How deep this concern for Israel really runs we may never know, for "everyone loves a winner," and Israel is favorably regarded today because of its informal but obviously friendly relationship to the Western nations.

Chapter 10   Prologue to the Future

*The future that awaits us American Jews is unpredictable.
It depends largely upon how we shall meet the challenge
of the present and avail ourselves of its opportunities.*[1]

A tremendous "population explosion" that is likely to bring the total population of the United States to 180 million people by 1960 is forecast by the United States Bureau of the Census.[2] The Bureau further projects a population of from 216 to 244 million by 1975, if the postwar boom in babies continues unabated. There is reason to believe that the marriage and birth rates will assure continuing population growth for decades to come. Though hydrogen bomb warfare and economic depressions may affect these prognostications, a steady increase in the rate of population growth is more than likely.

The continued growth of the "standard metropolitan areas" is therefore assured. By 1975 two-thirds of all the people in the United States will live in the metropolitan areas. A continued increase in the number of suburbs contiguous to central cities is certain.

The present upward economic trends are also likely to continue. Higher economic levels will make possible the fulfillment of many a middle-class family's desire for a better home, more playspace for the children, better schools, safer environments and a generally improved standard of relaxed living.

Jews, who constitute a large proportion of the economic middle class, will continue to move into the new suburban communities. The sources of strength and of weakness in suburban life, insofar as the Jews are concerned, therefore, deserve critical examination and evaluation. But first let us consider Jewish suburbia's evaluation of itself.

Ninety-six per cent of our respondents in this study are highly pleased with suburban life. Asked, "If you could do it again, would you move to the suburbs?" only eight persons answered "no." Those who expressed personal approval of suburbia also stated that they would urge their friends to move to their suburb. Seventy-two out of eighty-three suburban Rabbis, or 86.7 per cent, also expressed their belief that living in suburbia is "good for the Jews." Jewish community professional workers with offices in the central city, though pointing to certain problems and situations within suburbia that require solutions, were nevertheless unanimously in agreement that the Jews of suburbia are, in the main, living serene and happy lives.

Despite the generally acknowledged economic pressures which often result from taking up residence in the suburbs—mortgages, often more burdensome than were originally expected; costs associated with the furnishing of the home; the care of lawns, trees and plants; the added expenditures of insurance, foodstuffs and clothing—and about which suburbanites regularly complain, it is pleasant to know that they are happy in their new environment.

"How could we be unhappy in such a place? We have a beautiful new home, small, but really comfortable. Our children go to good schools. The teaching staffs have a fine reputation. True, the schools are crowded to the doors, but that, too, will be straightened out. What matters is that we are really *living*. There are lots of trees all over town. We enjoy watching each blade of grass come up, and we all pitch in to take care of it. We have gotten to know many people and have made some really good friends. And they're a good class of people in the whole neighborhood. If we hadn't come here, we would still be living in some neighborhood in the city, paying about as much in rent as we pay here for what we some day will own. We belong to the synagogue, ever so many clubs and the PTA. We think that, even though it isn't easy to pay for it all, this is much better for us. Here, at least, we feel like people!"

Such sentiments, though uttered in all sincerity, do not take into account the questioning and even negative attitudes toward suburbia which one hears in unguarded moments even from those who overtly sing its praises. In addition to the financial burdens, other factors prove to be an irritation.

"I'm getting sick and tired of being the family chauffeur. All I do all day long is taxi the kids to and from school, to and from Hebrew school, to and from doctors, dentists and piano lessons. I'm so sick of driving the car and spending all my time with the children that I would gladly give up the comforts of suburban living for a return to the city where the kids can walk to school under their own power."

"There are just too many organizations in this town and far too many things to do. I feel as if I were caught in a trap. So many of my friends belong to clubs of one kind or another—and they are all good, mind you. But what happens is that each of my friends wants me not only to pay my dues to her club but to be active in it as well. Frankly, I go broke just trying to be a good fellow and so what happens? My friends are getting cool to me and some are even angry."

"We got what we bargained for when we moved to the suburbs. But we got it in larger doses than I think is good for us. We are always on the go. The phone is always busy. People are always dropping in to invite you somewhere: 'Please come to *this* meeting!' 'Please come to *that!*' Always we are running to something; I'm just about fed up. I would like to be left alone for a while—just to catch my breath."

In the newer suburbs, especially when newcomers are establishing themselves, the tendency to "go places and do things" is very marked. The much desired "leisure" to which the new residents have looked forward is not easily obtained. At the price of becoming anonymous once again, as so many of these people were in the city, Jewish families often are obliged to shut themselves away from the organizations and people, however worth while, that would monopolize their time and energy. They simply refuse to affiliate with them.

The suburbanite complains, too, about the tendency to be with the same, limited group of people all the time, for this helps to create a type of provincialism that is really not wanted. Always in the company of the same people, "traveling" in the same crowd, exchanging ideas with the same persons, tends to create a deadening and narrowing effect which must ultimately prove injurious to the individual's growth and development.

Riesman [3] wisely comments in this connection:

We have the impression that the suburbanite, tied to his home as the doctor is to his practice, may actually be less likely to take off for a week-end in the country than the urban dweller whose janitor can look after his apartment and even the cat.

However, it is the social atmosphere, which helps to foster standards based primarily upon wealth and success, that disturbs many a suburbanite the most.

"I find that I am fighting a losing battle against the false standards that my children seem to believe are real values. I talk to them about how much I earn, and I even go to the trouble to explain where my money goes—but that seems not to matter. If the young people in the neighborhood have more of a weekly allowance than I give my son—and they do—then I am, according to my neighbors, depriving my son of what is his right. If the boy next door drives a car to school, nothing will do but that my son must have a car of his own. My daughter sees others wearing expensive clothes, and she somehow believes that unless she dresses the same way, she will be a 'nobody.' There is a boy on the block who is getting a Jaguar for his sixteenth birthday. Mind you—a Jaguar! And the kid hasn't even gotten his driver's license yet. What will he get for the seventeenth or eighteenth birthday? I say we're spoiling them. They have seen everything, tasted everything, had everything before they are twenty. And here we are talking about building a better world!"

These quotations are far from a complete catalogue of the arguments offered against suburban living.

Laymen and Rabbis who do not sing hymns of praise for suburbia, then, may have cause for their doubts and uncertainties. The joys of suburban life are, in many cases, not entirely unblemished by such false values as the worship of money and what it can buy, and the belief that because the "majority is always right," one should attempt to adjust to its standards, whatever they may be.

Although the suburb may provide numerous advantages in comfort, it also presents certain problems. Let us consider some of the most pressing of these problems.

I.

The synagogue-center, which in most cases encompasses a major proportion of the Jewish suburban community, provides ample opportunities for Jews, young and old, to identify themselves with their people and to join actively in a program for positive Jewish living. This is obviously a source of great comfort to those who are concerned about the future of Jewry in America. Not all students of the suburban scene may agree that a true revival of religion has taken place, but there *is* agreement that American Jews are actively affiliated with their religious institutions and centers. This, however, may create a danger:

Are Jews likely to become ghettoized in suburbia? Is the suburb in danger of becoming a gilded ghetto?

Fear has been voiced that further segmentation of the community along religio-ethnic lines will create both physical and spiritual ghettoes. Precisely because the temples so often provide full social, cultural and religious programs for the Jewish community—programs which are usually expertly directed, in contrast to the manner in which suburbia generally deals with these matters—Jews tend to stay very close to the Jewish groups and institutions. Some observers voice grave concern over this problem: There is apprehension that Jewish children will be associating almost exclusively with other Jewish children and that the opportunity for intercultural programs and associations will be materially reduced.

Jews who have recently moved into a suburb from an exclusively Jewish neighborhood in the city tend to create patterns very much like those they knew before. They desire to live near synagogues, temples and Jewish shopping areas. Since non-Jews tend to move out from such areas, suburbia may ultimately arrive at a condition which can only be described as ghetto-like.

Ghettoes tend to be created unwittingly; they are seldom deliberate creations. For example, the increasing present tendency to develop "residential club" communities closed to Jews, as is true in certain suburbs of Newark, forces Jews into other suburbs in greater numbers.

Ghettoes, even though they may be middle-class and suburban, can hardly be looked upon approvingly by Jews or Christians. The Jewish suburban community of today has been favorably compared with the old East European "Shtetl." Teller,[4] however, in a strongly worded critique, suggests that Jews in the Shtetl were in closer contact with non-Jews than are today's Jews in suburbia. Though this may be exaggerated, it does remind us that every effort should be made to prevent the isolation and segregation of Jews in suburbia.

Jewish communal leaders face the important task of reminding those who unwittingly tend to create such ghettoes that Jews should participate actively in the civic life of the suburb as a whole. This interest must express itself not only in political life but in the suburb's cultural, civic and social program, as well as in social action against delinquency, sub-standard housing and the general lowering of the moral tone of the community.

Each religious group in America has not only a legal right but a moral duty to preserve its distinctive values. No religious group in any community favors the loss of its identity through complete assimilation. Each denomination, therefore, seeks to preserve itself by providing healthful and culturally stimulating youth groups and activities. The synagogue, like all the others, attempts to provide opportunities for Jewish young people to meet under favorable conditions.

It is not such contact which induces ghettoism, but the tendency of the least informed to look upon all persons or groups other than their own as not just different, but inferior. Opportunities must therefore be created for Jews and non-Jews to meet and work together. Not only is brotherhood good in its own right, but the American ideal assumes that, out of such interchange of ideas and interplay of personalities, a culturally superior American people will develop.

This vexing tendency toward ghettoism is not easily solvable, yet we dare not for that reason ignore or minimize it. The development of a series of isolated Jewish suburban communities, provincial in outlook and ghetto-like in character, is not what any reputable Jewish leader desires. How to live equally in two great civilizations remains the major problem and the greatest challenge.

II.

Inadequate lay-leadership is another of the major problems that confront suburban Jewish communities. All too often, men who are chosen to assume leadership are totally unprepared for the task. These persons are usually well-intentioned, but inexperienced in Jewish communal work. They seldom possess adequate Jewish knowledge, and, not infrequently, they assume that the tactics of the market place may be applied with equal validity to local synagogual and religious problems and issues. Such "leaders," whether they are local merchants or professional men, tend to assume that the title which they acquire by virtue of their office confers on them a fund of knowledge concerning the Jewish way of life and makes them well nigh infallible in their judgments.

Genuine spiritual and qualitative progress is often impeded by this presumptive attitude. Although competition may have its virtues in the business world, it is obviously far less desirable in other aspects of community life, including the religious. The tendency to compete for Jewish member-family affiliations creates strain and suspicion, instead of the more desirable and needed harmony. Intra-communal relationships that make for divisiveness must be discouraged.

I have often noted that zeal for the growth of one's own congregation tends to foster this competitive spirit. Some Rabbis in suburban communities, often young and blissfully lacking in experience, have on occasion aided and supported their laymen in public feuds and differences. There is obviously a need for intensive workshops and seminars—to be sponsored perhaps by national Jewish organizations or, even better, by the central city community federations and Rabbinical councils—in which lay leaders and inexperienced Rabbis can be instructed in the intricacies and complexities of Jewish communal life. There is urgent need to point out the problems and possible dangers in community relations and to acquaint these leaders with the services and agencies already in operation which can help them meet specific problems.

Inadequate leadership obviously handicaps a community and slows down its natural growth. The creation of training schools for Jewish communal leaders is, therefore, a necessity. Such an organized effort, extended by central city federations and councils in association with established Rabbinical councils, would provide valuable and needed assistance to embryonic suburban communities.

The lack of experience in communal Jewish life is, however, only one of suburbia's present difficulties. Another is the general assumption among suburbanites that they can and should remain completely independent of the central city. Synagogual and lay leaders tend to insulate themselves against the leadership of the metropolis. They do not often take kindly to ideas and suggestions from this experienced source. They are like newlyweds, who so often are quite convinced that they can live their own lives completely independent of their parents and family. Although others may have failed in this attempt, they are certain that *they* will not require the wisdom an older generation can provide. Thus newly established suburban communities and their leaders often refrain from seeking guidance and counsel—until an obviously critical situation arises.

In certain core cities, Jewish metropolitan organizations seek to overcome this split by appointing or electing suburban Jews to their boards and executive committees. It is assumed that central city ideas and experiences will thus seep back into the suburban Jewish community. However, this procedure has not proved adequate, for the individuals appointed seldom serve as a liaison between suburb and central city. Their personal ties with the metropolitan Jewish organization are strengthened, but the suburban Jewish community gains little if anything in the process. On the basis of a study of community structure, I would suggest that the metropolitan organizations establish within each suburb or suburban area a replica of the core city organization in miniature, related to the central organization through representatives appointed or elected by the suburban Jewish community organization. The much-needed rapprochement, so basic and yet so often lacking, could thus be developed, while providing the suburb ample opportunity for self-expression and independence.

As we have noted elsewhere, the present tensions in community relations, though not always apparent, are nevertheless a fact. These tensions are likely to increase in the years immediately ahead. Experts in human relations are urgently needed now to assist each suburb in understanding the intercultural and interreligious problems that require immediate attention. It is important, too, that effort be made now to channel and solve the vexing issues of church-state separation and religion in the public schools. There is urgent need for a trained and discerning suburban leadership group, to be guided and counseled by the experienced leadership of the metropolitan and national Jewish organizations.

The Rabbi, though he is often regarded as suburbia's primary Jewish leader, is not always adequately prepared to meet the challenges presented by community tensions. He may, through his youth or inexperience, prove as inexpert in this area as are his lay leaders. Both, for the first times in their lives, are asked to serve the special interests and needs of their community, and they are often ill-prepared to do so.

Jewish metropolitan agencies often hesitate to do more than offer to provide some specific service for the new suburban community. The tendency to rebuff such advances is marked. New suburbs and their leaders appear to believe that they can meet most of their own community needs. In many cases, they find themselves mistaken. Their leaders are simply not fully aware of the cultural and religious needs of their own suburb.

Temple-centers in the suburbs often undertake to develop Hebrew educational school programs without a deep understanding of the basic objectives of Jewish education or the need for adequate school facilities, classrooms, trained teachers and satisfactory textbooks. Even when they consult the central city's bureau of Jewish education, suburban leaders, determined to maintain their autonomy, tend to accept only fragments of the counsel. As a consequence, many suburban Hebrew schools are confronted by a continuing series of crises, which are ultimately resolved only with the guidance of the central city educational bureau.

"How can one create a *desire* on the part of the synagogue's school committee to accept the curriculum which is generally regarded as the best in the area? Each school committee and many of the Rabbis work independently of the bureau. The result is that, in certain areas, you get—insofar as Jewish education in suburbia is concerned—organized chaos."

Suburban synagogues and temples are often unaware that expert guidance is also readily available to them through their national denomination organizations. A staff of counselors and national consultants who would visit these communities regularly to help the synagogue steer a steady course would prove invaluable. The national religious organizations, however, have not yet provided sufficiently large or adequately trained staffs to undertake this major responsibility.

III.

Although central city Jewish community councils and federations have not always managed to integrate suburban Jewish activities with their own organizational programs, they generally succeed in enlisting Jewish suburbia's support for fund-raising efforts. Aware of their financial needs, the metropolis has steadily moved forward in building up its army of campaign solicitors. Metropolitan Boston, for example, has incorporated thirty suburban communities, with a Jewish population of 40,000, in the metropolitan division of its Combined Jewish Appeal. This is true also of the federations and councils in New York, Cleveland, Chicago, Washington, Minneapolis and Los Angeles. However, these metropolitan areas are not yet able to provide, among other services, the many important family care and child services that many suburban Jewish families require. The development of decentralized suburban branch offices in far greater numbers is obviously necessary.

Although many national Jewish organizations, such as B'nai B'rith, Hadassah, Council of Jewish Women and the Zionist Organization, have established branches and chapters in suburban areas, core city *service* organizations have not yet developed completely adequate organizations through which to assist Jewish suburbia. The suburban synagogue continues to serve in many capacities for which its leadership is often inadequately trained, and it must continue to do so until an integrated program is fully developed for the suburbs on a highly professional basis.

The New York Jewish Federation reaches out into Long Island and its suburbs, as it has done for years into Westchester County, for financial support in its annual campaigns. However, the Jewish Social Service Association has yet to provide its many services in the newer and smaller suburbs.

The Jewish Community Council of Greater Washington has managed to include many of suburbia's leaders, including Rabbis, in key positions within the central organization. As a consequence, it has secured some cooperation and provided valued assistance on numerous occasions to the Jewish communities of Silver Spring, Bethesda and Chevy Chase. The Jewish Education Committee of this Council helps to set standards of Hebrew education in various congregational schools. It provides workshops for teachers, principals and Rabbis and offers helpful extension courses. Suburbanites, however, believe that an ideal integration between the central city and the suburb has not yet been attained.

Cleveland, through its excellent Jewish Community Federation, has also kept a watchful eye out for the welfare of suburban Jewish communities—understandably so, inasmuch as 85 per cent of the Greater Cleveland Jewish population lives in the suburbs. Both the Jewish Children's Bureau and the Cleveland Jewish Family Service Association moved their agencies in 1954 to Cleveland Heights.[5] In the case of the Euclid Jewish Center, the Federation has provided counsel, guidance, and service on request, and the Jewish Community Center of metropolitan Cleveland has paid a rental fee to the

Euclid Jewish Center for the use of its facilities in order to assure an adequate youth activities program in the area. The residents of Euclid are said to participate adequately in the annual Jewish Welfare Fund effort at fund-raising.

In Niles Township and Skokie, three Rabbis and certain lay leaders of the new Jewish community approached the Jewish community centers of Chicago for help in establishing proper recreational and educational facilities for the community. After a factual study of community needs was made, such assistance was provided.

St. Louis Park is so much a part of the Minneapolis Jewish community that, in all fund-raising efforts, the Minneapolis Federation of Jewish Service treats it as a section of Minneapolis, rather than a separate suburb. All other services, including family casework, are provided through a central office in Minneapolis. The Minneapolis Talmud Torah, as the result of a recent survey, established a branch of this noted Hebrew school in St. Louis Park.

On the West Coast, the Los Angeles Jewish Community Council is very much concerned with the needs of the suburban communities in both the San Fernando Valley and the San Gabriel Valley. There is, as yet, no central agency in the Council that supervises these San Gabriel Valley towns in the field of recreation, which is regarded as the problem and concern of each suburb. The Jewish Centers Association of Los Angeles, an autonomous agency, has operated an extension department since 1948 and has offered its assistance whenever called upon. The Los Angeles Jewish Family Service Agency has two caseworkers and a supervisor in its San Fernando Valley office, but none, as yet, in the San Gabriel Valley. Casework in the San Fernando Valley area differs from that of the remaining metropolitan community, with marital problems and referrals involving juvenile behavior made in greater numbers proportionately than elsewhere.

Well aware of the problems resulting from the rapid expansion of suburban communities, the Community Planning Committee submitted a report to the Board of Directors of the Los Angeles Jewish Community Council in which the following points were made:

The problem of extending adequate community services to the suburban areas is, in the committee's opinion, the major long-range problem confronting the Los Angeles Jewish community. . . . The Jewish population in the suburban areas has *more than doubled* in the same six years (1950-56). . . .

Complaints of inadequate service from the suburban areas have been steadily increasing. . . . Once the Welfare Fund Campaign is out of the way, the suburban areas feel that we forget about them. . . . Any new or expanded program for suburban areas should develop in the following fields:

A. Adequate Jewish education.
B. Group work service, especially to aid youth groups.
C. The setting up of some form of community organization for the separate suburban areas so that people interested in Jewish affairs may have a common meeting place and an organization for the expression of their needs and views.[6]

The Centers Association of Los Angeles has recognized the need for adequate youth programs and a general program of group work services in the suburbs. As a consequence, it is developing an agreement with synagogues, temples and other organizations throughout the area by which the temple pays for the cost of such services and the Association provides the necessary supervision.

The Bureau of Jewish Education of Los Angeles has provided a variety of services directly to suburban Jewish schools, giving not only supervision but also financial aid. In some cases it has actually helped to organize the suburb's Hebrew school.

The social service and family welfare needs of Jewish suburbia, if we are to base our conclusions upon this sample, appear as yet to be inadequately met. Problems of family life, vexing and trying situations with respect to juveniles, the weakness of many of the youth programs, concern over aged citizens—in fact, most of the problems so well handled by Jewish Family Associations and other professionally trained staffs—are hardly met on a basis that can satisfy the expert in these areas. We have already noted that Jewish suburbia, with its many new problems and tensions arising from religion in the public schools and from church-state relationships, has all too few direct connections with a central city agency from which it may gain guidance and direction.

Since the synagogue is the center of organized Jewish life in the suburb, community services may quite easily find their home within the synagogue building itself. Family and personal services could well be channelized through the synagogue. Thus, with the Jewish Family Service Society of central city (to single out one association) housed in the synagogue structure, trained psychiatric social workers and psychologists would become immediately available to suburban Jews. By decentralizing, Jewish central agencies could perform the tasks for which they are especially trained, establish strong ties between the suburb and the agency, yet reserve to the leaders of Jewish suburbia a real autonomy.

It is obviously necessary for the central city to effect a closer relationship with Jewish families and their temples in each suburb and, further, to create the liaison which will serve the best needs and interests of *both* suburbia and the central city. Long-range planning in this area is urgently needed.

The Area Council Plan developed by the Jewish Community Council of Los Angeles, though experimental, appears to have a good chance of establishing proper rapport between certain suburbs and the core city. Charles Zibbell,[7] Assistant Director of the Jewish Community Council of Los Angeles, describes the plan as follows:

The Los Angeles Jewish Community Council has a membership base of organizations (approximately 450 of them). Each of these organizations names representatives (one to five, depending on size) and it is these representative members that elect the governing body of 61. These organizations are spread throughout the greater metropolitan area. It was, therefore, decided to use this organizational base as a device for providing a basis for both a grass-roots decentralized area structure and integration with the central community organization. Thus, the San Fernando Valley Area Council was established based on a charter granted to it by the Los Angeles Jewish Community Council, which sets up the geographical area within which it is to operate. The organizational members of the Los Angeles Council which are located in the geographical area become the members of the Area Council Executive Committee. The Executive Committee, working in close concert with the staff of the functional agencies of the central community, establishes area sub-committees in such fields as community relations, Jewish education, agency services, etc. These committees become the sounding board for the particular problems of the area, and through interlocking membership with central committees are able to relate these problems to the overall metropolitan area. It also works in the opposite direction when these committee members bring to the suburban area the overall policies worked out by the central structure.

He adds:

In the very early days in the growth of the greater metropolitan area of Los Angeles, we found that the tremendous urgency behind our fund-raising effort pushed us out into the field into the farthest corners of the country. We acted almost like missionaries in our zeal to reach every Jewish family no matter where it was located.

Fund-raising, according to Zibbell, actually created new Jewish communities where there had formerly been individual Jewish families, each unmindful of and unrelated to the other.

I have been told of one incident in the community of Compton, which is roughly eleven miles from the center of downtown Los Angeles. One of our campaign field staff went into this community in order to organize a fund-raising effort. There were no Jewish organizations in town and there was serious question as to how many Jewish people lived there. He dug up a few families, started the ball rolling and when the first meeting was called at a local church, one hundred people arrived and regarded each other with utter amazement at the discovery that they were looking at fellow members of their Jewish community. When the wave of fund-raising ended, this community felt a need to continue as an organized entity and set itself up in a form of a Jewish center. This form of experience was repeated a number of times throughout the greater metropolitan area. The fund raisers . . . actually became catalysts for the crystallization of some kind of community structures in the areas that they touched.[8]

IV.

The economic investments which Jewish suburbanites make in the homes they buy and in the sundry comforts attendant upon living in their new community are as nothing compared with the great personal changes which occur in their new environments. These newcomers must establish new friendships and gradually acquire that informality in dress and manner which is generally associated with leisurely suburban life. Their children are enrolled in new schools with different curricula. Families become affiliated with synagogues and community organizations. The lives of parents are increasingly centered around their children. Life is family-oriented and it becomes highly important to be a "part of the group."

Given these new conditions for family living, one would expect such families to live on in their new suburb for many years. Yet this has not proved to be the case. On the contrary, the very mobility which has produced these suburbs has created many challenging and often frustrating situations. For before these new families have really settled in the suburb, they seem ready to move on again, searching for a new suburb that will represent greater wealth, hence a higher social status. Because homes can be sold easily, new homes in even the newer and more exclusive suburbs are being purchased and occupied for comparatively short periods of time. Suburban Jewish community leaders report that this transiency is a major problem affecting the organized Jewish life of the community. "These Jews are really here today and gone tomorrow."

An average of 20 per cent annual turnover in membership is reported in the congregations of Montgomery County. An examination of the records of several congregations in the Newton area, as well as the records of the Greater Boston Combined Jewish Appeal, indicate that the annual turnover in greater Boston runs about 10 per cent annually. The Boston suburbs of Sharon, Natick and Framingham have the same problem: their leaders are concerned because the number of families who really fix roots in the community appears to be declining.

In the suburbs like St. Louis Park it was recently reported that 10 per cent of the residents "plan to move." [9] The report explains that this is "a factor which might be expected when considering the number of small two-bedroom homes in relation to the age of the adults who live there and the increasing child population." St.

Louis Park and other Minneapolis suburbs have the highest proportion of families who have lived in their present residence for one year or less. The suburbs of the San Gabriel Valley also have a considerable degree of transiency, according to the accounts of community representatives. One in seven families (14 per cent) in the Los Angeles area reported in 1958 that they intended to move. In 1951, it had been one in five.[10]

Euclid records a high degree of transiency by families whose economic status has improved, as well as by those whose sons and daughters are approaching marriageable age. Parents in these families begin to express concern over the possibility of intermarriage should they remain in a predominantly non-Jewish environment.

"We want to get our children into communities where they will meet more Jewish boys and girls."

Transiency makes it difficult if not impossible for religious leaders within a suburban community to help the family integrate properly.

"You just cannot do much with people who are on the move. It takes time to get to know people and have them know you. Under the present circumstances, we must always fail with a large group because they never stay with us long enough to acquire our values or learn a new idea."

The ever-increasing mobility of suburban Jews should caution temples, religious schools and Jewish centers to erect structures that can be cleared of their indebtedness within ten to fifteen years. Far too many community buildings have found themselves bereft of their former members and supporters when, for one reason or another, the movement to another suburb or another location within the same suburb got underway. The current building trend, which so often involves vast financial commitments and expenditures for the erection of synagogues and centers, suggests that Jewish community leaders regard their institution as permanently attached to the community. The present tendency toward mobility makes this assumption highly unrealistic.

v.

The problem of intermarriage, too, is likely to become even more serious for Jews in the years ahead.

A recent statement [11] that "the rate of intermarriage tended to increase among the native born children of native born parents reaching a proportion of about 7.4 per cent of the population" accentuates the fact that intermarriage will increase whenever and wherever Jews live in communities that are not exclusively Jewish. Seven per cent of the Jews in the Los Angeles area have married members of another faith, according to a 1958 survey.[12] (This figure has not changed significantly since 1951.)

The recently completed study of greater Washington revealed that approximately 12 per cent of the households in this area "are mixed—that is, of the persons within them who are related by blood or marriage, at least one is Jewish and at least one is not." [13] This study points out too, that 11.3 per cent of the households in Montgomery County were "mixed." The proportion was even higher in suburban Prince Georges County (20.8 per cent) and highest in the suburbs of Virginia immediately adjacent to Washington (34 per cent).

Many suburban synagogues readily accept into membership Jews who have married non-Jewish women. Indeed, there are several suburban congregations whose president and vice-president are married to non-Jews. The support and public approval given to intermarriage by electing intermarried men to synagogue office means that such marriages are likely to increase in number. Given a continuation of "good times" and freedom from open anti-Semitism, we may expect the average rate of intermarriage for the nation to reach 10 per cent within the decade.

"Top positions of leadership in certain suburban synagogues rest in the hands of persons who have intermarried. If we can elect such persons to the highest post of our congregations, how long will it be before our youth understand that we are really not too serious about opposing intermarriage?"

Though most Jews applaud the new trend of fraternities and sororities toward non-sectarianism in their membership, occasional voices are raised in questioning concern, if not in protest.

"We are living in a society that must be termed 'open' and freer than it has ever been from narrow bigotries. But must Jews pay the price of giving up their identity as Jews through intermarriage that must result from such contacts in college fraternities or sororities? That is the way it looks to me."

Most Jewish parents want their children to maintain Jewish contacts. They do not favor the idea of intermarriage, primarily because it is their desire to perpetuate the Jewish people and the "religion of their fathers," however they may define that religion. There are many factors at work, including the very nature of democracy itself, that tend to increase the potential for intermarriage. Intensification of efforts to counter this situation, which Jews must regard as critical, must therefore occupy the most prominent place among the concerns of American Jews.

The Jewish community must become increasingly aware of its responsibility for the Jewish education of its youth throughout the standard metropolitan areas. At present, local federations, through their bureaus of Jewish education, help to set adequate standards in such matters as salary scales, conditions of employment, teacher qualification and curriculum. Metropolitan federations often provide funds for the maintenance of community Hebrew schools. The development of many new suburban religious and Hebrew schools, however, has diminished the central city's interest in Jewish education, inasmuch as these new schools are financed by the suburban congregations of which they are a part.

Jewish educators have already noted that many such schools, in spite of their founders' good intentions, are proving inadequate in terms of their educational standards, teaching staff, classroom facilities and curriculum. Such problems result not only from the inexperience and inexpertness of congregational officials, but from insufficient financing as well. The responsibility of the Jewish community for the education of youth throughout the area must, therefore, be clarified.

The rapid increase in the number of suburban schools has already resulted in a corresponding decrease in the number of pupils enrolled in the central city's Jewish schools. Slum clearance projects undertaken in many metropolitan cities also create vexing problems for the Jewish community: enrollment in the central city's Hebrew schools is considerably reduced as Jewish families move on to other areas. Jewish federations have already found it necessary to meet the deficits of such neighborhood schools because of their concern for Jewish education as the *right* of all children.

There is also the need, long recognized by Jewish educators, to provide for the further Hebrew education of boys and girls of high school and college age in the metropolitan area. The establishment of a centrally-located Hebrew high school, which the graduates of elementary Hebrew schools could attend for advanced studies, is essential to the cultural welfare of the total Jewish community. The manifold services that could be provided, including teacher-training courses and adult Jewish education programs, are self-evident.

Fortunately, Jewish federations in the metropolitan areas are beginning to give serious thought to these important problems. The sponsorship and guidance of Jewish education for the larger Jewish community, including the suburbs, should receive a high priority on its agenda.

Jewish organized life in suburbia is, with only a few exceptions, no more than fourteen years old. Since 1946, hundreds of thousands of Jewish families have entered upon a way of life which, if not entirely new, is certainly different in major respects from life in the central city.

When any person or group of people transplant themselves from one community to another, it is reasonable to assume that a variety of problems—organizational, cultural, social and spiritual— will present themselves. That the transition to suburbia has proceeded with comparative ease speaks eloquently for the ardor and purposiveness of its residents.

The Jews of suburbia have, to date, achieved a high degree of integration into the total life of their communities. They have also succeeded in attaining a high measure of identification with the Jewish people and its way of life. Weaknesses, imperfections and even decay and dissolution are readily apparent to the observer of the Jewish way of life in suburbia, to be sure. However, as has been noted throughout this study, there is much about which we may be highly pleased. Today, there are more Jews—young enthusiastic Jews—who have the will to be Jews than I have noted in over three decades of careful observance. There is ample reason to speak hopefully concerning their future.

Appendix

Estimates of temple membership were made on the basis of information received from suburban leaders with respect to the number of families who are affiliated with local congregations. These figures have been weighed against the total population of Jews in each of these suburbs. Paucity of factual material presently available concerning the number of Jews in the newer suburbs is unfortunate and makes it difficult to record the total Jewish population in America with any degree of accuracy. To complicate matters further, suburban families often retain their membership in urban synagogues.

The *American Jewish Year Book* figures are often outdated and, even more discouraging, seldom take account of the many suburban communities established since 1945. Even records for such old, well-established suburbs as Glencoe and Highland Park, Illinois, for example, are omitted. Despite these difficulties, however, an effort has been made to record what is known concerning forty-one of these suburbs.

ESTIMATE OF TEMPLE MEMBERSHIP AND JEWISH POPULATION
IN FORTY-ONE SUBURBS (1957)

Suburb	Number of Temple Member-Families	Estimated Total Jewish Population	Per Cent Affiliated
Alhambra (Calif.)	200	2,100	50
Baldwin (N.Y.)	350	2,625	48
Bay Shore (N.Y.)	500	3,325	54
Belmont (Mass.)	370	1,800	75
Bridgeton (N.J.)	200	1,000	80
Burbank (Calif.)	450	5,000	32
Elmont (N.Y.)	900	7,000	46
Encino (Calif.)	600	3,500	62
Englewood (N.J.)	950	5,500	60
Euclid (Ohio)	300	2,100	50
Fair Lawn (N.J.)	1,025	4,200	84

Suburb	Number of Temple Member-Families	Estimated Total Jewish Population	Per Cent Affiliated
Freeport (N.Y.)	480	4,800	35
Great Neck (N.Y.)	2,750	15,750	63
Highland Park (Ill.)	1,100	8,500	48
Kearny (N.J.)	300	2,000	55
Larchmont (N.Y.)	375	2,450	55
Laurelton (N.Y.)	1,050	12,000	32
Levittown (N.Y.)	880	5,250	54
Linden (N.J.)	615	3,200	80
Marblehead (Mass.)			74.8
Montebello & Monterey Park	550	5,400	50
Montgomery County (Maryland)			
Bethesda	220		
Chevy Chase	500		
Kensington	400		46.2
Silver Spring	621		
Wheaton	450		
Mount Vernon (N.Y.)	2,500	17,500	60
Natick (Mass.)	387	1,880	50
New Milford (N.J.)	800	2,000	45
Newton (Mass.)	3,651	20,000	62
Rockville Center (N.Y.)	1,500	7,350	73
Roslyn (N.Y.)	1,200	10,500	40
Rutherford (N.J.)	185	1,000	66
St. Louis Park (Minn.)	932	5,389	62
Sharon (Mass.)	650	3,600	65
Skokie (Ill.)	1,800	28,000	23
Swampscott (Mass.)	750	3,000	86
Wantagh (N.Y.)	1,000	14,000	25
White Plains (N.Y.)	2,700	13,000	77
Whittier (Calif.)	150	500	35

Notes

Introduction

1. Sylvia Fleis Fava, "Suburbanism as a Way of Life," in *American Sociological Review*, February, 1956, Vol. 21, No. 1, pp. 34-37.

2. Robert Park, *The City*, University of Chicago Press, 1925, p. 1.

3. David Riesman, "The Suburban Dislocation," in *The Annals of the American Academy of Political and Social Science*, November, 1957, p. 133.

4. Isador Chein, "The Problem of Jewish Identification," in *Jewish Social Studies*, July, 1955, Vol. XVII, No. 3, p. 29.

5. W. Lloyd Warner and Leo Srole, *The Social Systems of American Ethnic Groups*, Yale University Press, 1945, p. 28.

6. Albert I. Gordon, *Jews in Transition*, University of Minnesota Press, 1949.

7. Howard S. Becker and Blanche Geer, "Participant Observation and Interviewing; A Comparison," in *Human Organization*, Fall, 1957, Vol. 16, No. 3, p. 28.

8. See also Florence R. Kluckholn, "The Participant Observer Technique in Small Communities," *American Journal of Sociology*, 46, November, 1940, pp. 331-343.

9. Replies to the questionnaires were received from congregants in Newton, Sharon, Belmont and Swampscott, Massachusetts; Levittown, Hicksville, Westbury, Great Neck and Roslyn on Long Island, New York; Euclid, Ohio; Chevy Chase, Bethesda and Silver Spring, Maryland; Henrico County (Richmond) Virginia; Lincolnwood, Wilmette and Skokie, Highland Park and Glencoe, Illinois; St. Louis Park, Minnesota, and Alhambra, Arcadia, Altadena, San Marino, Temple City, San Gabriel, Monterey Park and Montebello, California.

10. The Rabbis of the following communities provided information that is included in this Study.

Baldwin, N.Y.	Covina, Calif.	Glen Cove, N.Y.
Bay Shore, N.Y.	East Meadow, N.Y.	Great Neck, N.Y.
Belmont, Mass.	East Rockaway, N.Y.	Hagerstown, Md.
Bethesda, Md.	Elmont, N.Y.	Hewlett, N.J.
Bridgeton, N.J.	El Monte, Calif.	Hicksville, L.I., N.Y.
Brookline, Mass.	Encino, Calif.	Highland Park, Ill.
Burbank, Calif.	Englewood, N.J.	Huntington, N.Y.
Cedarhurst, L.I.	Euclid, Ohio	Jericho, N.Y.
Chevy Chase, Md.	Fair Lawn, N.J.	Kearney, N.J.
Cliffside Park, N.J.	Franklin Square, N.Y.	Kensington, Md.
Closter, N.J.	Freeport, N.Y.	Larchmont, N.Y.
Colonial Hghts., N.Y.	Glencoe, Ill.	Lawrence, N.Y.

Laurelton, N.Y.	New Milford, N.J.	San Gabriel, Calif.
Levittown, N.Y.	Newton, Mass.	St. Louis Park, Minn.
Linden, N.J.	North Hollywood, Calif.	Sharon, Mass.
Livingston, N.J.	Norwood, Mass.	Silver Spring, Md.
Lynbrook, N.Y.	Nyack, N.Y.	Skokie, Ill.
Malverne, N.Y.	Oak Park, Mich.	South Orange, N.J.
Milford, Conn.	Ozone Park, N.Y.	Swampscott, Mass.
Millburn, N.J.	Rockville Center, N.Y.	Teaneck, N.J.
Milton, Mass.	Roosevelt, N.Y.	Temple City, Calif.
Monterey Park, Calif.	Rosedale, N.Y.	Wantagh, N.Y.
Mt. Kisco, N.Y.	Rosemeade, N.Y.	Westbury, N.Y.
Mt. Vernon, N.Y.	Roslyn Hghts, N.Y.	West Hartford, Conn.
Natick, Mass.	Rutherford, N.J.	White Plains, N.Y.
New Hyde Park, N.Y.	San Fernando, Calif.	Whittier, Calif.

11. John Dollard, *Caste and Class in a Southern Town,* Doubleday & Co., 1957, p. 21.

Chapter 1: America on the Move

1. Herbert Gans in *The Jews: Social Patterns of an American Group,* Marshall Sklare (ed.), The Free Press of Glencoe, Illinois, 1958, p. 205.

2. *U.S. News and World Report,* August 10, 1956. Based on U.S. Census records.

3. *The Municipal Year Book* (1957), p. 34.

4. Walter T. Martin, *American Sociological Review,* August, 1956, Vol. 21, No. 4, pp. 446-453.

5. As reported in *The Boston Herald,* April 28, 1958.

6. The ten cities are New York City, Los Angeles, Chicago, Philadelphia, Boston, Newark and environs, Cleveland, Washington, D.C., Baltimore and St. Louis.

7. Norman B. Ryder, "The Reproductive Rennaissance North of the Rio Grande," in *The Annals . . . ,* March, 1958, pp. 22-23.

8. David Riesman, "The Suburban Dislocation," in *The Annals . . . ,* November, 1957, p. 130.

9. By the State Commission Against Discrimination of New York, reported in the *New York Times,* November 19, 1957, p. 27 L.

10. *New York Times,* September 30, 1957, p. 25 L.

11. *New York Times,* May 9, 1957, p. 33 C.

12. Morton Grodzins, "Metropolitan Segregation," in *Scientific American,* October, 1957, Vol. 197, No. 4.

13. *Newsweek,* April 1, 1957, p. 36.

14. Warner and Lunt, *The Social Life of a Modern Community,* Yale University Press, 1941, pp. 55-56, 100-102, 234-235, 244-246, 261, 283-284, 290, 424.

15. David Riesman, "The Suburban Dislocation," in *The Annals . . . ,* November, 1957, p. 138.

16. See Chapter 4, "The Synagogue—Center of Jewish Life."

17. Will Herberg, *Protestant-Catholic-Jew*, Doubleday & Co., 1955, p. 274.

18. *American Jewish Yearbook* (1958), p. 14.

19. *Ibid.*, p. 15.

Chapter 2: Saga of the Suburbs

1. Max Lerner, *America as a Civilization*, Simon & Schuster, 1957, pp. 173-174.

2. This estimate was provided by the City of Newton and is based on its annual population poll.

3. Derived from the Assessment records of Newton, in which are recorded the names of all adults in this suburb.

4. From "Welcome Wagon" and real estate records. The Combined Jewish Appeal of Greater Boston maintains a record of contributors to its annual campaign who have moved from one area to another; this record was also consulted.

5. From a survey made by the National Jewish Welfare Board on behalf of the Hecht House, a Jewish settlement house located in Dorchester.

6. All real estate transactions for these years were examined, and the names of all Jewish families were recorded for this study. When in doubt, I turned to the brokers who had made the sale for further information. The real estate records indicate the size of the original mortgage in each case and include a record of down payment.

7. *New York Times*, September 30, 1957, p. 33.

8. Estimates of Levittown's Jewish population vary from 10 to 17 per cent.

9. Henry M. Christman, "Leaven in Levittown," in *The Christian Century*, August 28, 1957, p. 1015.

10. *Report of Committee on Community Organization*, Council of Jewish Federations and Welfare Funds, May, 1957, p. 3.

11. Two sources, The Cleveland Jewish Community Federation and Euclid's Rabbi, provided this information.

12. From the records of the temple in Euclid.

13. *World Almanac* (1958), p. 289.

14. Bureau of Labor Statistics, U.S. Department of Labor, July, 1957.

15. Stanley K. Bigman in *The Jewish Population of Greater Washington in 1956*, mimeographed, May, 1957, p. viii.

16. *Loc. cit.*

17. Department of Jewish Community Center Planning of the National Jewish Welfare Board, 1957, mimeographed, p. 1.

18. *The Jewish Population of Greater Washington in 1956*, p. 21.

19. Department of Jewish Community Center Planning, 1957, p. 1.

20. Mordecai M. Kaplan, *Judaism as a Civilization*, Thomas Yoseloff, Inc., 1957.

21. *A Survey of Niles Township*, prepared by the Jewish Community Centers of Chicago, February, 1956, mimeographed.

22. Supplement to *Survey of Niles Township*, 1957, mimeographed, p. 1.

23. *A Survey of Niles Township*, p. 4.

24. *Ibid.*, p. 3.

25. From a survey made by the Minneapolis Federation of Jewish Service, June, 1958, p. 26.

26. The suburbs along the San Gabriel Valley which have been studied include Alhambra, Arcadia, Baldwin Park, Covina, West and East Covina, El Monte, Monrovia, Montebello, Monterey Park, Rosemead, San Gabriel, San Marino, Sierra Madre, Temple City and Whittier. The author is indebted to many community leaders in greater Los Angeles, including the suburbs in the San Gabriel Valley, for the information provided herein.

Chapter 3: The Jewish Family

1. Henry E. Kagan, "The Jewish Family," in *CCAR Journal*, October, 1954, p. 10.

2. This material was obtained through informants in each of the major suburbs studied. Personal visits to these communities and innumerable conversations with persons in all walks of life resulted in the comments recorded here. Records of attendance and participation were obtained from the synagogues, temples and community centers in these suburbs.

3. *Community Self-Survey*, Minneapolis Federation for Jewish Service, June, 1958, p. 27.

4. *The Jewish Population of Greater Lynn, Mass.—a Demographic Study*, by the Jewish Community Federation of greater Lynn, November, 1956, p. iv.

5. *The Jewish Population of Greater Washington in 1956*, p. 8.

6. *A Study of Natick Jewry*, Associated Jewish Philanthropies of Greater Boston, August, 1957, p. 5.

7. All material incorporated in this study about the Brookline-Brighton-Newton Jewish Community Center was obtained from its executive director, Mr. Sidney Gale.

8. *Planning Survey Report*, Part 2, City of St. Louis Park, 1957, p. 9.

9. From the records of the Combined Jewish Appeal of Greater Boston. These figures were compared with those obtained from the "Welcome Wagon" in Newton, an organization which extends the greetings of the local merchants to new residents.

Chapter 4: The Synagogue—Center of Jewish Life

1. Mordecai M. Kaplan, *Questions Jews Ask*, Reconstructionist Press, 1956, p. 281.

2. Arthur Hertzberg in *American Jewish Year Book* (*1958*), p. 115.

3. National Council of Churches of Christ in the U.S., New York, December, 1957.——In 1800, about 10 per cent of the adult population of this country were church members. In 1900, according to the National Council of Churches, membership increased to 50 per cent. Herbert W. Schneider in *Religion in 20th Century America* (see 6, below) writes: "Not

much more than ten percent of the population acknowledge no religious affiliation whatsoever."

4. This figure, it must be noted, is an *estimate*. In most suburban communities, it is likely that some Jewish residents are affiliated with congregations in the central city. Because it has not been possible to ascertain the affiliation records of each synagogue or temple in the central city, the record of affiliation for suburban Jewish families may be incomplete. Also, in the newer suburbs formal affiliation with a synagogue takes place most often when children are old enough to attend Hebrew or Sunday schools. Thus, young parents with very young children and newlyweds with no children would tend to lower the average affiliation for each suburb. These figures then must be regarded as approximations. (See Appendix for estimate on forty-one suburbs.)

5. Mark Zborowski and Elizabeth Herzog, *Life Is With People*, International University Press, 1952, p. 68.

6. Herbert W. Schneider, *Religion in 20th Century America*, Harvard University Press, 1952, p. 4.

7. *Ibid.*, p. 24.

8. Max Lerner, *America as a Civilization*, p. 689.

9. Deuteronomy 8:3.

10. See *American Jewish Year Book* (1950), p. 154. Cf. *American Jewish Year Book* (1957), p. 152.

11. *United Synagogue Review*, February, 1949, Vol. 4, No. 6, p. 2.

12. Martin M. Cohen in *The Jewish Social Service Quarterly*, Fall, 1955, Vol. 32, No. 1, pp. 75-76.

13. See Chapter 2, page 53.

14. *Why We Build*, published by this congregation.

15. Philip Gilfix. See also Chapter 2, pages 25-26.

16. Annual Report of Temple Shalom of Newton, May, 1957.

17. Quoted in Simon Glustrom "Report on Fair Lawn" in *Conservative Judaism*, Winter, 1957, Vol. XI, No. 2, p. 30.

18. *A Study of the Natick Jewish Community*, Associated Jewish Philanthropies, Boston, 1957, mimeographed.

19. *A Study of the Lynn Community*, multigraphed, p. 44.

20. *American Jewish Year Book* (1958), p. 125.

21. *Report of the Bureau of Jewish Education of Los Angeles*, mimeographed, 1957.

22. *Jewish Community Council of Los Angeles, Study for 1953*, p. 52.

23. See Chapter 6, "The Search for Religion."

Chapter 5: The Round of Ritual

1. Mordecai M. Kaplan, *Questions Jews Ask*, p. 229.

2. Meyer Waxman, *Judaism: Religion and Ethics*, Thomas Yoseloff, Inc., 1957, p. 15.

3. The statements made by laymen with respect to ritual and observance have been compared with the opinions of the Rabbis in their communities.

4. *1958 Jewish Population Study*, Fred Massarik, Director, by The Los Angeles Jewish Community Council. This preliminary summary, published in 1958, will be completed and published shortly.

5. Rabbi Theodore Friedman, Congregation Beth El, South Orange, New Jersey.

Chapter 6: The Search for Religion

1. David G. Mandelbaum in *The Jews: Social Patterns of an American Group*, p. 519.
2. See Chapter 5, "The Round of Ritual," pages 128-147.
3. From an unpublished study entitled "The Riverton Study," directed by Dr. Marshall Sklare for the American Jewish Committee, and read from manuscript by this author (1958). Some respondents offered more than one answer.
4. See Chapter 5, pages 128-147.
5. One example of these changes is *The New Haggadah* for the Passover Seder, edited by Dr. Mordecai M. Kaplan, first published in 1941. Its foreword states that "The language and the concepts of the ancient rite need to be revised so that they go straight to the minds and hearts of the men and women of today." The traditional framework has been retained in this *new* Haggadah, and many innovations make the Passover experience even more meaningful for modern Jews.

In a similar development, many of the "Kibbutzim" or collective communities in the State of Israel have written new Haggadahs, relating the Story of the Exodus of the Jews from Egyptian bondage to their own exodus from European bondage (Nazi Germany and Tzarist and Communist Russia).
6. Marshall Sklare and Marc Vosk, *The Riverton Study, How the Jews Look at Themselves and Their Neighbors*, May, 1957.
7. Nathan Glazer, *American Judaism*, University of Chicago Press, 1957.
8. Mordecai M. Kaplan, "New Directives for Zionism" in *The American Zionist*, January, 1958, p. 7.
9. From a paper delivered by Dr. Kaplan before the Rabbinical Assembly of America, April 30, 1958, at Kiamesha Lake, New York.
10. Erich Fromm, *Escape from Freedom*, Rinehart & Co., 1941, pp. 21-22.
11. Bernard and Nathan Lander, the former, Professor of Sociology at Hunter College and Head of the Graduate Division of Yeshiva University; the latter, a Sociologist at Brooklyn College, New York. This statement was made in a paper delivered before the Synagogue Council of America in April, 1957.
12. Zohar 73, VB.
13. *Ibid.*, III 73a.
14. See Alfred O. Hero, World Peace Foundation Study, "Current World Affairs Behavior of Americans," Boston, 1959, p. 73.
15. B. Talmud, Pesachim 50b.
16. Abraham Heschel, "The Task of the Hazzan," in *Conservative Judaism*, Winter, 1958, Vol. XII, No. 2, p. 1.

Chapter 7: Tension and Unrest

1. Leo Pfeffer, *Creeds in Competition*, Harper & Brothers, 1958, p. 4.
2. A.D.L.—*Reports on Social, Employment, Educational and Housing Discrimination*—April-May, 1958, Vol. 2, No. 2, p. 29.
3. *Ibid.*—January-February, 1959, Vol. 2, No. 5. All ten pages of this national report are devoted to the issue of discrimination in housing.
4. For much of this information, the author is indebted to several

Jewish agencies working in the area of prejudice and intolerance. The help of numerous "field-men" of the Anti-Defamation League (whose reports, particularly on the subject of suburban unrest, were made available) and many others whose experienced eyes and ears recorded incidents leading to concern, unrest and tension is also gratefully acknowledged.

5. *New York Times*, April 8, 1958, p. 17.

6. *Ibid.*, April 11, 1958, p. 27.

7. This material was obtained from the mimeographed committee report of the special Parent-Teachers Association Committee appointed to deal with these problems.

8. The *Milton Record*, Milton, Mass., May 3, 1957.

9. *Survey of Niles Township*, 1957, mimeographed, p. 5.

10. *Ibid.*, p. 5.

Chapter 8: The Homogenized Society

1. Arthur Schlesinger, Jr., in *Saturday Review of Literature*, June 8, 1957.

2. Max Lerner, *America as a Civilization*, pp. 260-261.

3. *Changing Times*, September, 1957, p. 29.

4. See William Whyte, Jr., *The Organization Man*, Simon & Schuster, 1956; David Karp, *Leave Me Alone*, Alfred A. Knopf, Inc., 1957; John C. Keats, *The Crack in the Picture Window*, Houghton Mifflin Co., 1957.

5. Quoted in the *New York Times*, June 12, 1957, p. 36 L.

6. Eric Fromm, *Escape from Freedom*.

7. A. H. Maslow, *Motivation and Personality*, Harper & Brothers, 1954, p. 338.

8. Robert Hutchins in the *New York Times*, June 14, 1957, p. 23 L.

9. Max Lerner, *America as a Civilization*, p. 689. See also Chapter 4, page 91.

10. Rabbi Ira Eisenstein, in Anshe Emet Bulletin, Chicago, 1958.

11. See Chapter 3.

Chapter 9: The Larger Community

1. Dr. Abba H. Silver, in an address delivered before the 26th General Assembly of the Council of Jewish Federations and Welfare Funds, New Orleans, November 14, 1957.

2. *The Jewish Population of Greater Washington in 1956*, p. 12.

3. *Community Self-Survey*, Minneapolis Federation for Jewish Service, 1958, p. 79.

4. See Chapter 3.

5. Alfred O. Hero, "Current World Affairs Behavior of Americans," World Peace Foundation, 1959.

6. Bernard Barber, *Studies in Leadership: Leadership and Democratic Action*, Alven W. Gouldner (ed.), Harper and Brothers, 1950, pp. 477-504.

7. John M. Dumas, "Apathy—Our Fifth Column," National Municipal Review, 1947, Vol. XXXVI, pp. 494-496.

8. Bill Cunningham in *The Boston Herald*, August 31, 1957, p. 11.

9. Herbert H. Lehman, "Economic Justice," in the *Bulletin of the Religion and Labor Foundation, Inc.*, Columbus, Ohio, June-July, 1951, p. 5.

10. *Christian Century*, May 30, 1956, Vol. 73, No. 22, p. 663.
11. Bernard Canter, editor of the *Friend*, London, May 18, 1955.
12. *New York Times*, June 8, 1957, p. 21.

Chapter 10: *Prologue to the Future*

1. Mordecai M. Kaplan, *The Future of the American Jew*, The Macmillan Co., 1948, p. 536.
2. *U.S. News and World Report*, November 28, 1958, p. 72.
3. David Riesman, "The Suburban Dislocation," in *The Annals . . . ,* November, 1957, p. 138.
4. Judd Teller, "The Changing Status of American Jewry," in *Midstream*, Summer, 1957, Vol. III, No. 3, p. 9.
5. We note with satisfaction that the Jewish Family Service Association in Cleveland, Ohio, recently invited three suburban congregations—Fairmount Temple, Park Synagogue and Suburban Temple—to participate in a pilot project seeking to establish how best to meet the family counseling needs of these congregation-families. The project, begun April 1, 1958, is scheduled to continue until June 1, 1959. As part of this project, a professionally trained member of the family counseling staff is available for consultation about personal or family problems at each of these synagogues.
6. Irving Hill, *Report of Community Planning Committee*, annual report of the Los Angeles Jewish Community Council, January 27, 1957, pp. 13-15.
7. Charles Zibbell, in an address at the Council of Jewish Federations and Welfare Funds Regional Assembly, January 11, 1958.
8. *Ibid.*
9. *Community Self-Survey*, Minneapolis Federation for Jewish Service, June, 1958, p. 50.
10. *1958 Jewish Population Study*, Fred Massarik, Director, by the Los Angeles Jewish Community Council, p. 5.
11. *American Jewish Year Book* (*1958*), p. 11.
12. *1958 Jewish Population Study*, Los Angeles, p. 13.
13. *The Jewish Population of Greater Washington in 1956*, p. 124.

Index